JIHAD IN BROOKLYN

THE NYPD RAID THAT STOPPED AMERICA'S FIRST SUICIDE BOMBERS

JIHAD IN

BROOKLYN

THE NYPD RAID THAT STOPPED AMERICA'S FIRST SUICIDE BOMBERS

SAMUEL M. KATZ

NEW AMERICAN LIBRARY

New American Library
Published by New American Library, a division of
Penguin Group (USA) Inc., 375 Hudson Street, New York, New York 10014, USA
Penguin Group (Canada), 10 Alcorn Avenue, Toronto,
Ontario M4V 3B2, Canada (a division of Pearson Penguin Canada Inc.)
Penguin Books Ltd, 80 Strand, London WC2R 0RL, England
Penguin Ireland, 25 St. Stephen's Green,
Dublin 2, Ireland (a division of Penguin Books Ltd.)
Penguin Group (Australia), 250 Camberwell Road,
Camberwell, Victoria 3124, Australia (a division of Pearson Australia Group Pty. Ltd.)
Penguin Books India Pvt. Ltd., 11 Community Centre, Panchsheel Park,
New Delhi - 110 017, India
Penguin Group (NZ), Cnr Airborne and Rosedale Roads,
Albany, Auckland, New Zealand (a division of Pearson New Zealand Ltd.)
Penguin Books (South Africa) (Pty.) Ltd., 24 Sturdee Avenue,
Rosebank, Johannesburg 2196, South Africa

Penguin Books Ltd., Registered Offices: 80 Strand, London WC2R 0RL, England

First published by New American Library, a division of Penguin Group (USA) Inc.

First Printing, January 2005
10 9 8 7 6 5 4 3 2 1

LIBRARY OF CONGRESS CATALOGING-IN-PUBLICATION DATA:

Katz, Samuel M., 1963–
    Jihad in Brooklyn : the NYPD raid that stopped America's first suicide bombers / Samuel M. Katz.
    p. cm.
    ISBN 0-451-21443-9 (trade pbk.)
    1. New York (N.Y.). Police Dept. Emergency Service Unit. 2. Terrorism investigation—New York (State)—New York—Case studies. 3. Suicide bombings—New York (State)—New York—Prevention—Case studies. 4. Terrorism—New York (State)—New York—Prevention—Case studies. I. Title.
HV8079.T47K38 2005
364.152—dc22

Set in Bembo
Designed by Ginger Legato

Printed in the United States of America

This book is dedicated to the memory of the fourteen NYPD Emergency Service Unit officers killed in the terrorist attacks against New York City on September 11, 2001.

SERGEANT JOHN COUGHLIN
SERGEANT MIKE CURTAIN
SERGEANT RODNEY GILLIS
DETECTIVE JOSEPH VIGIANO
POLICE OFFICER JOHN D'ALLARA
POLICE OFFICER VINCENT DANZ
POLICE OFFICER JEROME DOMINGUEZ
POLICE OFFICER STEPHEN DRISCOLL
POLICE OFFICER RONALD KLOEPFER
POLICE OFFICER THOMAS LANGONE
POLICE OFFICER BRIAN MCDONNELL
POLICE OFFICER PAUL TALTY
POLICE OFFICER SANTOS VALENTIN
POLICE OFFICER WALTER WEAVER

Author's Note

Shortly after the September 11, 2001, attacks, when I spent some time with members of the NYPD's Emergency Service Unit talking about what they had endured "that" day and what it was like on the "pile" searching through the smoldering debris, I understood that it was important that the story of the "Brooklyn Job" be told. I had known about the incident in Park Slope for some time, and I personally knew the cops who had led and executed that daring and lifesaving raid in Brooklyn, yet in what context could that story be told in the wake of the most lethal terrorist attack ever?

A federal law enforcement official whom I knew and trusted told me that in light of 9/11 I *had* to write a book about the Brooklyn Job. "Forget the terrorists," he said. "Their motives and desires are unimportant. To get into their heads legitimizes what they tried to do. Fuck 'em! This was perhaps the one night in policing where everything went right. Egos, bullshit, and bureaucracy were all flushed down the toilet so that the cops could do the right thing. Had the NYPD's Emergency Service Unit not intervened the way it did that hot summer's night in July 1997, we would today be referring to the subway tunnels underneath the river as Ground Zero!"

He was absolutely right. This is a cops' story. One of sacrifice and determination and I-told-you-sos. Four years after the bombing of the World Trade Center and four years before 9/11, an incident occurred that, for the American law enforcement radar, should have been a watershed incident in how this nation—especially law enforcement—deals with terrorists, and it now needs to be told.

This is the story of that one night when the NYPD and its elite Emergency Service Unit did what it does best—save lives!

10-13 ... Shots Fired ...

Captain Ralph Pascullo didn't remember if he had yanked the keys out of the ignition when he stormed toward the cabstand. Everything was moving way too quickly for him—he wondered if this was suspended animation or some other adrenaline-induced surreal out-of-body experience, the likes of which he had always read about. The orange glow from the streetlights seemed to pulsate. The rotating red light on the dashboard of his Chevy Caprice pierced his peripheral vision with throbbing flashes. He was bothered by the uncomfortable reality of the silence on the street—something so uncommon for the northern end of Fourth Avenue in Brooklyn, even at 4:50 A.M. He had been on hundreds of tactical operations in his twenty-five years as a cop, but this one felt different, and it was worrisome. A coarse dryness crusted into his throat. It felt like the grind of a shoe on the hard pavement. Pascullo found it hard to swallow and regulate the heavy beating of his heart, trapped now in the Kevlar cocoon of his heavy body armor. Time moved in freeze-frame seconds, almost as if his mind were photographing the events with a powerful yet slow-moving motor drive, but he could still feel himself rushing toward the cabstand in a furious fluid motion. Out of the corner of his eye he saw the six cops, the informer, and the translator rush into the building; they looked, he thought, like soldiers marching nervously on a patrol behind enemy lines. From the corner of his other eye he saw his old partner, his Glock 9mm semiautomatic at the ready. It was reassuring to know and trust the trigger to your right. It was a sign of just how dangerous this night was that a one-star chief was leading a raid.

Pascullo's hands were sweating in the humid wash of New York City in July, but his hands would have been sweating even if this were the dead of winter. How many police commanders send their men on what all agreed was tantamount to a suicide mission? This wasn't the military, after all. There was no such thing in the NYPD and the Emergency Service Unit as "acceptable losses." This "hit," Pascullo knew, was historic—how bloody was something he would have to wait and see.

Pascullo gripped his shotgun tight, too tight, as he hoisted the wooden stock into his shoulder and shoved the barrel, which when aimed at you looked big enough to fire beer cans, at the overweight Arab negotiating the backgammon board on the garbage-strewn sidewalk. The Arabs, six in all, must have thought the unmarked police vehicles were on a narcotics assignment, or were out to arrest a robber, rapist, or murderer in one of the adjacent buildings. Perhaps the Middle Eastern tunes pulsating from a taped-up radio were annoying the neighbors, but in Brooklyn—especially in Park Slope—the residents knew better than to dial 911 for quality-of-life offenses. The Arabs were shocked when Pascullo used his Ithaca 37 shotgun as a 12-gauge broom sweeping four of the men off their stools and onto the ground. "Don't move," Pascullo demanded, using a grinding whisper to keep the men kissing the sidewalk, "and don't fucking talk!"

The Arabs appeared confused and agitated. They were scared shitless. Those who didn't move fast enough were yanked by their hair or shirt collars and thrown to the ground in a harsh and unforgiving tackle. Pascullo looked around to see if the Arabs had any wires or cell phones in their hands—anything that could signal the Palestinians in the apartment that the police were there. Two of the men wet themselves. Chief Kammerdener took his Glock and placed it into the neck of the young Arab who showed a brief sign of possible resistance, and then covered the Arabs, now lying on the sidewalk with their hands over their heads, to make sure none of them moved.

Pascullo could hear his heart thumping. He hoped his old partner wasn't listening. He tried to breathe and regulate the oxygen entering his upper torso but found it hard to do. He didn't want to remove his weapon from the Arabs, but he was tempted to glance at his wrist and check out the time. Securing the cabstand had taken precious few seconds, but time stood still. Pascullo wondered if the entry team had been inside the location for ten seconds or ten minutes. Silence was a bad sign, he thought. Or, perhaps, the apartment was empty—the cops would find nothing and walk back to the street to talk about yet another bullshit job on the midnights. *If this is nothing,* Pascullo mused, *these guys will be talking for months about the raid that never was.* Pascullo smiled for a brief second, knowing that the cops in ESU had a notoriously cruel sense of humor and it would take him a long time to live down so much hype and fear over nothing. But then a gunshot echoed into the night, followed by two more. *Shit,* Pascullo thought as he glanced over at Kammerdener, *this is for real.*

If shots were fired Pascullo was supposed to remain on Fourth Avenue to cover the Arabs from the cabstand. Kammerdener was counting on him to stand fast, but Pascullo couldn't remain behind while his men were involved in a shoot-out with potential terrorists. Pascullo grabbed his 12-gauge shotgun and locked it into his shaking hands as he rushed into 248 Fourth Avenue, not knowing what to expect and, because of radio silence, unable to telegraph his arrival on the scene.

The vestibule was dark and grimy, and the path toward the alley covered in filth; rats, some as large as cats, scampered across the floor to escape the heavy stomps. Smashing the door into the courtyard open, Pascullo raised his shotgun to engage something—

anything—he might encounter in the darkness. He glanced toward the ground floor apartment where he heard chatter and movement. He heard three more shots and he saw the flash of the bullets being fired. Who was shooting? Were his men dead? Six men on the team and six rounds fired. *Fuck!* he thought. *What was happening?*

If the terrorists were true to their word and would, indeed, blow themselves up once confronted by the police, how long was it until the courtyard turned into a fireball? When would the heat and force of the blast envelop him and rip across his body armor? Pascullo attempted to feel the thickness of his Kevlar assault vest, realizing that the heavy and cumbersome layer of protection adorning his torso was barely capable of protecting him against bullets—a bomb would rip the vest, and everything inside it, to shreds. How long would it take from the moment the suicide bomber flipped his switch to the time of the blast? The questions cascaded uncontrollably from Pascullo's brain. As he raced toward what—in his mind—was a certain kill zone, Pascullo wondered just how long it actually took to die in a blast. . . .

The Fedayeen on Freedom's Door

Morning couldn't have come fast enough to the son from Hebron. Dawn's first light on the American continent was something he had dreamed of for years. The bright sun towering from the east this September morning illuminated the arrivals hall in a cascading burst of energy and light. The passengers getting off their transatlantic flight seemed groggy and lumbering, laden down by jet lag. The West Bank native walked merrily past the people on his flight, looking at the robust chubby faces of the airport workers and cognizant for the first time of just how close he was to his ultimate objective.

The march toward passport control was a long stroll past signs advertising the virtues of Molson Golden, the Toronto Blue Jays, and Niagara Falls. The airport was clean, well lit, and so carefree; the terminal was so different from home. The Palestinian stood on line at passport control along with men and women who spoke a myriad of languages and wore everything from the finest suits one could acquire in Frankfurt and London to the same *shalwar kameez* that their fathers and grandfathers had worn in the slums of Peshawar. The sign at the arrivals hall in Toronto's Pearson International Airport read WELCOME TO CANADA in both English and French, and that greeting was reiterated by the immigration officer who smiled as he accepted the Palestinian's passport and papers and said, "Welcome to Canada. What's the purpose of your visit here?" The Palestinian, calm and deliberate, handed the immigration officer his packet—a passport and a single-entry, T-1 visitor/student visa that allowed the young man with a hollow smile to stay in Canada as long as he was enrolled in university. The immigration officer's stamp pounded the entry mark into the young man's passport with a single stroke. And without any additional fuss or formality, Gazi Abu Mezer, whose anger and ambition were so well contained on line at passport control, was ushered into North America with a smile and a "Have a nice day."

It was September 14, 1993.

Gazi Abu Mezer walked out of Terminal Three at Pearson, fumbling with a bulky suitcase he had bought in the Kasbah of his hometown, and glanced at a copy of the *Globe and Mails* piled knee-high at a newsstand. The photo was of Israeli prime minister Yitzhak Rabin and PLO chairman Yasir Arafat locked in a historic hand embrace on the White House lawn as a gleeful President Clinton looked on in pride and joy. The handshake, designed to inaugurate a historic period in the Middle East, had occurred less than a day ago and Abu Mezer knew that Rabin's treachery and Arafat's betrayal would not go unpunished. Hamas, Mezer knew, would not tolerate the selling out of the Palestinian people.

Gazi Ibrahim Abu Mezer was born on October 2, 1973, in Hebron, in the occupied West Bank. The West Bank of Abu Mezer's youth was a volatile mix of resistance and opportunity—passion and violence. The wedge of land on the west bank of the Jordan River had—up until Israel's lightning military victory in the 1967 Six-Day War—been the jewel in the crown for the Hashemite Kingdom in neighboring Jordan for nineteen years. The West Bank had been awarded to the Palestinians in the historic November 29, 1947, United Nations vote partitioning Palestine into Jewish and Arab states, though Palestinian leaders rejected any arrangement that denied them complete control of Palestine—from the Mediterranean to the Jordan River—so the offer of statehood was rejected.

During the 1948 war of Israeli independence, the British-trained and British-led Arab Legion rushed across the Allenby Bridge over the river Jordan to help eradicate the Jewish state shortly after its creation. When the war ended in March 1949, the battle lines became cease-fire lines, which in turn became the de facto boundaries of the fledgling Jewish state. Yet Jordan's King Abdullah did not relinquish control of the West Bank to the Palestinians when the fighting stopped—Jordan simply annexed the terrain and assumed control over its inhabitants. The West Bank and its major cities of Jenin, Nablus, and Hebron, and most importantly the eastern half of Jerusalem (including the walled Old City), became a driving force in the economy of the kingdom.

But the West Bank was on a fractured fault line at the epicenter of the Arab-Israeli dispute. Thousands of Palestinians fled their homes in what would become Israel to escape the brutal fighting of the 1948 war—they fled to Lebanon, Syria, and the Gaza Strip, and they fled to the West Bank, where men and women, many of whom were educated professionals, found that they had abandoned their homes never to see them again only to end up in godforsaken refugee camps administered by the United Nations. In Bethlehem, Ramallah, and elsewhere throughout the West Bank, the camps sprang up as living reminders of the *al-Nakba*—the horrific tragedy of Israeli statehood that had befallen the Palestinian people. The refugees were an underclass, especially among West Bank natives who had lived in the area for generations. The refugees nestled with their Ottoman-era leases linking them to a parcel of land and keys that were to open their front doors. But amid the suffering and the anger, there were no outspoken aspirations for a Palestinian homeland in the West Bank under Jordanian control, only silent wishes. On the whole life was comparatively good.

Violence was inevitable, however. Israel, during the first years following independence, was in no position to even foster territorial notions of seizing the West Bank; after 1948, Israel was a bankrupt nation barely holding its own, having lost some six thousand soldiers and civilians out of a population of six hundred thousand in the struggle for independence. Armistice lines had been drawn, but the border area surrounding the zigzag seam line separating the West Bank from Israel was a frontier without fences or fortifications, and infiltrations were commonplace.

Most infiltrations were perpetrated by small-time cow thieves who raided the border agricultural settlements seeking livestock. Other infiltrations were far more insidious. Egyptian intelligence had supported the creation of Palestinian guerrilla groups that would attack Israeli border settlements with hit-and-run shooting and bombing campaigns; Egyptian and Jordanian intelligence provided these guerrillas, known in Arabic as the Fedayeen, or "Men of Sacrifice," with weapons, training, and intelligence. From 1953 to 1956, they carried out dozens of attacks, killing hundreds of Israeli civilians.

Israel's response to the Fedayeen attacks was biblical justice—an eye for an eye became the standard operating procedure. For every Fedayeen attack, the Israel Defense Forces (IDF) launched an even larger retaliatory strike of its own. Most revenge attacks targeted Jordanian military and police posts along the border; punishing those who allowed, or turned a blind eye to, the infiltrations across the frontier was a favorite strategy, but invariably civilian targets were hit, too. Border towns in the West Bank that sheltered the Fedayeen were seen as fair game. A special Israeli retaliatory commando force, known as Unit 101, was even created to specifically deal with the Fedayeen. The unit, founded and commanded by a young swashbuckling officer named Ariel "Arik" Sharon, was designed to be creative and unconventional. The unit consisted of the very best soldiers inside Israel yet answered to few, and the end results of its operations were often bloody messes. In 1953 a Unit 101 operation against the West Bank town of Qibya left sixty-nine people dead after Sharon's sappers blew up forty-five houses in the village with the residents still inside them. Israel was lambasted internationally for the Qibya operation, and commando strikes against the West Bank ceased shortly thereafter when Unit 101 was disbanded.

For nearly a decade, the West Bank remained quiet. Life inside the West Bank during the years of Jordanian rule can be classified as prosperous, yet precarious. As part of the Jordanian kingdom, the West Bank enjoyed a high standard of living that was a cut above life anywhere else in the Arab world with the exception of Beirut and the upper-class neighborhoods of Cairo. West Bank business flourished; the Jordanian dinar, one of the strongest currencies in the Arab world, drove industry and trade throughout the region. Universities flourished in the West Bank, as well, ranging from Birzeit University near Ramallah to a multitude of smaller specialized colleges and Islamic universities in Hebron, Nablus, and Jenin. Tourists, too, ventured to the West Bank under Jordanian rule. Christian pilgrims retraced the footsteps of Christ in Jerusalem's Old City and they traveled to Bethlehem to see where Jesus was born. On the surface, everything appeared to be normal.

But the West Bank was, after all, the West Bank. Jordanian security services made sure that expressions of Palestinian nationalism did not threaten the rule of King Hussein, the grandson of King Abdullah, who had been assassinated by a Palestinian zealot at the steps of Jerusalem's al-Aqsa mosque in 1951. Jordanian rule was often threatened by the Fedayeen and, in 1965, the new phenomenon that established a West Bank base of operations—Fatah.

Fatah—the guerrilla movement headed by Yasir Arafat—was the largest armed faction of the Palestine Liberation Organization in 1964; it had bases in Syria, along the Golan Heights, in Gaza, and in the West Bank. Like those of the Fedayeen a decade earlier, Fatah attacks launched from Jordanian territory in the West Bank sparked harsh Israeli retribution. Each attack, counterattack, and counter-counterattack raised the level of overall violence between Israel and her neighboring Arab state and brought the region ever closer to full-scale conflagration. By May 1967, the terrorist tit for tat had, indeed, brought the Middle East to the brink. In May 1967, following a particularly brutal terrorist attack in northern Israel, the Israel Air Force retaliated against Syria. Syrian warplanes were sent to intercept the approaching Israeli aircraft, but within minutes, in one of the most lopsided dogfights in history, thirteen Syrian MiGs had been blown out of the sky. Outrage in the Arab world was massive and the call to war was sounded in Damascus, Cairo, and Amman. Egyptian president Gamal Abdel Nasser ordered United Nations peacekeepers out of the Sinai Desert and he rushed the pride of the Egyptian military into the demilitarized zone. Syria mobilized its forces for war, as did Jordan; in fact, the Jordanian military was placed under overall Egyptian military command. War seemed inevitable.

The Israeli belief was that this would be *the* war of Israeli national survival—the Israeli military was outnumbered one hundred to one on the battlefield, and in Tel Aviv, schoolchildren dug mass graves preparing for this inevitable and ultimate conflict. Yet the Israeli military opted to strike first, and on June 5, 1967, the Israel Air Force launched a massive preemptive air strike against the Egyptian, Syrian, Jordanian, and Iraqi air forces; within three hours, Arab airpower was reduced to smoldering shells of million-dollar fighters and bombers destroyed on runways. Without airpower the Arab armies were at the mercy of the Israeli army.

When the smoke cleared on the West Bank on June 10, 1967, and cease-fires were agreed to by all the combatants, Israel had quadrupled its size. The Israel Defense Forces occupied the entire Sinai Desert, won from Egypt; the Golan Heights, from Syria; and, of course, the West Bank, from Jordan. West Bank Palestinians were trapped, once again, in the throes of conflict.

The Palestinians believed the propaganda emanating from Cairo, Damascus, and Baghdad that the Jews would be pushed into the sea and once and for all destroyed in this final conflict. "Liberation awaits you," West Bank residents were promised. In the town of Jenin, in the north central West Bank, the people believed that the approaching Israeli army units entering the city were, in fact, a lead column of Iraqi armor coming all the way from Baghdad. Town residents threw rice and flowers at the soldiers, thinking them to be their saviors. When the soldiers, confused by the greeting, informed the residents that they were Israelis, the residents fled in panic. Some openly wept in the street.

In Gaza, where the local Palestinian population lived in absolute poverty under Egyptian "administration," the new world of June 10 was one of humiliation, yet angry reservation. In the West Bank, the home of over one and a half million Palestinians, what many thought of as the heart and soul of Palestinian nationalism was now occupied by the Israeli military. An Israeli military administration assumed the day-to-day control of the Palestinian inhabitants throughout the West Bank—from those living in villages that still looked the same way as they had four hundred years earlier under Turkish rule, to the major towns such as Ramallah. Israeli currency became the staple of the lively souk markets, and Israeli soldiers and appointed administrators were responsible for everything from running the schools to collecting garbage.

The Israelis did not know what to make of their newfound conquest. Israel had gone from a small speck on the map only eleven miles wide at its narrowest point to a regional superpower with a military that could vanquish anything that the oil-rich Arab states could throw at them. Yet occupying the land of a million inhabitants in the West Bank and nearly a million more in the Gaza Strip was not part of Israel's grandiose plan. There were many inside the ruling Labor Party who argued that the land seized in conflict should be bartered back to the Arabs in exchange for a lasting peace. The Arabs and Israelis were reticent about dealing with one another, let alone scripting the blueprint for a peace accord. In September 1967, the Arab League met in Khartoum, capital of Sudan, and convened its famous "Three No" Summit: there would be *no* cessation of hostilities against Israel, *no* negotiations with the Jewish state, and *no* recognition that Israel even existed; in the Arab media, Israel was referred to solely as the "Zionist Entity."

Against this backdrop Israel began to hold on to its newly seized territories as security buffers separating its major population centers from Arab armies across the Jordan River. Israel also established settlements—what hard-line members of the Knesset used to call "facts on the ground"—inside the West Bank and Gaza Strip.

For Israel—as it had been for Jordan after the 1948 war—the jewels in the West Bank crown were the Old City of Jerusalem and the Haram al-Sharif, the Temple Mount. The Haram al-Sharif, peaked by the Dome of the Rock and the al-Aqsa mosque, was the third-holiest spot in Islam; it was from here, Muslims believed, that the prophet Abraham ascended to paradise. To Jews the Temple Mount, or Har Ha'Bayit, as it is known in Hebrew, was where the holy temple had stood guard over the Jewish kingdom until it was destroyed once by the Assyrians and then again by the Romans. Jerusalem was religiously, spiritually, and politically the heart and soul of ancient and modern Israel. The city had been split during the 1948 war like East and West Berlin. East Jerusalem, including the Old City, became part of Jordan's West Bank. West Jerusalem, carved around the no-man's-land of the Old City and its adjacent neighborhoods, became the capital of modern Israel.

When Israeli paratroopers stormed across the minefields and barriers separating Jordan and Israel on the second day of the 1967 war, the battle for the holy city was fierce yet one-sided. Within one day, Jordanian defenses had crumbled and Israeli paratroopers in their camouflaged fatigues reached the Western Wall of the Old Temple at the outer fringes of the Temple Mount. The wall, also known as the Wailing Wall, was the holiest site in Judaism and its capture became a source of religious pride—and awakening—for Jews around the world.

Nowhere, perhaps, was this fervent religious awakening felt more than in the city of Hebron. A little over twenty miles south of Jerusalem, Hebron is a city whose name, in both Hebrew and Arabic, is derived from the word "friend"; in Arabic, Hebron is known as Beit al-Khalil, the "House of the Beloved," since Isaac, the beloved son of Abraham, was born and educated in what would become this major city of 130,000 inhabitants. Unlike the cities of modern Israel, such as Tel Aviv and Netanya, which are recent creations of the Zionist vision, Hebron has always been a city with a strong and vibrant Jewish population. Jews lived in Hebron through Roman, Crusader, Mamluk, Ottoman, and British rule. In August 1929, much of the Jewish community in the city fled after Arab riots killed sixty-seven Jews during the first of many Palestinian uprisings. A small and ultrareligious Jewish community remained behind in Hebron, since the city was, according to tradition, where Abraham was buried; Abraham, along with his wife, Sarah, as well as his descendants Isaac and Jacob and their wives, Rebekah and Leah, is buried at the Tomb of the Patriarchs. Jews flocked to the tomb on pilgrimages to pray; Muslims built the al-Ibrahimi mosque alongside the tomb, as well.

In April 1968, almost a year after Israel captured the West Bank, sixty Orthodox Jews booked rooms in Hebron's Park Hotel for the Passover holiday. They never left. Amid violence and Palestinian protests, the squatters were eventually moved to an Israeli army outpost on the outskirts of town. That outpost would, in 1971, become the town of Kiryat Arba, an Israeli city of some six thousand families smack-dab in the middle of the religious battle for Hebron. Residents of Kiryat Arba wandered through the dangerous Kasbah of Hebron carrying their Uzi submachine guns to the sneers and hatred of the local residents, who saw their religious rights challenged by interlopers armed to the teeth and protected

by the might of the Israeli security services. Hebron became a bat-
tleground of religious will amid a political landscape of mistrust
and hatred.

Gazi Ibrahim Abu Mezer was born into this climate of religious
conflict over the soul and control of a city. The youngest of seven
children, Gazi Abu Mezer came from a well-educated middle-class
family living in a modest home in the center of town. Like those
of children living in Belfast or any other contested city, Mezer's
formative years were marked by the "struggle." By all outward appearances the Israelis held Hebron, like other towns in the West
Bank, firmly in control and yet governed the Palestinian population with varying degrees of kindness and opportunity. Palestinians
were free to work inside Israel—where their wages were light-
years higher than anywhere else in the Arab world—and to study.
Tourists flocked to Hebron to pray at the Tomb of the Patriarchs
and to purchase the city's famed glassware; the economy, as evident
by the bustling activity inside the city's market, thanks to the
tourists and Israeli bargain hunters, was strong. People prospered
and the restaurants were always filled with people to feed who
spoke a Babel of languages and paid in a multitude of currencies.

Safeguarding this activity was an all-encompassing Israeli military and Border Guard security blanket. Soldiers patrolled the city
twenty-four hours a day, seven days a week. Every facet of day-to-
day life required Israeli permission. Anyone seeking a permit to
build an addition to his home, or to travel, required the permission
of the Israeli civilian authority, which in turn meant an okay from
the Shin Bet, Israel's domestic counterintelligence and counterterrorist agency. Often, an okay from the Shin Bet required information in return. The Byzantine nature of Middle Eastern commerce
dealt with cash, betrayal, and survival.

Although the Shin Bet and the Israeli army controlled the
physical security of Hebron, the various Palestinian terrorist fac-

tions truly ruled the city. Each and every one of the Palestinian liberation groups—factions headquartered in Beirut, Damascus, and Baghdad—had cells and functioning military platoons and battalions operating in the West Bank and Gaza, especially in Hebron. The factions, like street gangs determined to carve out turf for themselves regardless of what the authorities had to say about it, controlled various neighborhoods, streets, and even apartment buildings; territory was often fought over with gun battles, and terrain was marked by graffiti. The factions financed their operations by extorting a tax from city residents and through stolen-car rings, narcotics dealing, and brothels. At night, when the soldiers and policemen—and even the Shin Bet—retreated to the HQ building at the entrance to the Kasbah, the armed men, often in masks, would emerge to rule the streets.

Neighborhood residents knew which of their neighbors belonged to which organization. Owning a gun—which risked hefty prison time—or any other identifying paraphernalia marking a young tough as a "member" was a badge of honor. Hebron was the type of city where force earned respect and the factions were all about violence. In the days before cell phones and digital pagers, school kids were often recruited by the factions to serve as messengers. A child could earn a few liroth by carrying a message from an operative in an apartment to his contact selling poultry in the market. Many of the messages originated from coded statements read over radio stations in Damascus or Amman, which were, in turn, transformed into written orders dispatched on food wrappers, matchboxes, and packs of cigarettes. Young kids with guts and promise were recommended to join one of the youth gangs run by the factions.

According to his family, young Gazi Abu Mezer supported the Popular Front for the Liberation of Palestine, or PFLP.[1] The PFLP was a pan-Arab Marxist group preaching a communist revolution throughout the entire Arab world beginning with the liberation of

Palestine. It is unclear whether or not a teenage Gazi nurtured communist ideals. But the PFLP, founded and run by Dr. George Habash, a Greek Orthodox physician turned revolutionary, fielded some of the most brutal gangs operating inside the West Bank.

The gangs, with such names as the Black Panthers and the Red Eagles, perpetrated acts of terror against Israeli soldiers and policemen as well as against civilians. They specialized in torturing and murdering men—and women—who they suspected collaborated with the Israeli authorities. Men unfortunate enough to be suspected of being a *Ma'Shtap* were dragged from their homes, blindfolded, beaten, forced to sign a confession after a nightlong interrogation (meaning torture) session, and then shot and set alight; the terrorists would routinely pull the pin on a hand grenade and place the device underneath the smoldering corpse so that when Israeli security officials investigated the crime scene, the grenade would explode. Women, primarily prostitutes and young girls who might have dishonored their families, were tortured and raped to extract a confession. Their bodies were mutilated before they were executed.

Gazi, like any young teenager growing up inside Hebron during the years of occupation, would have been no stranger to violence and death. The bloodshed was, in fact, only beginning. By the time Gazi turned fifteen the West Bank was ablaze.

On the night of November 25, 1987, a Palestinian terrorist, doped up on amphetamines, flew through the silent dark night from southern Lebanon into Israel on a motorized hang glider. The terrorist's objective that night was to kill everyone living inside an apartment building in the town of Ma'alot, yet the gunman proceeded to attack an army outpost down the road. In a blaze of drug-induced fury, he killed six Israeli soldiers and wounded some sixty more before being killed. To the Israelis, the incident was but another in a long series of bloody assaults they had had to endure at the hands of Palestinian terrorists. To the Palestinians, however, and in particular those living under Israeli occupation in the Gaza Strip and West Bank, the attack was viewed as a symbolic opening salvo in the true war of Palestinian liberation—for the first time in years Israeli soldiers were targeted. Joy over the attack escalated into demonstrations—both organized and spontaneous—against Israeli occupation. Palestinian flags, outlawed under Israeli security codes, began to appear on the streets of the West Bank's towns and villages. Kids began setting tires on fire and hurling rocks at Israeli troops. The demonstrations, and subsequent violence, became known as the Intifada, or "Uprising."

The Intifada coincided with a new phenomenon sweeping through Gaza and the West Bank—fundamentalist Islam.

The rage of Islam had been brewing inside the souls of the Palestinians living in the crosshairs of the Arab-Israeli conflict since 1948, when Egypt's Muslim Brotherhood—a forebear of what would become al-Qaeda—sent a brigade of holy warriors to Israel to destroy the Jewish state. The message of the Brotherhood became entrenched in Gaza, where poverty pervaded the one million inhabitants living in the cramped squalor of 140 square miles. In Gaza, where Egyptian rule was brutal, the calls for an Islamic revolution began to appear as the sole salvation for the Palestinian people. The Egyptian military arrested hundreds in Gaza who displayed fundamentalist sympathies, including a young crippled cleric named Ahmed Yassin, who had permanently injured his spine while frolicking on the beach with friends. Yassin, a brilliant scholar who dedicated his life to the study and pursuit of Islam, realized that the Palestinian people could count on only Islam and themselves if they were to ever be liberated. Hamas, the acronym of "Islamic Resistance Movement" in Arabic, was born.

The spread of fundamentalist Islam coincided with the signing of the 1979 Camp David Peace Accords between Israel and Egypt,

and the Iranian revolution. Palestinians saw Egyptian president Sa-
dat's selling out to Israel—the Sinai Desert in exchange for a peace
treaty—as a typical Arab betrayal of the Palestinian people. The
Camp David Accords were proof to many that secular Arab regimes,
in Cairo, Amman, Damascus, and even the PLO in Beirut, were
simply out to bankrupt their principles and the faith of their
people and cut the best deal they could arrange with the infidel
Jewish state. Egypt, the beacon of Arab military might and political
thought, had capitulated. No other political system could be trusted
to deal with the Israeli problem, it was argued in the mosques and
religious centers of Gaza, Hebron, and Nablus. Only Islam held the
key. . . . Only Islam could liberate Palestine.

The dream for an Islamic liberation of Palestine was enhanced
by the Iranian revolution. The Ayatollah Khomeini's uprising against
a pro-Western and corrupt monarch became a source of great inspiration and pride inside the Gaza Strip and West Bank; it did not
matter that the Iranians—Shiites—and the Palestinians—Sunnis—
had historically been at odds with one another.

In the wake of the Iranian Islamic resurgence the number of
mosques in the West Bank nearly doubled. In 1978, the Islamic
University in Gaza, considered by many to be a headquarters of
operations for the Brotherhood, was opened. At that time, as well,
immigration laws in Europe and the United States were relaxed; in
America, an increasing percentage of those allowed entry were
Muslims from the Asian subcontinent and the Arab world. Many
were Palestinian. Many of these newcomers to the United States
had opted to leave their homes to escape religious persecution.
They established a series of mosques and cultural institutions
throughout the United States—many in large urban areas, such as
New York City, Chicago, and Los Angeles. Many of these immigrants would establish successful businesses and excel in varied professional and academic careers.

In 1978, supported by funds coming in from Palestinian émigré communities in North America, Sheikh Ahmed Yassin formally established Hamas and registered it with the Israeli military authorities in Gaza. The Shin Bet viewed this new Islamic organization as a political counterweight to the other Palestinian factions. The Israelis allowed Hamas to open schools, clinics, and other institutions throughout Gaza. Membership in Hamas grew with each passing week of firebrands' sermons and promises of religious salvation from the poverty and pervasive misery of life under the Israeli gun; *zakat,* or charity, one of the pillars of Islam, was openly distributed to the poor and disillusioned. Unlike Fatah or the Popular Front, which helped only those who paid a hefty tax, Hamas helped virtually everyone who needed assistance. Hamas did not present itself to the Palestinian people as a corrupt organization. It did not indulge in illegal criminal activity; Hamas gangs, in fact, much to the Shin Bet's amusement, violently attacked Fatah and PFLP drug dens and brothels.

Secretly, though, Hamas did not pursue a solely benevolent course. Hard-core followers of Yassin established small groups, or cells, that gathered intelligence and sought out weapons. In 1982 Yassin was arrested by the Shin Bet and charged with terrorist conspiracy. He was released three years later as part of an exchange of fifteen hundred terrorists for three Israeli POWs in 1985. Yassin returned to Gaza and decided to push his Islamic revolution into a full-speed assault toward open conflict. Yassin ordered emissaries to set up an organizational operations center in Amman, where the Muslim Brotherhood had made considerable political gains, and had offices opened throughout the world. These branches were to gather in funds and support from the sizable Palestinian and Islamic communities that were well established throughout Europe and North America; the European headquarters site became London and the U.S. headquarters was in Virginia. The organization received donations from Saudi Arabia and even Shiite Iran. With a free flow of cash, Yassin and his terrorist commanders were able to establish military cells, communications networks, and stockpiles of weapons and explosives. By the time the Intifada erupted, Hamas had become a dominant religious and military force to be reckoned with in the West Bank.

Yassin was able to build a strong network of social and resistance entities courtesy of cash—a lot of it. Initially, most of the Hamas financial assets came as a result of donations made by wealthy businessmen in Saudi Arabia and the Gulf States. According to conservative Israeli intelligence estimates, Hamas networks in the West Bank alone operated on a stipend exceeding one million dollars a year. The funds were filtered through foundations and charities, highly laundered, until they made it to the cells and operatives in the field. Hamas separated its political wing from its military operations in Gaza and the West Bank; in Gaza, the force was known as the Izzedine al-Qassam Brigades, and in the West Bank, the Hamas military force was called the Abdullah Azzam Brigades. The Azzam Brigades, named after the West Bank–born Islamic cleric who traveled to Afghanistan in 1979 to set up a base of operations for the Islamic volunteers fighting the Soviets alongside Osama bin Laden, was especially strong in Hebron.

Gazi Abu Mezer was—like all Palestinian teenagers during those tumultuous Intifada years, when schools were closed, citywide strikes paralyzed complete economies, and Israeli roadblocks limited which Palestinians could travel and where—an active participant in the uprising. "There wasn't a kid around with two healthy arms and legs who didn't throw Molotov cocktails, stones, or fire a zip gun at Israeli forces," reflected Colonel M., a veteran IDF commander who operated in Hebron in 1990. "If a kid didn't participate in the conflict, he was considered an outcast and a traitor."[2] One hundred kids could be standing at the entrance to the Kasbah in Hebron hurling rocks and bottles at Israeli forces ordered to stand down and absorb the blows, yet the moment the Israelis were ordered in and arrests were made, those seized suffered a difficult ordeal.

Gazi Abu Mezer was arrested twice for his Intifada activities—once in 1990 and once in 1991—and he spent a week in Israeli security detention each time. Little is known of Mezer's time while incarcerated, but it couldn't have been easy. Suspects rounded up spent days without the chance to see parents or representation—they were fed, interrogated, and unleashed into a general population of bombers, murderers, thieves, and other criminals. Although the treatment that a Palestinian detained by Israel might be subjected to was more humane than the treatment he would receive at the hands of security officials in Jordan, Egypt, Syria, or Iraq, the experience must have been a grueling ordeal. Detention facilities were also ripe recruiting stations for Hamas. Teenagers swept up in Israeli dragnets, sitting in a corner and weeping after wetting themselves in detention, were consoled and reassured by the men from the Azzam Brigades. Whereas Fatah and PFLP men would routinely fold under questioning, the Hamas operatives refused to succumb to the tricks—and torture—of the Shin Bet. The men from Hamas remained silent when pressed for answers and they refused to cry when beaten. They were symbols of defiance and inner strength.

Although Mezer's family, in interviews given later, commented that Gazi was always a good and happy child, the weeks of being detained without charge by the Israelis changed him. His expression became a dour one. He became angry and spoke of leaving Hebron.

About thirty miles away from the tumult of Hebron, along a circuitous path that skirted Jerusalem to the north, lived another teenager also affected by the chaos of the Intifada. His name was Lafi Khalil and he was born on October 24, 1974, in the town of Ajoul, an upscale suburb of Ramallah. Ajoul was the kind of place that, had it been in any other part of the world, would be the hometown that produced doctors, lawyers, and professionals. Ramallah, situated just a few miles north of Jerusalem, was known as the Beverly Hills of the West Bank, and the small villages that made up the city's suburbs were where many of the West Bank's richest and most prominent families came from. Unlike Hebron, where religious passion flowed through the arteries of the city's inhabitants, Ajoul was a secular village where Christians and Muslims lived side by side. Because of its affluence, and because of its proximity to Jerusalem, where many of the town's residents worked, support for the Intifada was muted. Parents made sure that their kids went to school—when the schools were open—and fathers and mothers dreamed that their sons and daughters would travel far from the bloodshed to advance their studies in the great universities in Amman, Cairo, or Beirut.

"He was a balanced person who had always been friendly with everybody," Lafi's uncle, Suhail Mifleh Khalil, said of his nephew.[3] Lafi Khalil lived an anonymous and typical childhood growing up in the West Bank's most lavish precinct. He never involved himself in politics or rebellion, family members would later comment, and he was always a good student. There are no Israeli reports of his ever being detained, arrested, or monitored for security-related offenses. In fact, his academic history indicates he was always a good student and was even on the honor roll.

Hamas, however, had slowly infiltrated even the most opulent suburbs and villages throughout the West Bank—including Ajoul. Many Palestinians who had emigrated from the territories years before to find freedom and fortune in America were the most fervent supporters of Sheikh Yassin's religious movement. They donated hundreds of thousands of dollars into the Hamas coffer, and provided support and covert assistance to the organization; they returned to the land of their birth to buy homes and invest their fortunes. Many of those Palestinians came from places like Ajoul,

Bir Naballah, and the dozens of other villages that dotted the greater Ramallah vicinity. Hamas posters soon began to appear along the walls in the village; Hamas graffiti, calling for the death of the Jews, were scribbled along stone fences. At night, the men of the Azzam Brigades removed their Uzi submachine guns and M16 assault rifles (stolen from the Israeli military or purchased from Israeli criminals) from their caches and patrolled the village in black masks and green bandannas adorned with Islamic sayings. To parents with dreams of having their children escape the madness, the Hamas squads were a daunting and foreboding reality. A village that had been left unscarred by the Arab-Israeli conflict was now becoming its front line.

Hamas operatives used to enjoy telling their Israeli interrogators that there was nothing that anyone could do to them since they were living in a sort of purgatory, with one foot in prison and one foot in the grave. And to thousands of young and angry Palestinian men who were infatuated by the notion of waging a holy war against Israel, the call to arms was an infectious and inescapable force.

Yet both Gazi Abu Mezer and Lafi Khalil appeared determined to escape purgatory. Even though they lived only thirty miles from one another, neither knew the other one growing up; in the tribal-minded world of the territories, any world outside your street or village was considered foreign. Yet both young men were united by a common dream to escape, one way or another, the hell of the West Bank. Both young men dreamed of somewhere else. Both men dreamed of the United States of America.

America, America

There wasn't a Palestinian in the West Bank who didn't know what 27 Nablus Road in East Jerusalem was. The address, like 1600 Pennsylvania Avenue, was a symbol of promise and power. It was where a Palestinian could fill out forms, pray, and hope. It was a place where dreams were made and hopes dashed. It was the consular section of the U.S. Consulate in East Jerusalem.

In the local slang, the school-like building made out of neatly chiseled blocks of Jerusalem stone near the American Colony Hotel was called the "Hill of Shattered Dreams." It was where a family head, armed with his birth certificates, high school diploma, college transcripts, and other personal documentation could attempt to get one foot through the door out of the West Bank and into the United States. People gathered outside the building just after dawn each and every day—Monday to Friday—for the three hours—eight thirty a.m. to eleven thirty a.m.—when applications were processed; it was important to get to the consulate early to get a good spot on line and hopefully not have to wait too long. It was rumored that those who came in near closing were subjected to clerks who were tired, angry, and in no mood to hear sob stories. It was best to come early.

The consulate filled up pretty quickly each business day. The reception area was usually filled to capacity with men dressed in suits they purchased in Amman weeks before that they hoped could make a good impression, while others wore the traditional *galabiyah* and rags that their fathers had worn before them. Many were taking care of the endless forms needed in the bureaucracy of immigration, ensuring that they had filled out everything correctly. Some were married to American citizens; others had spouses, siblings, or children who were green card holders. Some, the small minority, had jobs waiting for them in the Midwest or in a major city, reserved for them by either a corporation or a relative. Others, simply burned-out by the rigors of day-to-day life in the West Bank, were hoping for a small miracle that would qualify them for an immigrant visa to live and work in the United States.

Of course anyone with security-related offenses against his record, meaning terrorist charges, had no chance of receiving a visa. The American background checks were stringent, and the Shin Bet and the Israel National Police records were exemplary. Thousands were disqualified for their past crimes—Gazi Abu Mezer among them.

For every system that requires forms filled out in triplicate, notarized school records, a "no arrest" certificate from the police, and a doctor's exam, there arc ways to cheat and manipulate your way through it. Those whom the State Department and the Immigration and Naturalization Service (INS) might have viewed as nondesirables could always come to the United States courtesy of the side door—the long and poorly secured border with Canada. Unlike the United States, which vetted potential immigrants with layers of scrutiny and requirements, Canada was a large and underpopulated nation that made it much easier for immigrants of all economic and political persuasions to receive an accommodation. Whereas the U.S. State Department would automatically knock out political-asylum requests from people whose fears did not meet a list of criteria, Canada's open-door policy made it a conceivable reality for anyone who could tell a tall tale and feign discrimination to get an official invitation to settle or study there.

Gazi Abu Mezer would, indeed, make it to the United States, but it would have to be from the north.

Unlike the U.S. State Department, the Canadian government did not have an office catering to the Palestinian population in the West Bank and Gaza—those hoping to study or work in Canada had to travel to Tel Aviv, to the Canadian embassy on Nirim Street, where diplomats and consular representatives were more than happy to assist immigrant hopefuls on their applications. On May 19, 1993, Gazi Abu Mezer took a *sherut* cab from a Palestinian stand in East Jerusalem to Tel Aviv in order to apply for a Canadian student visa from the Canadian embassy. Tel Aviv might have been only sixty miles from Hebron, but in reality the two cities were centuries apart. Tel Aviv was a modern, bustling metropolis with skyscrapers, shopping malls, gridlocked traffic, beaches, and a nightlife that could have been the envy of a European city; if you removed the automobiles and Coca-Cola signs from the Hebron of 1993, as well as the TV antennae, what was left would look pretty much the same way it did four hundred years prior. Before the Hamas suicide bombings commenced and details of Israel's top secret negotiations with the PLO in Oslo became public knowledge, a West Bank Palestinian could travel to Tel Aviv undisturbed—tens of thousands did, in fact, to work in the country's construction industry and menial-labor market. Security checkpoints, ferreting out Palestinians entering Israel from the West Bank, were minimal. The caveat was, though, that the Palestinians had to be back in their homes by dark.

The Canadians were benevolent when it came to helping those seeking to live or study in the provinces. Embassy employees guided Abu Mezer through the process. There were no security questions to be asked, no mention of the Popular Front, Hamas, or time inside a Shin Bet lockup.

With his Canadian application signed, sealed, delivered, and being processed, Abu Mezer stood on line outside the Israeli military headquarters and security facility in Hebron to obtain a travel permit. Even though West Bank residents were entitled to obtain Jordanian passports, a Palestinian couldn't cross the Allenby Bridge over the Jordan River to travel to the Hashemite Kingdom, or depart Israel's Ben Gurion International Airport, without the signed and stamped approval of the local military governor. Whether or not the Israeli military granted a travel permit depended on numerous factors: was the applicant involved in terrorist activity and would he make contact with terrorist groups in Jordan or elsewhere in the Arab world? Was he wanted for any crimes? Sometimes the decision on whether or not to permit a Palestinian to travel was arbitrary.

The fact that he was detained—yet never charged—on two separate security violations might have forever hindered Abu Mezer's attempts to get out of the West Bank, but on July 6, 1993, Mezer was issued a travel document from the Israeli government allowing him to travel to any country that would grant him a visa; he would be permitted back into Israel provided that he returned to the country no later than July 5, 1994.

The travel document was Abu Mezer's catch-22 official invitation to Canada—the Canadian government did not check an applicant's criminal record when determining whether or not to grant a visa, and they considered the fact that Abu Mezer was issued an Israeli travel permit to be proof that he was a solid citizen. On September 10, 1993, the Canadian embassy in Tel Aviv granted Mezer a one-entry, T-1 visitor/student visa. The visa permitted him to stay in Canada as long as he was enrolled as a student there.

Just exactly where Gazi Abu Mezer received the funds to travel to Canada, let alone the means to live there and rent an apartment or buy food, remains—like so many aspects of Gazi Abu Mezer's life—an absolute mystery. Terrorist groups did sometimes finance someone wishing to flee the territories in exchange for a favor down the road. It was a very Byzantine arrangement, but it was practiced all the time. "It was very much like that scene in the movie *The God-father*," Y., a former Shin Bet agent, explained, "when Marlon Brando tells that undertaker, after agreeing to do a favor for him, that 'one day, and that day may never come, I might call upon you to do a service for me. . . . ' Well, that's how things worked in the territories, especially when someone needed cash or help from one of the terrorist groups. Get me this, get me that, help me travel overseas, and if you ever need something from me, don't hesitate to ask."[1]

It was, in retrospect, fitting that Gazi Abu Mezer left the Middle East on September 14, 1993—the day after Israeli prime minister Yitzhak Rabin and PLO chairman Yasir Arafat stood for what would become the timeless image of the two of them shaking hands on the White House lawn. September 13 would be a day that would forever change the Middle East and cause every fanatical element—something there is no shortage of there—to respond with violence. September 13 was the day that propelled Hamas from a group that Israel still didn't consider a major threat to her national security to one of the most zealous and homicidal terrorist organizations in the world. Yet by the time Hamas began to rally public support against the peace accords between Israel and the PLO by staging violent demonstrations, waving swords in the air and promising to liberate Jerusalem and kill the Jewish presence in the holy land of Palestine, Gazi Abu Mezer was flying over the Atlantic. Masked men, holding the Koran, vowed to fight the peace treaty with the blood in their bodies and the fire in their souls. It would have been a good show for Abu Mezer to see, though by the time the Israeli military was breaking up the display near the al-Ibrahimi mosque, Gazi Abu Mezer was in a cab heading toward downtown Toronto. From there his next stop would be America, by any means at his disposal.

According to his request for a student visa, Gazi Abu Mezer wanted to study business administration. Instead he enrolled in a few English-language courses. He lived hand to mouth, renting rooms in the city's Middle Eastern neighborhoods, where transients from

Lebanon, Syria, Egypt, Algeria, and Morocco, as well as Palestinians, converged. Very little is known about his activities in Toronto, with a few exceptions.

On September 23, 1993, less than two weeks after arriving in Canada, Gazi Abu Mezer climbed the stairs of the Osgoode subway station on the Yonge-University-Spadina Yellow Line, and walked the few blocks to the U.S. Consulate General on University Avenue. There, he queued several times to get the proper forms needed to apply for a visa to enter the United States—ostensibly to visit as a tourist.* Having made it to Canada with little difficulty, Abu Mezer must have thought that his path to America would be equally obstacle free. The U.S. State Department and the Immigration and Naturalization Service did not believe the twenty-year-old Palestinian's story that he would return to Canada within the required time frame of the requested visa and issued a routine refusal of the application. There were many factors that could have influenced the State Department's decision, such as his age, lack of family and finances, or the fact that he was originally from the West Bank. Regardless of the reason, Abu Mezer was not permitted to enter the United States legally. There were, of course, other ways in.

On November 12, 1993, Gazi Abu Mezer filed an application with the Canadian Immigration and Refugee Board to be considered a Convention Refugee, or CR, in Canada; CR status, similar to the classification for political refugees in the United States, is awarded to individuals who demonstrate a well-founded fear of persecution in their home country for reasons of race, religion, nationality, membership in a particular social group, or political opinion; in a world of small and ugly wars, this made almost anyone from the Third World a prime candidate. A CR applicant is allowed, under the guidelines of Canadian law, to remain inside

---

* At the time, visa requests were destroyed after one year of the initial paperwork submission, so the exact nature of Abu Mezer's request is not known.

Canada while his or her case is pending, with one caveat: if the applicant leaves Canada while the case is in the works, Canada is *not* obligated to reaccept him back into the wide and warm embrace of the Great White North. Grudgingly, Canadian security officials admit that CR status is as good as gold;[2] an individual who receives CR status is afforded virtually all the rights handed to Canadian citizens—with the exception of voting.

Canada has one of the highest approval rates for political-asylum applicants in the world.

In June 1994 the Canadian Immigration and Refugee Board held an initial hearing on Gazi Abu Mezer's application and determined that the young Palestinian did, indeed, meet the necessary criteria to qualify for CR status. On July 5, 1994, Gazi Abu Mezer formally applied for political asylum in Canada.

Little is known of Gazi Abu Mezer's years in Canada—his time in the country is, according to some Canadian Security Intelligence Service officers, "enigmatic."[3] He enrolled in English-language courses in Toronto and worked at odd jobs. He also managed to enter the Canadian criminal justice system. Gazi Abu Mezer was arrested twice in 1994—once on an assault charge and the other time for credit card fraud.[4] He was sentenced to a year of unsupervised probation for each charge.

Leaving Toronto for the wide-open spaces of British Columbia, Gazi Abu Mezer had followed the advice that was popular chatter in the Arab coffeehouses, falafel stands, and other Middle Eastern haunts of Toronto—namely, if one wanted to smuggle himself into the United States, the border in the Midwest and Pacific Northwest wasn't guarded as proactively as the regions around Ontario. Canada was an easy point of entry for illegals entering the United States. While heavily armed Border Patrol agents attempted to stem the tide of illegal aliens crossing the Rio Grande from Mexico along the southern frontier, most portions of the border separating the United States from Canada weren't even marked off by fences. The border was a region of commerce and goodwill. To get from one side of the border to the other a traveler needed only to show a driver's license; often, driving a car with the state's corresponding license plates was enough.

For a veteran of the Kasbah who had survived the occupation and the Intifada, and the temptations of the various terrorist factions, crossing an unsupervised border *should* have been a piece of cake. Much of the invisible frontier was isolated, or in rural areas where watchful eyes were nowhere to be found. It was, as one INS agent who worked the border separating Canada from North Dakota would comment, "the easiest place in the world to disappear into."[5]

For twenty-nine months Abu Mezer languished as a transient in a nation where foreigners from every walk of life, every race and religion, were offered every opportunity in the world. For a survivor, one with skill and a determined spirit, Canada could have been the promised land. But it appears that Canada was never on the young Palestinian's agenda. Not with America there for the taking.

Gazi Abu Mezer's first attempt to cross the border came in 1996.

According to a report compiled by the Department of Justice, Office of the Investigator General, Gazi Abu Mezer's name first became a blip on the U.S. law enforcement radar in February 1996. Connie Dennison, a constable with the Royal Canadian Mounted Police, stopped and questioned an Arab named Haikal Khaldon in Winnipeg, Manitoba, after he had come back and forth across the U.S.-Canadian border. The border was a notoriously easy crossing between Emerson and Pembina, North Dakota; Khaldon said he lived in Minneapolis, Minnesota, and was meeting a young Palestinian named Gazi Abu Mezer in Winnipeg to discuss opening a business. Mezer was never arrested, detained, or questioned, but his name was inserted into a federal law enforcement computer system. At the time there was no centralized and coordinated database recording all immigration-related criminal questionings along the U.S.-Canada border.

There were numerous established crossing points along the thirty-five hundred miles of border between the United States and Canada controlled by regional INS and U.S. Customs Service field offices—they were spread out in such places as Houlton, Maine; Swanton, Vermont; Buffalo, New York; Detroit, Michigan; Grand Forks, North Dakota; Havre, Montana; and Spokane and Blaine, Washington. The "Blaine Sector" was considered one of the easiest to cross illegally. Traffic in the sector—tourist and commercial— was frenetic. Over 1.5 million people crossed the border points annually, along a sector that covered some one hundred miles of frontier spread from the Puget Sound on the west coast of Washington to the Cascade Mountains in the central part of the state.* Because it was so heavily traveled, INS records indicated that there were more arrests in that area than in any other stretch of border between the two nations. Resources assigned to the sector, however, were not great—fewer than twenty-five agents and supervisors secured the vast and rough terrain. There were times that the frontier was completely unmanned between midnight and morning's first light. To make traffic flow, INS and Customs Service agents attempted to limit inspections of vehicles—for both contraband and illegal aliens—to seconds. Aliens attempting to cross from Canada into the United States believed that the area was so busy with legitimate traffic that inspecting agents and patrolling law enforcement units were bound to be sloppy and make mistakes— especially since so many Canadians worked in the United States and commuted across the border daily, as did numerous Washington State residents who worked in neighboring British Columbia.

---

*It is interesting to note that in December 1999, in another terrorist incident originating in the Arab émigré community in Canada, an Algerian named Ahmed Rassam attempted to cross the border into the United States in Port Angeles, Washington, with a carful of explosives, planning to blow up parts of Los Angeles International Airport (LAX) in what would become known as the Millennium Plot.

Penalties for illegals crossing over in the sector were also reported to be the most lenient along the border. Most of those apprehended—with the exception of wanted felons—were returned voluntarily. "The policy was one of 'Tough luck, mate, but we got you,'" claimed a Canadian law enforcement official. "It was as if both sides said, 'Better luck next time.'"[6] Other illegals were released on their own recognizance, or given time periods—generally thirty days—to leave the United States on their own.

Gazi Abu Mezer's first attempt to enter the United States was an unsuccessful one. On June 23, 1996, he was picked up around Ross Lake, a rugged patch of wilderness that looked like the perfect backdrop for a Hollywood western, in the North Cascades National Park in Washington State. The terrain was beautiful yet, for a novice, treacherous—the lake, and its surrounding water traps, could easily swallow a man who did not know how to traverse the hills, gullies, and mazelike forests. At about five p.m., according to the INS report, tourists enjoying the splendid wildlife and nature summoned help from the Ross Lake Resort for a young man, believed to be in his twenties, along the lake. Ninety minutes later, two National Park Service rangers spotted Gazi Abu Mezer being assisted by bewildered tourists who were ferrying him to the southern shore of the placid body of water. He was disheveled, agitated, and frightened. Abu Mezer was suffering from hypothermia.

The two rangers, eager to assist, first asked Abu Mezer for some ID. His response was a line he would repeat throughout his failed efforts to enter the United States: "I am a Palestinian and a citizen of Jordan." He also said that he was traveling with a friend who had separated from him over seven hours earlier. Abu Mezer had crossed the border with a friend, Jamal Abed, who, authorities suspect, was the smuggler bringing the Palestinian across. Abed had a Washington State driver's license and an address in Seattle, but he was a Canadian immigrant; he was Kuwaiti born—citizenship wasn't a birthright in Kuwait—with a Jordanian passport, which led authorities to suspect that he was possibly Palestinian. When he was apprehended a short while later, the rangers found six hundred dollars in cash on Abed, which they believed was the fee Abu Mezer paid to be taken across the border. Abu Mezer told the rangers that he was camping with his friend, but that the two had gotten lost in the wilderness.

"Facilitators," as the men who smuggled the illegals across the border were called, were not hard to find in British Columbia—a province known as a stepping-off point for those hoping to enter the United States illegally. A gateway for the Chinese, British Columbia was also a favorite point of departure for Indians, Pakistanis, Bangladeshis, Africans, and Middle Easterners seeking the promised land of the fifty states. In the ethnic food haunts all along the path to Vancouver, bulletin boards listed the pager numbers of men who, for a nominal fee, could guarantee a border crossing. The signs, often handwritten with perforated slips for the facilitator's telephone information, were in a multitude of languages and offered services for a range of fees depending on the number of people needing to cross the border. If a facilitator was savvy, able to rough it up a bit along the rugged border areas, the trade was incredibly lucrative and risk free. And, when caught, facilitators—and their cargo—faced virtually no jail time at all.

The following morning the Park Service handed Abu Mezer and Abed over to Special Agent Dave Hatton from the Border Patrol.

The policy in cases such as Abu Mezer's arrest was that the alien be fingerprinted and checked through the national criminal justice computer, and if his record was clean, he was to be either deported or voluntarily returned to Canada. Although deportation was viewed as the more legally prudent option in dealing with someone who had transgressed the law, the number of available beds in the nearby detention facility often determined how much to the letter the law was carried out. Beds were always scarce. Four years earlier INS had permitted Ramzi Yousef, the mastermind behind the February 26, 1993, bombing of the World Trade Center in New York

City, to be released on his own recognizance after arriving at JFK International Airport with a bad Swedish passport; although Yousef's claim that he had come to the United States in order to seek political asylum was not believed by investigating agents at the airport, there were no beds left at the INS detention center, and as a result Yousef was let go until a hearing could be scheduled before an immigration judge. Although the bombing of the World Trade Center and the widely publicized hole in the INS bureaucracy that had allowed Yousef to penetrate America's borders with little difficulty had caused lawmakers to demand that scrutiny at the country's border crossings be intensified to keep terrorists out, the Border Patrol and INS were still operating under the traditional view that keeping illegal aliens out of the United States was purely economic. National security was *still* not a factor. The agents working the border looked for illegals out to steal jobs, and drug traffickers plying the lucrative routes back and forth across the border with Asian heroin heading south and methamphetamine going north. No one bothered to look out for terrorists.

Neither Abu Mezer nor Abed had a criminal record in the United States and there were no outstanding warrants for either's arrest. After checking with his counterparts in Canadian Immigration at the border crossing in Huntington, British Columbia, to discuss the Abu Mezer case, Special Agent Hatton was informed that Abu Mezer had been admitted to Canada as a student and that Abed had permanent-residence status in Canada. Both men, through Canadian eyes at least, were okay.

On June 24 Abu Mezer was reluctantly returned to Canada but not before the Border Patrol agents instinctively thought it prudent to fingerprint the young Palestinian—just in case. . . .

Five days after his armed escort back to Canada, Gazi Abu Mezer was once again on the move south toward the United States. On June 29, 1996, Border Patrol agent Neal Clark apprehended

Mezer again as he attempted to enter the United States some sixty-
five miles west of Ross Lake. This time Abu Mezer didn't rely on
the advertised—and expensive—talents of a shepherd. This time,
he tried it solo.

Gazi Abu Mezer donned a tracksuit and a Walkman, and jogged
through Peace Arch Park, a large open area next to the port of entry in Blaine, Washington. When he thought it was clear he simply
crossed the border at a mild trot. Abu Mezer claimed to be a Canadian citizen when confronted by Agent Clark, who wasn't fooled by
the Palestinian's charade; having seen and heard it all before, Clark
must have been amused by the comical image of the young man
jogging, his eyes racing around in every which way looking for the
law as he crossed the invisible line separating Canada from the
United States. At first Abu Mezer told the Border Patrol agent that
he was a Canadian citizen, but the Palestinian's acting skills—and his
command of English—left much to be desired. The story quickly
changed. As Agent Clark folded his arms and listened to Abu Mezer
stammer, the story got better. Without the duress and fear of an Israeli lockup and a chin-wag with a Shin Bet, Abu Mezer surren-
dered his masquerade and his will to the American border inspector.
At first Abu Mezer recanted his Canadian tale and admitted that he
was a student. Then, moments later, he was a Canadian Convention
Refugee, and realizing that the word "Palestinian" might arouse
suspicion, Abu Mezer told the agent that he was an Israeli. Abu
Mezer told Agent Clark that he would love to show him his identifying documents, but they were in his car parked on the Canadian
side of the border. But that story, like all the tales not holding tall in
the wind that afternoon, soon collapsed. Mezer was carrying 500
dollars in U.S. currency, and 260 dollars in Canadian bills. He was
led back to the Blaine station house in handcuffs.

It took only the briefest of radio exchanges for the Border Patrol
agents to realize that Abu Mezer had been arrested just days earlier.

Abu Mezer had committed a misdemeanor crime after being voluntarily returned several days earlier. But there was no point in pressing
the matter further. It would have been pleaded down to a nothing
charge. The Palestinian would have spent weeks and thousands of
dollars of taxpayer money to, in the end, apologize and walk across
the border once again. A judge would have probably laughed the
case out of court. Gazi Abu Mezer spent all of sixty minutes in the
United States that warm June day. He was walked grudgingly across
the border at the Douglas port of entry back to Canada.

Border Patrol agents wrote several reports about the Abu Mezer
arrest, and the Palestinian was linked to what the law enforcement
officials feared was an alien smuggling ring. The belief was that the
young Arab male was nothing more than a human pincushion tasked
with checking out which spots in the sector were easiest to cross.

For nearly seven months Gazi Abu Mezer fell off the face of the
map, disappearing into the émigré communities of British Columbia, no doubt plotting his next attempt to cross the border into the
United States. To this day exactly how the young Palestinian supported himself remains a mystery.

On the evening of January 14, 1997, Border Patrol agent Dar-
ryl Essing pulled into the Bellingham bus station, some twenty-five
miles from the Canadian border and Blaine station, working the
four-to-twelve shift. Because he was the only Border Patrol agent
working that night along the much traveled boulevards of the
illegal-alien highway, Agent Essing concentrated his efforts on
popular hangouts where undocumented aliens tended to gather.
Fast-food hangouts were favorite targets of the INS agents who
worked the shift, as were areas where drugs were sold and
women—and young boys—sold their bodies. Greyhound bus stops
in the area that connected the small towns with Seattle, Tacoma,
and the state's other cities were the most lucrative targets when an

agent wanted to make surefire arrests. The night buses were the best. The illegals loved to move in the darkness.

The three Middle Eastern men chattering away as they prepared to board a bus to Seattle lit up Agent Essing's radar like a neon sign. The men, nervous and looking like they didn't belong, were soon pulled to the side and questioned by the Border Patrol agent. The questions were simple; the answers were truly Byzantine. None of the three Arabs could satisfy the experienced agent's curiosity about their immigration status. When confronted by Essing, the three rolled their eyes upward and began to stammer out tales of why they were waiting for a bus in Washington State. The stories were ridiculous and the men seemed more agitated and frightened with each new question. The three were placed up against the wall, frisked, and then handcuffed until backup from the local sheriff's office could arrive and help bring them back to the Bellingham Border Patrol station. The three men arrested that night—Fires Taleb Mohammad, an Iraqi citizen, Mohammad Khalil from Jordan, and Hebron native Gazi Abu Mezer—were processed by the agents. Agent Essing knew that this was going to be a long night.

The arrest was a blow to the young Palestinian's dreams. How wonderful a feeling it must have been, after initial failure, to have finally made it undetected into the United States. He had crossed the border without worrying about a lake or twisting his ankle jogging. This time he didn't need to pay a facilitator, nor did he have to worry about drawing attention to himself as he waited for the right moment. He was walking on American soil and closer than he had ever been to fulfilling his dream of forever leaving Canada behind. But twenty-five miles into a journey that by now was nearly four years old, Gazi Abu Mezer was once again lowering his head in order not to whack his skull as he entered the backseat of a police car, arrested for a third time while trying to enter America. How could a survivor of the Israeli occupation not successfully slink past a virtually unprotected border?

This time, however, the catch-22 of evaporated Canadian benevolence gave the Palestinian the "in" he had so desperately sought for so long.

Because of his arrests in the United States and because of his criminal history in Toronto, the Canadians informed the U.S. Border Patrol that Abu Mezer would not be welcomed back—not this time. Deportation, therefore, would be back to the West Bank through the Israelis, and this scared Abu Mezer immensely. Gazi Abu Mezer admitted to being a Palestinian and, for the first time since his arrival in North America, he confided that he had been arrested and jailed for throwing rocks at Israeli soldiers. Perhaps Abu Mezer felt that relinquishing the burden of his past to the Border Patrol might buy him sympathy, and perhaps that would make someone turn a blind eye; after all, in the Middle East, sympathy accompanied by a tall tale and a healthy bribe was enough to make worlds turn. Yet Abu Mezer's confessional did nothing more than raise red flags. An Iraqi, a Jordanian, and a Palestinian—traveling together—spelled only one word to a law enforcement agent—terrorist.

In the perfect world—where by-the-book actually meant something—the typical procedure for dealing with an individual in Abu Mezer's position with his track record would be deportation. Once again Gazi Abu Mezer had reached the gates of the promised land only to be cast away.

Gazi Abu Mezer was charged with the misdemeanor offense of EWI, or Entry Without Inspection; charging the Palestinian with a misdemeanor was pure tactics—if he was ever caught trying to enter the United States illegally again, the charge would then become a felony and guarantee him time in federal lockup and a no-questions-asked backseat on a TWA Boeing 767 to Tel Aviv in handcuffs next to two deputy U.S. Marshals. A fifteen-thousand-dollar bond was recommended for Gazi Abu Mezer—five thousand dollars more than for the two other Arabs—because of his alleged smuggling-ring ties and criminal record. The amount, though, could have been a million dollars—in Seattle, aliens have to pay the full bond amount, because bail bond companies will not issue bonds in deportation cases due to the high risk of flight. Abu Mezer, without the resources to defend himself and without hope of beating the system in a deportation proceeding, declared the need to claim political asylum on the grounds that his life was threatened should he return to Israel. The Palestinian had turned the tables on his captors. He now had a chance to fight.

There would be several hearings in Abu Mezer's legitimate attempts to remain in the United States. Throughout January 1997 INS attorneys and a federal immigration judge bickered on Abu Mezer's status in repeated motions. At a January 27, 1997, hearing the judge signed an Order of Deportation to Canada, with the understanding that if Canada would not accept Mezer, the INS could reopen the case and Mezer would have the opportunity to initiate an asylum claim. Canada, however, refused to take the Palestinian back, so deportation proceedings to Israel were initiated. Yet after three years in North America, Gazi Abu Mezer had learned the system. He knew that anything involving a court or a magistrate delayed the works like a wrench tossed into a gearbox. If he could remain in the system, somehow involved in one court proceeding or another, he would have a chance. Living in the West Bank taught young kids that life was lived on a day-to-day basis. If you could live one more day, be there to fight one more day, you never knew what might happen. Gazi Abu Mezer was not about to surrender and head back to Israel without a struggle. Being returned to Israel with a Canadian and American criminal record would have red-flagged him as a case to be watched and monitored. For a man who lied his way to Canada and Whatcom County, Washington, the fear of being returned to the clutches—and questions—of the Shin Bet was genuine.

It was here, when he was almost certain to head back to Israel, that Abu Mezer formally made his plea for political asylum. Whether or not the request was granted was immaterial. The Palestinian was determined never to head back to the West Bank again.

In a hearing on February 6, 1997, Abu Mezer requested that his bond be reduced: "It's too high," he told Judge Anna Ho, according to INS reports. The purpose of bond, of course, was to guarantee that the defendant would actually appear at his proceeding— the amount of bond demanded by the court depended on the crime, the defendant's record, and other mitigating circumstances, such as his links to the community, and family and employment ties. On paper, Gazi Abu Mezer was a poster child for those "held without bond." With no links to the community and a dubious criminal past, Abu Mezer should have been wearing orange coveralls and eating bologna sandwiches in the Seattle federal lockup until his trial, but Judge Ho believed his claim that he had a group of friends in Seattle who would help him post bond, and that he had relatives living in Chicago. Judge Ho, in her infinite wisdom, reduced the bond to five thousand dollars. No one from the U.S. Attorney's office or the INS ever bothered to check out Abu Mezer's claim.

On February 14, 1997, as Abu Mezer was busy filling out his motion for asylum, Hussam Abu Eisheh, an illegal alien from Jordan and a Seattle cabdriver, posted a five-thousand-dollar cashier's check to settle the Palestinian's bond. Abu Eisheh had a Seattle address and a social security number; he had overstayed a student visa after dropping out of Indiana University of Pennsylvania. According to reports, Abu Eisheh, at Abu Mezer's request, contacted his uncle working in Saudi Arabia and requested that seven thousand dollars be sent to a drop-off point in Seattle; once the bond was paid, the remaining two thousand dollars would be used to get the Palestinian as far away from the Pacific Northwest as possible. The money transferred from Saudi Arabia to Seattle was sent courtesy of an ancient and ultrareliable money transfer system known as *hawala;* the word comes from the Arabic root *hawal,* meaning "change." *Hawala* is the transferring of money without actually moving the cash physically—it is a remittance system built on trust and the extensive use of connections such as family relationships or regional affiliations. Transfers of money take place based on communications between members of a network of *hawaladars,* or *hawala* dealers. In Arab—as well as Pakistani and Indian—enclaves throughout the United States and Canada, someone needing to transfer money back home, or to have money sent over from the old country, could walk into a café or a storefront and send money courtesy of a handshake, a phone number, and the knowledge that the system of trust and reputation had been successfully working for thousands of years; the *hawaladars* earned a modest commission for their services, and customers could send thousands of dollars across continents without ever establishing the first page of a paper trail. For illegal aliens and those on the run, those who could not open up a savings account or get a credit card, *hawala* was a financial matter of life and death.

After posting his bond, Abu Mezer could have disappeared into the vast emptiness of the United States, but he remained in Seattle to fight his case. On April 7, 1997, in papers prepared by a court-appointed attorney and filed with Judge Ho, Gazi Abu Mezer detailed his case for never wanting to go back to the West Bank. He claimed that his family's business and home in Hebron were destroyed by the Israelis in 1980 and that he had been participating in anti-Israeli incidents and demonstrations since he was fourteen. The asylum plea detailed that he had been arrested on July 31, 1990, on security violations and held for forty days, and that he was also arrested on November 25, 1990, and held for nearly three months on administrative charges; to bolster his claims, Abu Mezer supplied the court with two documents from the International Committee of the Red Cross in regard to his incarceration. Mezer claimed that while in Israeli custody he was tortured and sexually abused. Abu Mezer also claimed that he lost part of a finger when an Israeli soldier shot him in 1989.

Yet most telling were the tidbits Abu Mezer revealed about himself and Hamas. Abu Mezer claimed that his father had insisted that he spend time at local mosques to learn about Palestinian history and culture and while at the local mosque he met members of Hamas. The Israelis, in turn, routinely harassed him and raided his home, searching for any ties to Hamas, and he was pressured by agents of the military administration to inform on Hamas or otherwise face detention and torture. Abu Mezer wrote that he feared for his life if he was returned to the occupied territories, in part because Israeli authorities believed he was associated with Hamas; "I was not a member of Hamas," he added, "but I knew of persons who were."

INS and the U.S. Attorney's office did not find anything alarming about Abu Mezer's mentioning of Hamas, even though by 1997 Hamas had redefined Middle Eastern terrorism with a slew of suicide bombings and was, since 1995, one of twelve terrorist organizations whose U.S. assets could be frozen if they were found to be raising money for terrorist groups that threatened the Middle Eastern peace process. INS attorneys believed at the time that Abu Mezer's Hamas claims were nothing more than bravado; the words "persecution for being attached to an organization with fundamentalist religious ties" were attorney favorites when pleading asylum cases. Abu Mezer stressed that his family sent him to Toronto so that he could try, among other things, to get to the United States.

The paperwork for Abu Mezer's motion was sent by Judge Ho to the State Department for further review. Like with anything ground through the never-ending federal bureaucracy, the State Department returned the letter two weeks later with a sticker on the packet stating:

> The Department of State's Office of Asylum Affairs does not have factual information about this applicant and will not be making specific comments on this application. Adjudicators may wish to refer to current Country Reports

on Human Rights practices, or if produced for this country,
to our Profile on Asylum Claims and Country Conditions.

The State Department office, designed to handle 150,000 asylum requests a year with a predominantly part-time crew, had dropped the ball. There was no check of Abu Mezer's ties to Hamas, no investigation into his claims or his true political leanings and affiliations—there wasn't even a record check from the State Department's Consular Lookout and Support System, or CLASS, the unclassified computerized lookout system maintained by the Bureau of Consular Affairs. Gazi Abu Mezer's case was falling through the cracks and he had sought a way out.

The hearing for Abu Mezer's asylum plea was moved to June 23, 1997, and assigned to a new judge. Part of Abu Mezer's bond plea was that he make each and every one of his court appearances. On June 1, 1997, Abu Mezer telephoned his attorney and told her that he wanted his case transferred to a court in New York City; ten days later he requested that his asylum application be withdrawn, and stated that he had traveled back to Canada. INS and Abu Mezer's attorney settled on a sixty-day grace period in which Abu Mezer could prove that he was back in Canada or face immediate deportation but the settlement—the absolute definition of government drowning in toothless bureaucracy—was nothing more than a waste of time. Gazi Abu Mezer, the twenty-four-year-old Palestinian wanderer who claimed to know members of Hamas, was in New York City.

Backdoor Entry

4

Lafi Khalil didn't have to enter the United States through the back door of the Canadian frontier on a darkened June evening—he arrived courtesy of a Boeing 747, and walked smack through the main entrance.

The West Bank that Lafi Khalil was determined to leave was a world apart from the territories that Gazi Abu Mezer abandoned in 1993. Abu Mezer's West Bank was an occupied land in the throes of a full-scale religious war. Lafi Khalil's West Bank was controlled by an autonomous Palestinian Authority, where displaying the Palestinian flag or a photo of Yasir Arafat was no longer a crime. The West Bank was on the verge of statehood and, in so many ways, on the verge of absolute bedlam.

The handshake between Israeli prime minister Rabin and PLO chairman Arafat signaled the beginning of the end of Israeli occupation of the West Bank. On July 1, 1994, in a display that many Israelis found even more unlikely than the handshake on the White House lawn, Yasir Arafat returned to the Gaza a triumphant leader whose exile had strengthened his resolve. Hundreds of thousands greeted Arafat's return to Palestine. The Israeli occupation of the Gaza Strip, with the exception of a few "to be negotiated later" settlements, had come to an end twenty-seven years after it had begun. In the West Bank, nearly forty thousand Palestinian police, security agents, presidential protectors, and secret policemen that had trained in Jordan and Egypt were ushered into the major cities and towns as Israeli forces withdrew. Ramallah, the new Palestinian capital of the West Bank, Jenin, Nablus, Hebron, Tulkarem, and Qilqilya were no longer occupied. The Palestinian Authority, the settling seeds of what would eventually govern the future Palestinian state, collected taxes and garbage, mailed letters, administered schools, and managed citizen complaints. The West Bank that Gazi Abu Mezer left no longer existed.

Opposition to the peace accords was strong inside the ranks of Israel's right wing and in the hearts of the revolutionaries and religious fundamentalists on the Palestinian side of the fence. The act of a madman was bound to dictate events that would grip the entire region in bloodshed. On February 25, 1994, Dr. Baruch Goldstein, a Brooklyn-born physician living in Kiryat Arba, walked into Hebron's Tomb of the Patriarchs in his army fatigues with a Galil assault rifle and calmly and methodically launched a murderous fusillade at worshippers—primarily fathers and their sons—praying in the Muslim side of the shrine. Before the Palestinians could bludgeon the deranged man to death, the doctor from Brooklyn managed to kill thirty men and boys; he wounded nearly one hundred more.

Hamas took the grief and outrage over the Hebron massacre and turned it into a religious rationale behind raising the ante of violence in the Arab-Israeli conflict to a new and disturbing level. Forty days after the carnage inside the al-Ibrahimi mosque—the traditional Islamic mourning period—suicide bombings came to Israel.

Martyrdom and the whole notion of suicide attacks was something of an anomaly for Hamas—sacrificing one's life in the execution of a religious war was, after all, a tactic that Hezbollah, Lebanon's Shiite terrorist group, had perfected and copyrighted. Hamas, a Sunni Muslim organization, had never espoused sacrifice and martyrdom in any of its religious edicts or initial attacks against the Israelis. Two years before, though, a chain of events had already been put into motion that would change Hamas and the Middle East forever.

On December 13, 1992, three Hamas terrorists posing as Orthodox Jews kidnapped Nissim Toledano, a Border Guard police officer, as he walked to work in Lod, a city near Ben Gurion International Airport. Toledano was tortured, his body mutilated and then executed; his mangled corpse was tossed into a West Bank gully. The brutal dissection of the young police officer embodied an evil that the Israeli government was completely unprepared to address; the attack, and similar strikes before, embodied a statement from the Hamas covenant that was coming true: *"Israel exists and will continue to exist only until Islam will obliterate it, as it obliterated others before it."*

The government of Prime Minister Yitzhak Rabin responded by ordering the security services to assemble the top 415 Hamas leaders in Gaza and the West Bank and to deport them to the abyss north of Israel's security zone in southern Lebanon; the Hamas leaders were blindfolded, bound, and placed on buses that drove them to Israel's northern border. The men arrested included doctors, lawyers, clerics, engineers, and day laborers. They were the top policy makers inside Hamas, and the deportations crippled the organization. In their exile the deportees entertained CNN and other network news teams who flocked to their tent encampment on a snow-covered hill. At night, though, the deportees were visited by Hezbollah instructors and Iranian intelligence agents. The deportees learned that suicide bombings had forced the United States to buckle at the knees in Beirut, and the tactic had worked with equal effect against Israeli troops in southern Lebanon. Suicide bombings, the Hezbollah commanders promised, would have an equally devastating impact when introduced into the streets of Israel. When, under intense American political pressure, the Israelis returned the deportees to their homes, the message of suicide attacks was brought back to the territories and instilled inside every Hamas operational cell.

Unlike Fatah and the other popular fronts, groups that had been fighting the Israelis in the occupied territories since 1967, Hamas had very limited access to the raw materials needed for building improvised explosive devices. When the bombing campaign was sanctioned by the organization's top leadership, the explosive devices that the Hamas terrorists wore on their bodies or carried inside satchels had to be built from scratch. "The Engineer," a bomb-building technician named Yehiya Ayyash, was enlisted to build the bombs from store-bought materials—hydrochloric acid, hydrogen peroxide, detergents, acetone, a battery, nails, and tubes could produce a chemical agent that was highly combustible with enormous explosive power. Less than ten dollars' worth of material, a little know-how, and a homicidal desire could turn a shopping spree to a hardware store into a kill zone.

The first suicide bombing attack in response to the Hebron's Tomb massacre came on April 6, 1994, when a young Palestinian crashed a car full of explosives into a school bus in the northern Israeli town of Afula; the blast killed eight teenagers and parents and wounded fifty others. A week later a Hamas suicide bomber blew himself up inside a crowded commuter bus in central Israel. The attacks were bloody and without warning. "There is no way to stop someone who knows the time and place of his destruction," Y., a senior Shin Bet agent, commented. "This is a form of warfare where the security services have virtually no chance of winning."[1]

From April 1994 to June 1995 sixty-two Israelis were killed in six suicide attacks. The bloodiest two would have profound effects on the thinking of Gazi Abu Mezer and Lafi Khalil.

On October 19, 1994, a nineteen-year-old Palestinian blew himself up on board the number five bus that ran straight down the heart of Tel Aviv's most traveled street. The bus was targeted during rush hour, when the bomber could be certain that there would be standing room only available to the straphangers heading to work. Twenty-one were killed by the blast; over one hundred were seriously wounded by the incinerating fire, suffocating smoke, and indiscriminate shrapnel fragments flying in a million directions at three thousand feet per second. The targeting of a bus in a downtown section of Israel's major metropolis was considered by Hamas a measure to paralyze the economy of Tel Aviv. Body counts were important. Symbolic gestures were invaluable.

The second precedent-setting attack by the terrorists, this one perpetrated by the Iranian-backed Palestinian Islamic Jihad, introduced a new tactic to the suicide-bombing vernacular—the "double tap." On January 22, 1995, a suicide bomber wearing an Israeli army uniform blew himself up in front of a snack kiosk at a junction where soldiers assembled before heading to their bases in the West Bank. The blast was massive, and killed six soldiers and wounded thirty more. As those who could walk—or crawl—pulled themselves out of the kill zone, and the first responders—the cops and firemen—rushed in to help provide emergency medical care, a second bomber, also dressed as an Israeli soldier, detonated a large kit bag he was holding crammed with homemade explosives and nails used as shrapnel. The fireball was followed by the blinding hell of suffocating black smoke and the red spray of blood and tissue spewed into the air. Twenty-two Israelis were killed in the double-tap attack. The tactic would become a terrorist favorite.

The peace accords between the Israelis and Palestinians had, for the first time in fifty years, brought promise to the region, but the suicide bombers had turned the potential for peace into a graveyard. The Palestinian Authority had pledged to stop Hamas, though Arafat's security forces were reluctant to move against the Islamic militants. Arrests were made only after intense political pressure from both Jerusalem and especially the Clinton White House, and even then the incarcerations were little more than publicity stunts; Hamas detainees were often held in vague forms of house arrest where they could communicate with subordinates and superiors.

Israel, therefore, had to stop Hamas on its own and the campaign became a covert—and sometimes bloody—exercise in hunting the suicide bombers and terminating them, and their handlers, before they could strike. The Shin Bet, once the most intimidating and feared force on the West Bank, was reduced to gathering intelligence from the sidelines—monitoring cell phone traffic, attempting to extort information from informants, and seeking new means to gather intel on individuals now under complete Palestinian jurisdiction. Much of the effort to stop the suicide bombings fell to Israeli military and counterterrorist units that routinely crossed the invisible demarcation lines between Israeli and Palestinian-controlled territory to "snatch" fugitives and Hamas suspects and, in their own special way, to inflict terror and uncertainty into the young men who made up the compartmentalized cells planning to perpetrate the next major attack.

The suicide bombings would have made life difficult for a young Palestinian like Lafi Khalil. Palestinian youths, unemployed men, and women and children were often summoned to join in mass celebrations following each bloody suicide bombing. The mood of vengeance and euphoria was infectious during the Hamas-run demonstrations. Young men were often swept up in the frenzy of celebrating the carnage.

Ajoul was one of the 450 West Bank villages that were considered "Zone B" under the division of territory labeled by the Oslo Peace Accords, a zone in which Palestinians controlled civil matters, while Israel retained control over security issues. Palestinian secret policemen ruled the towns and villages and handled everything from collecting taxes (those who didn't pay were beaten, tortured, and tossed into a jail cell for six months) to maintaining political unity (anyone caught bad-mouthing Arafat's rule was beaten, tortured, and tossed into a jail cell for six months). The

Palestinians employed fourteen separate security forces to keep their people in line. "At night," the saying would go, "if you weren't dragged out of your bed kicking and screaming by Arafat's people, then it would be the Israelis. . . ." Israeli counterterrorist units routinely raided Zone B.

By the summer of 1995 Lafi Khalil had had enough. He enlisted his parents' support to obtain the money needed to take a bus to Amman, across the Allenby Bridge, in order to arrange a Jordanian passport. The need to travel across the Jordan River, enduring the body cavity searches and other indignities of passing through Israeli security at the bridge, was just another one of the mind-numbing obstacles that Palestinians had to deal with just to run routine errands. Without a passport, however, Khalil couldn't travel anywhere outside the homogenous bubble of the Arab world. The indignity was necessary. A passport was a golden parachute to a Palestinian. It provided the promise of potential escape should matters deteriorate further, and in the West Bank life always seemed to take a downward spiral.

On June 26, 1995, Khalil obtained a Jordanian passport in Amman; it was valid for two years. Several days later, with his travel documents in hand, Khalil once again crossed the Allenby Bridge, was strip-searched by Israeli security personnel at the border, and was then allowed back into the West Bank.

The Jordanian passport would come in handy.

In the summer of 1995 Hamas perpetrated two lethal suicide bombings—one in a Tel Aviv suburb and the other in Jerusalem—that diminished already wavering Israeli public support for Prime Minister Rabin's peace accords with Yasir Arafat. Every bloody limb picked up by emergency crews from a bomb site was another ten thousand Israeli voters fed up with affording any permanent peace to a Palestinian Authority that pledged to fight terror but stood impotently by as Israelis were killed. On November 4, 1995, Prime Minister Yitzhak Rabin was assassinated by an Israeli Jew, a college student, who vehemently opposed the surrender of "Greater Israel" to the Palestinians; Rabin's Shin Bet protective detail was convinced that any attempt on the prime minister's life would come from an Arab assailant. To prove to the Israeli public that it was still a counterterrorist organization capable of safeguarding the citizens of Israel, the Shin Bet rebounded from the assassination fiasco and assassinated the master Hamas bomb-building engineer in his Palestinian Authority–protected hideout in Gaza. Hamas, once again, vowed revenge, and forty days after Ayyash was killed, the revenge bombings commenced.

In a span of one week, in several gruesomely devastating attacks, Hamas and the Islamic Jihad killed nearly one hundred Israelis. The political fallout was an earthquake. In the May 1996 elections, the nightmare reality that was the Oslo Accords was voted out of office. Right-wing Likud Party chief Benjamin Netanyahu became the Israeli prime minister. Prospects for peace now seemed to be nothing more than an evaporated fancy. Many Palestinians—and Israelis—realized that the situation was only going to get worse. Lafi Khalil decided enough was enough.

To a young Palestinian seeking a way out of the West Bank, America was always the fantasized final destination. Tens of thousands of Palestinians had settled in the United States—in Oklahoma City, in Omaha, in Phoenix, in Paterson, New Jersey, and of course in places like Detroit, Chicago, and New York. There was always someone—a neighbor, a friend, a cousin—who had a friend or a cousin who found fortune and freedom in America. But getting the money to travel to the United States was a daunting obstacle few young Palestinians, even those from prominent families, could overcome. Getting the proper paperwork to set foot in the United States legally—or illegally—was something else entirely.

Palestinians were masters at scamming—whether it was hooking up their homes to the Israeli electrical grid or skirting taxes owed to Arafat's collectors. People forced to live life day by day were experts—as a matter of pure survival—at bucking the system. Entire industries of scammers, forgers, manipulators, and smugglers supported this survival system. In any of the major towns or refugee camps in the West Bank—and around Palestinian areas of Jordan, Syria, or Lebanon—there were as many peddlers selling visas, forged birth certificates, and counterfeit U.S. dollars (a Hezbollah specialty), as there were legitimate businesses.* Khalil needed some under-the-table assistance if he was going to successfully get to America.

In the fall of 1996, inside a Ramallah currency exchange storefront, Khalil paid a modest fee of several hundred dollars and then handed his Jordanian passport to a man named "Abu Shanab." Shanab, who made his living acquiring visas for Palestinian émigré hopefuls, obtained a valid Ecuadorean entry visa stamp on the Jordanian passport; in all likelihood, Abu Shanab bribed a worker at the embassy, which was located in Tel Aviv, for the precious stamp. The visa was dated November 14, 1996, and afforded Khalil multiple entries into Ecuador for a ninety-day period up until February 6, 1997.

On November 25, 1996, Khalil took a cab from Ajoul, through several Israel Defense Forces roadblocks, to the American consular office in East Jerusalem. Armed with a Jordanian passport, he believed that obtaining a transit visa that would enable him to fly into the United States en route to Ecuador was nothing more than a formality. Vice-consul Kathleen Riley interviewed Khalil to process his request for a C-1 transit visa; the C-1 enables travelers to stay in the United States for up to twenty-nine days while transiting to a third country. The interview was brief—not lasting more than three minutes, a Department of Justice investigation would

---

*In the Palestinian Authority the black market economy of forgeries, stolen merchandise, payoffs, and counterfeit material was state run. In April 2002, following the "Operation Defensive Shield" reinvasion of the West Bank, Israeli military units uncovered an entire industry of credit card and currency forgery presses, as well as chop shops for stolen vehicles, all within the walls of Yasir Arafat's Muqata compound in Ramallah.

later reveal. Transit requests to South America were common—many Palestinians seeking green pastures away from the fighting sought their fortunes in the vast South American heartland (there were strong Arab, primarily Lebanese, communities in Argentina, Brazil and Paraguay).

Khalil, in broken English, explained to Riley that he needed to fly through the United States in order to visit an uncle in Ecuador; Khalil said that he intended to be in the United States for only one or two days. Acquiring the visa was imperative. Any traveler heading to the United States needed a visa when leaving Israel, even if the traveler was continuing on to another country; airlines faced stiff fines if they transported a passenger without the most basic of entry visas. Vice-consul Riley believed Khalil's tale to be genuine; he didn't even have to show proof of a ticket to Ecuador. The visa was his.

In early December 1996, Khalil once again traveled to Jordan. He defiantly presented his *hawiyya,* or identity card, to the Israeli soldiers at the entrance to the Allenby Bridge and then displayed his Jordanian ID the moment he entered the Hashemite Kingdom. At just before midnight on December 6, 1996, Lafi Khalil walked into the high-security departure area of Terminal Two in Amman's Queen Alia International Airport. Security at the airport was always tight. Travelers walking into the terminal were directed into two lines—one for men and the other for women. Male travelers were subjected to pat-down searches even before handing their luggage to the screeners for an X-ray check. If a male traveler was from a suspect country, or acting in any way suspiciously, he would be *talked to* by agents from the GID, Jordan's General Intelligence Department. Women, too, were patted down by a female police officer and sometimes forced to endure a cavity search behind a screen before they could check in their luggage. Queen Alia Airport was a dizzying and cavernous hall basked in the flickering eye-squinting illumination of fluorescent lights. Security personnel—uniformed and plainclothes—intermingled with secret service agents and other intelligence operatives who carefully worked the crowd to thwart any possible terrorist attack.

Lafi Khalil stood on a long line of men, women, and children struggling with heavy cases checking in to the early-morning KLM Royal Dutch Airlines flight to Amsterdam and, after a day-long layover in Schiphol Airport, a connecting leg to New York City's John F. Kennedy International Airport. Before Khalil could board his jet, though, a five-dinar (approximately nine-dollar) exit fee had to be paid, and there were three different passport controls— all manned by different branches of the Public Security Directorate and GID—that had to be negotiated. Nothing was carefree and easy in the Middle East. But getting his visa to transit through the United States had been Khalil's most formidable obstacle. The obstacle course of security and scrutiny at Queen Alia was a mere formality for the exuberant Palestinian. He was now only a day away from landing in America.

Lafi Khalil landed triumphantly at New York's John F. Kennedy International Airport on the afternoon of December 7. He walked off the Boeing 747 and trotted toward passport control. All passengers deplaning from an international flight must pass the checks of a "primary immigration inspector," who reviews passports and customs declaration forms. Passengers whose documents are suspect are vetted by secondary inspectors, who take the passengers aside and interview them, examine their belongings, and run computerized criminal checks. From an INS point of view, however, Khalil was one hundred percent good to go. His visas—both the C-1 transit entry permit and the Ecuadorean stamp—were legitimate. But waiting on line at passport control, Khalil would receive a bureaucratic gift from the heavens. The primary INS inspector, burdened by an endless row of passengers coming off an endless armada of flights from locales as diverse as Frankfurt and Karachi, mistakenly stamped a B-2 visa inside Khalil's passport; the B-2, a tourist visa, allowed the Palestinian to legally stay in the United

States for six months. The only distinction between the B-2 and C-1 visas is a relatively small, typewritten entry that is easy to mistake.

Regardless of the stamps in his passport, Khalil's intentions were clear—he was inside the United States with no intention of leaving.

Khalil, with prearranged family contacts, did have a connecting flight to catch that afternoon. He grabbed his Ramallah-purchased suitcase and walked toward Terminal Nine, the American Airlines hub, where he boarded a connecting American Eagle flight to Syracuse, in upstate New York.

The native of Ajoul had made it in.

5

The Borough of Kings

The call to afternoon prayer slices through the heart of the thoroughfare. All along the avenue, from the store selling thin sheets of the sweetest apricot paste this side of Aleppo to the snack stand offering heaping bowls of hummus dashed with fava beans and olive oil, the muezzin's call is heeded by the faithful. The men entering the mosque speak a dozen dialects whose origins stretch from the western tip of North Africa to the desolate mountain peaks of southern Yemen. Some are old, still wearing the suits cut for them in the souk in Alexandria thirty years ago that they manage to, somehow, still fit into; others are young, connected to their ancestral homes solely by the tales of their fathers and visiting relatives from the old country.

Outside, on a street bustling with shoppers and passersby, melodies emanating from a passing car serenade one and all with a traditional favorite from Fairuz about the Beirut she knew and loved. The smells are of lentils cooking, falafel frying, and cigarette smoke drifting into the air from men twisting their mustaches as they play involved games of backgammon—*sheshbesh*—well into the night. In social clubs, where only members are permitted, men smoke water pipes and sip coffee laced with cardamom as they sit and read the sports page and the controversy over a last-minute goal scored by the Port Said "Masry" Football Club in its win over the Qanah Football Club from Ismailia. The talk, regardless of time of day, is always about politics. The debates are animated and often contemptuous; depending on which side of the political or religious spectrum one might be from, the names Arafat, Mubarak, al-Assad, Nasrallah, and Yassin are spoken with reverence or bloodthirsty disdain. It is here that one finds many photos of Israeli prime ministers, past and present, with target crosshairs painted over their faces. Freedom of speech and religion is, after all, a constitutional right in this portion of the Middle East known as Brooklyn's Atlantic Avenue.

Up and down Atlantic Avenue, one of the main thoroughfares in the Borough of Kings, one could close his eyes and, with ears perked and senses finely tuned, firmly believe that he was somewhere in the Middle East. But one could also travel to any number of neighborhoods in Brooklyn and swear one was in China, Mexico, the former Soviet Union, eastern Poland one hundred years ago, Haiti, Cameroon, Puerto Rico, the West Indies or a dozen other nations and cities from far distant shores. Brooklyn, New York, has always been about immigrant landings and American dreams. Neighborhoods were carved up like atlases along ethnic lines at the turn of the twentieth century, when the tenement sprawl of Manhattan created opportunity and homes for newcomers to a continent whose arms were wide open. Jews remained with Jews, Italians strove to live with Italians, and Poles wished to remain with their own. Each community built fortresslike facts on the ground—schools, churches, synagogues, bathhouses, restaurants, cafés, businesses—and built its political power that catered to its own special needs. Even after the immigrants died off and the first generation born in the U.S. assimilated and moved to suburbia, neighborhoods retained their ethnic battle lines. Today, Orthodox Jewish bastions of Williamsburg and Crown Heights look and feel much like they did nearly a hundred years ago, Greenpoint remains Polish, and Bay Ridge and Bensonhurst remain Italian. African-Americans, streaming north from the South in search of better lives, have left their cultural stamp on neighborhoods like East New York and Bedford-Stuyvesant. As new groups reached the United States in subsequent waves of migration, neighborhoods would soon adopt and reflect their religious and ethnic mark. The Russians, primarily Russian Jews, discovered Brighton Beach and turned it into Little Odessa.

Middle Easterners found the enclave around Atlantic Avenue. Atlantic Avenue is a borough-wide artery that runs east to west from the always clogged Van Wyck Expressway in Queens (the connection to JFK International Airport) to the East River in Brooklyn. Atlantic Avenue runs through the two boroughs and links a hundred cultures and a dozen neighborhoods along the way. Atlantic Avenue was always a central artery pumping vibrancy into Brooklyn. In the late 1800s Atlantic Avenue became a major commercial center, thanks in large part to the Brooklyn Bridge; the thoroughfare became a fashionable shopping area sparked by waterfront commerce and manufacturing firms. By the 1930s, the industries and jobs afforded by the riverfront made the area a favorite of Middle Eastern immigrants; thousands of people, primarily Christians, emerged from the backwaters of the Nile Delta, the crowded squalor of Algiers, the ancient cities of Damascus and Aleppo, in search of a better life for themselves and their children in the promised land of America. The Middle Eastern exodus consisted of established families from the big cities who brought their fortunes with them, along with poor farmers and laborers whose rough hands had worked so hard just to eke out a living under harsh conditions, who saw promise and equality when passing through New York Harbor past the Statue of Liberty. They came from Morocco, Algeria, Tunisia, and Egypt. Thousands came from Syria, Lebanon, and the Arabian Peninsula. Arabic became a staple of the Atlantic Avenue landscape.

The religions of the region were equally represented with this new wave of immigration: Copts and Maronites established churches,

Jews—primarily Syrian Jews—established synagogues, and the Muslims—both Sunni and Shiite—established mosques.

The tapestry of the Middle East and the Arab world proved welcome and promised opportunity in a borough fabled for turning the American dream into a reality. Assimilation wasn't necessary. The community was self-sufficient. One could easily walk though Atlantic Avenue and the surrounding streets leading to Fourth Avenue with eyes closed and believe—without stretching the imagination for a moment—one was in Beirut rather than in Brooklyn.

It was impossible to remove the political and religious passions of the Middle East from the Brooklyn enclave. A Christian shop owner from Lebanon would proudly display framed photographs of Bashir Gemayel, the Phalangist warlord assassinated by Syrian intelligence agents for his alliance with Israel in September 1982, with the same reverence that African-Americans held for portraits of Martin Luther King. A Syrian shop owner down the street would hang photos of President Hafiz al-Assad behind the cash register, even though the dictator was officially labeled a supporter of terrorism by the State Department; up until the U.S. embassy was seized in Tehran in 1979, Shiite storekeepers hung photos of the Ayatollah Khomeini in their bodegas next to the mirrored advertisements for Budweiser and Michelob.

And everywhere one looked on Atlantic Avenue, the flag of Palestine waved proudly.

It was impossible to escape the political and religious passions of the Middle East and the Arab-Israeli conflict on Atlantic Avenue. Businesses owned by Palestinians, or who thugs thought were Palestinians, were firebombed; the famed Tripoli restaurant was often attacked by Jewish Defense League vigilantes.

There were always concerns in New York City that terrorists—sleeper cells and active operatives—found safe haven inside the

Arab community of Atlantic Avenue. Detectives working the squads in the Eighty-fourth and Eighty-eighth Precincts used to joke that they could always tell when something blew up in the Middle East, even before it would reach the news or the papers, because an FBI surveillance van, usually masquerading as a cable TV repair truck, would be parked outside one of the many social clubs in the area. During the 1980s, at the height of the war against the Soviet Union in Afghanistan, several mosques served as storefront covers for Arab and Muslim volunteers being processed for combat in central Asia. In 1990, when Sheikh Omar Abdel Rahman, the blind cleric who had been on the U.S. terrorist watch list for his role in the 1981 assassination of Egyptian president Anwar el-Sadat, entered the United States, he came through Brooklyn first before settling down across the Hudson in Jersey City. When, on September 1, 1992, a Kuwaiti-born Pakistani named Ramzi Yousef managed to slip through the fingers of the INS at New York's John F. Kennedy International Airport, his first stop was Brooklyn. Yousef, one of Osama bin Laden's first emissaries of the global jihad, had been sent to New York City to lead the cell that would bomb the World Trade Center on February 26, 1993. Many of the conspirators involved in the World Trade Center bombing plot lived in Brooklyn, as did others involved in the al-Qaeda-inspired "Day of Terror" plot to blow up multiple New York City landmarks, including 26 Federal Plaza and bridges and tunnels across the East and Hudson rivers.

Shots fired in the Middle East often claimed victims across the Atlantic in Brooklyn. When Brooklyn-born Dr. Baruch Goldstein went berserk inside the al-Ibrahimi mosque in Hebron, rage in the Arab world was absolute. Palestinian Authority chairman Yasir Arafat's Fatah Party declared, "Oh, brothers, we promise not to let this pass. We will declare war after this aggression." There were large-scale demonstrations in Baghdad, Beirut, and Benghazi. Yet the first shots of vengeance were fired in Brooklyn. At ten thirty a.m. on the morning of March 1, 1994, Rashid Baz, a Lebanese immigrant driving on the Brooklyn Bridge, opened fire on a van transporting fifteen rabbinical seminary students from Manhattan to Brooklyn; Baz was armed with a Glock 9mm semi-automatic pistol and a Cobray 9mm submachine gun. Baz initially opened fire with the machine gun, but pursued the van across the bridge, firing with his Glock as he drove. Two students were shot in the back of the head by Baz's barrage of gunfire; one of the injured, Aaron Halberstam, would die four days later. Baz, who had a Druze* father and a Palestinian mother, at first told police that the shooting was the result of a traffic dispute. He was convicted of the murder and the attack and sentenced to 141 years behind bars; two other Arab associates of Baz's, who assisted him in hiding the evidence from police, were convicted of minor offenses. Testimony at Baz's trial indicated that the motive behind the shooting was the Hebron massacre.

There was a reason why Atlantic Avenue was so attractive to those on the political and religious fringe of violent fanaticism—it was as perfect a place as could exist in New York City where a traveler on a mission could teeter on the brink of oblivion and disappear.

The businesses established to cater to this immigrant population made this parcel of Brooklyn so attractive to illegals, wanderers, and those on the run. If a newcomer from the Middle East didn't have an apartment or the legal means to get a phone, travel agents, some

---

*The Druze faith was born in eleventh-century Egypt where a local ruler founded the new sect; one of this new sect's first prophets was a spiritual leader named al-Darazi, from which comes the name "Druze." The Druze faith centers around Muslim pillars of the prophet Muhammad's being the messenger of God, yet it emphasizes inner and hidden layers of meaning. The Druze believe in the reincarnation and transmigration of souls, and they are great believers in secrecy; only the *ukkal*, or knowledgeable ones, are allowed access to written texts discussing the faith, while the *juhhal*, or nonbelievers, are not allowed to even glance at the Druze holy books explaining the tenets of the religion. Followers of the faith must display more than piety in being considered a knowledgeable one—only those who display stellar moral character are allowed access to the secrets of religion. Indeed, the Druze religion emphasizes moral and ethical virtues quite heavily. One of the examples of moral character is the concept of *taqiyya*, which calls for complete loyalty by its adherents to the government of the country in which they reside.

with a dusty model of a Yemenia Airways Boeing 727 in their window, offered cheap calls back home to the Middle East for a modest fee. Dozens of storefronts, from jewelers to bargain basement apparel stores selling counterfeit copies of the most fashionable Adidas and Nike sneakers and tracksuits, would arrange, through *hawala,* for funds to be transferred back and forth across the globe. In the falafel and pizza stores, cafés, restaurants, and mosques, 917 area code pager and mobile-phone numbers were listed on photocopied pages with perforated edges, offering everything from off-the-books jobs to immigration help. Flyers stapled to wooden posts and taped to walls offered services from brokers in the old country willing to settle family estates. There were also ads from matchmakers interested in setting up illegal Arab men with older, perhaps unattractive, American women for marriages of green card convenience.

Many of the ads and flyers offered places to stay—sometimes for as little as fifteen dollars a week—for men in need of a bed to sleep on and a sink to wash up in. The rooms dotted the borough far from the prying eyes of INS agents, New York City housing inspectors, and even the Board of Health. It was an underground system of alcoves, dingy rooms, and closets turned into living spaces for people who had no papers, little money, and no choice. The rooms, often shared by as many as six to eight souls, were small, dark, and dirty. The inhabitants didn't mind. They weren't expecting a duplex on the Upper West Side when they came to New York City. They craved a place to close their eyes where anonymity was guaranteed. The Immigration and Naturalization Service wasn't too interested in the Arab underground, anyway. Arab immigrants didn't take jobs away from Americans on the unemployment line, and Middle Eastern illegals weren't high profile enough for the INS teams that scoured the borough in white and green vans looking to round up undocumented aliens, primarily searching the areas where Mexicans, Hondurans, and Guatemalans settled.

The illegal Middle Eastern population consisted primarily of young men—students who never had any intention of going back and who survived working odd jobs for cash in the hundreds of local businesses. Local Arab businesses hired only local Arab workers—mainly undocumented ones. Those who knew how to drive a car—New York State driver's licenses weren't really required—were the lucky ones. The wages were low, and the conditions were abhorrent. If an illegal was lucky, the store owner would let him sleep in the rat-infested basement where the goods were stored. The work week was often seven days long. It wasn't paradise, but it was better than being back in the Middle East.

A tribal system of self-reliance existed in the community. The Lebanese relied upon fellow Lebanese; Syrians called upon their countrymen for support, and the burgeoning Yemeni population called upon the brothers and sisters from Aden and Sanaa for support. Palestinians gravitated toward other Palestinians. There is no official record of when and where Gazi Abu Mezer and Lafi Khalil actually met. Both men drifted to Brooklyn in the summer of 1997 and gravitated to the Atlantic Avenue area. Once they arrived, like many other young men on the run from INS before them, they could walk into any number of businesses with names reflecting their Palestinian heritage and ask for a job. The conversation often started with the shopkeeper inquiring about the newcomer's accent. "Where are you from?" "Is that a Nablus accent I hear?" The conversation would then drift into "Do you know Abu Salem from Ramallah?" It seemed that everyone in the West Bank knew everyone else, and everyone knew one of someone's relations or friends in Brooklyn. By the time the conversation was over, the newcomer was either wearing an apron around his midsection and working a broom or was armed with a sliver of paper and a telephone number written on it. "Ask for Mohammed," the shopkeeper would say. "He always needs strong men to help with the business."

Gazi Abu Mezer worked odd jobs requiring no skills and little English. Lafi Khalil, according to his relatives in Ajoul, was ill when he arrived in Brooklyn. Abu Mezer, according to people who knew him in and around the lower end of Park Slope, where he lived, went from rooming house to rooming house, angry about his lack of economic opportunity; the two men apparently spent much of their time hanging out around the neighborhood, usually spending hours on the phone. Pay phone scams were popular among immigrants without phones at home and without the means to get cellular service. Buying a stolen AT&T or Sprint calling card number was easy. It often took months for the victim to realize that his number had been swiped, and by that time, tens of thousands of dollars in calls to Nigeria, the Dominican Republic, the West Bank, India, or China could have been charged to the account. Once the calling card number was canceled, the user would simply obtain another number for a small fee. It is not known whom Mezer and Khalil called or where the calls were going to.

Abu Mezer and Khalil regularly complained about how poor they were to local neighborhood merchants who got to know them.[1] Khalil was less concerned about his financial portfolio and far more interested in getting laid. Khalil used to finger through Spanish-language soft-core pornography magazines in the local bodegas as well as stand on the corner in the summer, yelling "Hey, baby" to the young women walking by in tank tops and shorts. According to Dean Shahin, a Palestinian who roomed with the two in a boardinghouse catering to illegals, Khalil used to spend most of his earnings from odd jobs around the block by going to the Big Top Lounge and Club 44, both strip clubs, near Times Square in Manhattan before it became Disneyfied.[2]

Both men weren't particularly religious and their behavior on the streets did not reflect the pattern of indoctrination usually associated with profiled Islamic zealots. Yet they did, according to witnesses and reports, find comfort and community in a location known for radical Islam, anti-Israel diatribes, and anti-American sentiment: the al-Farooq Mosque. The mosque, located at 552–554 Atlantic Avenue in between al-Qaraween Islamic Books and the Land of Paradise Gift Shop, was a center of radical Islamic thought in Brooklyn. Federal law enforcement officials believe it to have been a major spiritual and operational al-Qaeda hub in the United States before—and after—the September 11, 2001, terrorist attacks. The al-Farooq Mosque, one of the approximately 150 mosques inside the confines of New York City, was established in 1976. In 1980, the mosque opened the al-Aquasa Islamic School, which taught Arabic and Islamic studies to youngsters, primarily on weekends, and began to provide other social services for the community, as well. Yet during the late 1980s a shadowy organization known as the al-Khifah Refugee Center began raising money for Arab volunteers traveling from the United States and elsewhere in the world to fight the Soviets in Afghanistan and processing their travel. Under the auspices of al-Khifah, the Mektab al-Khidmat, or the services, facilitated much of the logistics for operations in Afghanistan. One of the Imams of the al-Farooq Mosque was none other than Sheikh Omar Abdel Rahman, who was asked to leave in 1991 after his anti-American rhetoric became too much even for the mosque directors. In fact, virtually every one of the Arab terrorists involved in attacks against the United States in the 1990s made his way through the dimly lit mosque, including individuals with strong ties to al-Qaeda charged with both the World Trade Center bombing and the August 1998 bombings of the U.S. embassies in Nairobi and Dar es Salaam, Tanzania. One of those men, Ali Mohammed, a young Egyptian army officer who found his way to the mosque after coming to Brooklyn, held military-training classes in the basement of the mosque, where the al-Khifah offices were located; the curriculum included topography, survival, military strategy, and weaponry.

For a pair of young Palestinian drifters eking out a day-to-day existence in a city where they were members of a non-English-speaking minority, the al-Farooq Mosque was the type of place where their fears of being picked up by the cops and sent back to the West Bank were replaced by nationalistic self-esteem and anger. Signs posted on the window of the al-Qaraween Islamic bookshop next door said ALLAH IS GREAT—MAY JUSTICE COME TO THE INFIDELS.[3] Both Abu Mezer and Khalil were reported to have prayed at the mosque frequently—primarily on Fridays. They would have walked into the storefront vestibule, on a dirty checkerboard tile floor, past a locked garbage-can-like tin drum that served as the collection box,* and then taken the elevator to the second or third floor, where sermons and classes were being held. The sermons, from local Imams and visiting scholars from the four corners of the Middle East, were reported to be fiery; many inside the mosque were from Yemen, and their allegiance to the preachings of men like Abdullah Azzam and Osama bin Laden was well-known. Blame for much of the world's woes was directed squarely at Israel's feet and since the United States was Israel's major military ally, America, too, was to blame for so much suffering and injustice.

To the two newcomers from the West Bank, the sermons were a reaffirmation of everything they had fled—the fear, the hatred, and the reality that whether they were on the West Bank running from the Shin Bet or in Brooklyn hiding from immigration, they, the Palestinians, the Muslims, were always in the crosshairs. The sermons could often fill a content soul with rage and they could make an angry young man full of fear hell-bent on action.

Literature was also handed out in the mosque—flyers exhorting the new call for a jihad, pamphlets urging the release of the "prisoners of war" seized for their role in the bombing of the World

---

* According to FBI indictments following the September 11, 2001, attacks, the mosque was suspected of raising significant amounts of cash for al-Qaeda inside the United States.

Trade Center in 1993, and demands that Sheikh Omar Abdel Rahman be released—immediately! The literature was infectious—propaganda of the highest order intent on turning moderate believers into passionate zealots.

The two Palestinians, seeking the American dream only to live a lonely and impoverished life, existed on a precarious sustenance of day labor. Their anger was festering.

A chance for the two to better their lives came in, of all places, the quiet backwater world of rural North Carolina.

Word of mouth was the only reliable form of communication for people who lived in the underground world of Atlantic Avenue. In early July Walid Museitef, the owner of the IGA Grocery in the quiet rural town of Ayden, North Carolina, asked a cousin of his in Brooklyn to spread the word inside the illegal community of Atlantic Avenue that he wanted to open another store in the area and that he needed reliable workers. Both Khalil and Abu Mezer volunteered and took a Greyhound bus from the Port Authority on Eighth Avenue and Forty-second Street for the twelve-hour trip to Greenville, several miles from Ayden. For nearly three weeks the two worked in—and mainly hung around—the sleepy town, which was a world away from the grime and despair that could be felt on Atlantic Avenue. The soft summer nights of gentle breezes did little to appease the two Palestinians. Khalil was interested only in finding a woman; Abu Mezer wanted money.[4]

The two Palestinians appeared to find some elements of life in North Carolina appealing. A photo of Abu Mezer later discovered in Brooklyn showed the young Palestinian smirking, a red-and-white-checkered kaffiyeh Arab headdress worn as a scarf, as he held a 12-gauge shotgun over his head in celebration. Gun stores intrigued the two. In the West Bank a Palestinian caught with a firearm would be rushed straight to Megiddo Prison for detention, trial, and a subsequent ten-year prison sentence. Here all you needed was cash and you could have an Uzi of your very own. Bullets, semiautomatic handguns, and even .50-caliber pistols— virtually every firearm was available in the beautiful country back roads of North Carolina, where bumper stickers read YOU CAN TAKE MY GUN AWAY FROM ME WHEN YOU PRY IT FROM MY COLD DEAD FINGERS.

So impressed were the two with the local gun shops that they reportedly came home with a souvenir—gunpowder.

The three weeks in the Tar Heel State did not appease the two West Bank natives. Restless, horny, and out of cash, they took the bus back to New York City. They were seen in the Borough of Kings on Monday, July 28, 1997. Those who saw them would later comment on how resentful and angry they seemed upon their return.

The two Palestinians found a place to stay in a dilapidated two-story shacklike structure behind an apartment building and storefronts at 248 Fourth Avenue, between President and Carroll Streets on the northwest fringes of Park Slope, one of Brooklyn's oldest and most cherished neighborhoods, near its border with the Atlantic Avenue enclave. For anyone driving along Fourth Avenue looking for the address, the building was out of sight and—the tenants hoped—out of mind. Hidden behind a brownstone storefront that was home to the Family Car Service, a livery taxi company that dispatched cabs for the many local residents who did not have cars of their own, the building where so many newcomers to Brooklyn lived on a weekly scale was completely invisible to anyone on the street, from a mailman delivering a package to a building inspector or an INS agent looking for something else.

In order to get to the three-room box apartment, one had to enter 248 Fourth Avenue and walk through the hallway toward an outer alleyway that connected to a courtyard where the building stood. The courtyard reeked of urine and decaying garbage. Rats the size of small dogs punctured discarded milk cartons and

Chinese take-out containers in search of food. Garbage, from bicycle chains to old slippers, was strewn about everywhere. It was impossible to walk into the courtyard without stepping in a pile of filth. Flies hovered over the stench and refuse around the clock. In the heat and humidity of New York in July, the courtyard looked and felt like a disease-ridden patch of the Third World.

Inside the three-room apartment, conditions weren't much better. The interior smelled like mold mixed in with the overpowering essence of a bus station restroom that hadn't been cleaned in months. The summer heat made conditions inside all the more suffocating. The bathroom and shower setup was filthy. A yellow film covered the tile, and rust covered the fixtures. Alongside the kitchen, two mattresses were thrown on the floor. There was no furniture in the kitchen other than a small wooden table, a stool or two, and a sink that made the porcelain in the bathroom appear to be pristine. A few dirty dishes were always in the sink; the remains of rice, yogurt, and cheese caked onto the plates had hardened like rock. Gnats and mosquitoes buzzed incessantly around the sink. The refrigerator motor hummed and knocked. It was empty, though the overpowering stench of what used to be inside hinted of something having gone terribly rancid. It was the type of refrigerator that one usually saw discarded on a street corner with its door removed.

The bedroom, which Abu Mezer and Khalil lived in, consisted of two mattresses, a table, a flickering sixty-watt table lamp, and a television set someone had discarded on Atlantic Avenue that, with a bit of tinkering, found new life inside a dingy, dark, laughable excuse for an apartment. The only bit of decoration in the place was a prayer rug.

Security and privacy inside the apartment were virtually nonexistent. A fifteen-dollar lock and a wooden door were all that separated the residents from the dangers of the outside world. None of the illegals had bank accounts, ATM cards, or plastic money. What they earned cleaning toilets, clearing asbestos from pre–World War

II buildings, and washing dishes they kept on their person, or under mattresses. At any moment—in the early morning or well after midnight when the dim lights used to write letters home were extinguished—crooks known to prey on those who couldn't call the police for help could burst in and take weeks or even months of savings. Those who lived in the small rooms were incredibly mistrustful of anyone from the outside. They never spoke of how much money they saved, or where they kept their stash. No one could be counted on.

In the apartment there were no cubicles or curtains offering privacy. The walls were paper-thin. The Spanish curses from the Mexican illegals fighting in an adjoining apartment were heard with crystal clarity inside the Palestinians' home; when the Pakistani neighbors next door laughed out loud, the flowing cadence of Urdu filled the room as well. The complex was a virtual United Nations of languages, cultures, racial features, and cooking smells; where a newcomer came from mattered little to the greedy landlords who thrived on the meat market of illegal aliens—the only thing that counted was that the week's rent was paid in advance. An agent working for the landlord—believed to be a Pakistani gentleman—was responsible for finding men to fill the rooms and pay the weekly fee.

The Egyptian

One of the tenants inside the grungy rooms behind 248 Fourth Avenue was Abdel Rahman Mosabbah, an Egyptian and another newcomer to the promised land. Unlike most of the others seeking temporary room inside the squalor of underground Brooklyn, Mosabbah was one hundred percent legal: he was armed with a green card, which permitted him to live and work in the United States. He was full of dreams and aspirations that were completely within reach and completely legal. Mosabbah could have worked on Wall Street, in a Starbucks, or even for the Metropolitan Transportation Authority driving a subway train. He could have taken any job open to any American in the city. He had a green card. Of course, English-language skills were a different story.

Abdel Rahman Mosabbah's journey to Brooklyn originated in a spot on the map so remote and ancient that the two worlds couldn't have been farther apart. Mosabbah was born in the village of Alaqal al-Bahari, some 350 miles south of Cairo along the Nile in the area around Luxor where the pharaohs once reigned. Alaqal al-Bahari was the kind of sleepy, neglected, out-of-the-way village that save for the slightest markers of technology looked the same way in 1997 as it had in 1497. Donkeys pushing wooden carts ornately decorated with the traditional blue paint scheme to ward off the evil eye plodded through the village's main dusty street. Old men smoking cigarettes and drinking sweet tea debated politics and Islam; young children, dressed in tattered rags, kicked homemade soccer balls around. Most homes did not have running water. Disease, too, was a part of daily survival—everything from bilharzias, a debilitating disease of the bladder and intestines carried by worms, to cholera, typhus, and malaria. It was the kind of village where Islamic fundamentalism was strongest. Where the local mosque was the pulsating heart of the community and where the word of the Imam was the word of God.

In backwater Alaqal al-Bahari men worked in the fields, or behind the wheel of a truck, or in one of the many other low-paying industries that sustained families below the poverty line in a nation of over seventy million people where the disparity between rich and poor was mind-boggling. Egypt was a land where the rich got richer thanks to political connections, baksheesh, and the small community of privileged families maintaining their hold over everyone else. The poor, on the other hand, had practically no chance for success. Poverty helped fan the fires of fundamentalist Islam. "Only Allah has salvation for you against the enemies who have made you poor," the clerics would preach, as they blamed America and Israel for the ills of society. Poverty and the hatred festered by the clerics were a trap for many young Egyptians doomed to the same impoverished fate of their fathers.

Mosabbah's parents were determined not to let their son fall into the wicked cycle of despair. They always felt that he was special—if anyone in the large extended family was to succeed, the patriarchs felt, it would be Abdel Rahman. Born in 1966, Mosabbah was sent to study in Cairo, in university, where he specialized in linguistics. His dreams were to find a wife and to build a worry-free life for himself and his children. Egypt offered little promise and virtually no future. His eyes were fixated west, across the ocean, in America.

Besides being smart and known for his honesty and unbendable character, Mosabbah was also lucky. He fell in love and married and, in 1997, won perhaps the most prized possession known to anyone outside of the fifty states: the DV-97 permanent-resident green card.

To a young newlywed from small-town Egypt, the official designation of the State Department's green card lottery was a mind-boggling manuscript of official bureaucratic confusion:

> The congressionally mandated Diversity Immigrant Visa Program is administered on an annual basis by the Department of State and conducted under the terms of Section 203(c) of the Immigration and Nationality Act (INA). Section 131 of the Immigration Act of 1990 (Pub. L. 101-649) amended INA 203 to provide for a new class of immigrants known as "diversity immigrants" (DV immigrants). The Act makes available 50,000 permanent resident visas annually to persons from countries with low rates of immigration to the United States.

The DV Program was an absolute lottery with odds often as daunting as hitting a multi-state Powerball with a hundred million dollar jackpot. The annual DV Program makes permanent-residence visas available to persons meeting the simple, but strict, eligibility requirements. Applicants for Diversity Visas are chosen by a computer-generated random lottery drawing. The visas, however, are distributed among six geographic regions, with a greater number of visas going to regions with lower rates of immigration, and with no visas going to citizens of countries that have sent more than fifty thousand immigrants to the U.S. in the past five years. Within each region, no one country may receive more than seven percent of the available Diversity Visas in any one year.

There was one caveat in the already slim-to-none chance of getting in through the lottery. Any applicant hoping for the State Department to consider the paperwork *must* have completed either a high school education or its equivalent, or two years of work experience.

In 1997 some five million applicants around the world traveled to U.S. embassies to fill out the paperwork needed to apply for the coveted green card, the permanent-resident status allowing a newcomer to live in the United States. Some three thousand in Egypt qualified. Abdel Rahman Mosabbah was one of the lucky souls. Early in the morning of July 14, 1997, Abdel Rahman Mosabbah thought himself to be the luckiest man on the face of the earth when, after an eleven-hour nonstop flight from Cairo, he walked off of a Boeing 747 straight into the international arrival hall at New York City's Kennedy Airport.

Mosabbah had always dreamed of working hard, earning a just salary, providing for his new wife, and building a family. America offered so much promise for these restrained fantasies. The moment his aircraft began its approach over the eastern shores of Long Island before landing, the dream suddenly appeared to be a reality. Mosabbah looked older than his thirty-one years; the Egyptian sun that had tanned his olive skin to a darkened brown had wrinkled his face. His jet-black hair, cut short, was combed neatly; a mustache covered his upper lip. Yet as he walked through the INS barrier at passport control armed with his permanent-resident visa, Mosabbah could have been mistaken for a twelve-year-old kid. The smile must have been that strong.

Mosabbah decided to leave his wife behind in rural Egypt with his family while he obtained a foothold in the American dream; he must have realized that the first few weeks and months in the New World would be challenging, trying, and perhaps downright dangerous. Egypt was a land rife with dangers and threats; if crime and poverty weren't enough to contend with, the corruption and brutality of life inside a nation at war against Islamic militants were.

Police officers could not be trusted. They could steal from and abuse virtually anyone they determined to be a victim; the higher the rank, the more insidious the larceny and cruelty. Payoffs could always thwart an arrest or a beating. That was the unfortunate reality: anyone merely suspected of a terrorism offense, or the slightest connection to a possible terrorist cell, or even being a passing acquaintance of someone whose name was connected to al-Jihad (the group headed at least spiritually by Sheikh Omar Abdel Rahman) or al-Gama'a al-Islamiyya (the Islamic Group) could be extorted into paying for his freedom. Al-Gama'a was particularly popular among university students, and anyone with a degree or higher education always sparked police interest. According to an Amnesty International report titled "Egypt: Torture Remains Rife As Cries for Justice Go Unheeded," thousands of arrested individuals have been subjected to torture over the last decade or so at the hands of the state security services and the police. Regular torture, to extract a confession or even a name or an address, includes electronic shocks, beatings, whippings, being strung upside down and beaten while suspended from one's wrists and ankles, and being suspended in contorted positions. Security suspects are also subjected to death threats, as well as the threatened or actual rape and sexual abuse of themselves as well as their mothers, fathers, spouses, siblings, and children. Torture is an equal-opportunity way of life—for men and for women.

Many individuals are held incommunicado—their whereabouts not known for weeks and sometimes even months.

There was hesitation before Mosabbah felt it right to bring his wife to the U.S. What were the conditions like? Could the authorities be trusted? Was crime rampant? Whom could he trust? For someone coming from a place where anyone could be picked up and detained without a charge, anyplace new would have appeared daunting. Mosabbah wanted to establish a home and some security before inflicting the change of lifestyle on his wife.

A newcomer to the United States from a land like Egypt must have found the dizzying pace of New York City absolutely incredible. The speed of the human and vehicular traffic, the noise, the language—everything was foreign.

Like many newcomers to a new world, Mosabbah was armed with small notes scribbled on tattered papers with names, phone numbers, and addresses of possible places to stay, and leads on where to find a job. Everyone in the old country knew someone who knew someone who might know a cousin of someone who could help arrange work and a place to stay. On his own, Mosabbah would never have known how to start looking for employment or where to find a room to stay. The network, the invisible army of contacts, cousins, do-gooders, and fee-driven facilitators, was there to help.

The Egyptian's family had helped to finance his trip and he came to America, like the millions who came from far and distant shores through Ellis Island in years past, with only pennies in his pocket. His luggage consisted of the bare basics—some canned foods and sweets from Cairo; why bring the burdens of home when, as legend had it, there was gold on the streets of America? Mosabbah hoped to bring his wife over in a few months—once the money for an airline ticket and an apartment was saved. In the interim, he hoped to find a warm bed to sleep in.

That bed, thanks to word of mouth, was in the two-story shack behind 248 Fourth Avenue along with the Palestinians Abu Mezer and Khalil, and a fellow Egyptian named Mohammed Chindluri.[1] It wasn't much, but Mosabbah was a hardworking man with a dream and patience. The humidity was stifling, even to the native of southern Egypt, where temperatures in the shade routinely breached the hundred-degree envelope. In Egypt, at least, the nights bathed the body with a constantly refreshing breeze; in Brooklyn, nights with ninety percent humidity sucked breathable oxygen out of one's lungs. The roaches inside the apartment were large and pesky. The rats were fearless. The conditions, Mosabbah hoped, would get better. He must have been grateful that his wife was not there to see that this was part of the American dream.

An American nightmare was waiting, though. On July 28, the two Palestinians returned from the Carolinas.

There was little camaraderie between the four men in the apartment. They lived side by side but each in his own world. The roommates came from different mind-sets. "Egyptians tend not to like Palestinians because they think the Palestinians to be trouble-makers," reflected D. F., a Jordanian security officer with vast experience in working with both sides, "and the Palestinians tend to think of the Egyptians as stupid, because Palestinians like to think of themselves as the smartest people in the Middle East."[2] Egyptian colloquial Arabic differs greatly from the Palestinian version of the language; the two cultures laugh at different jokes, eat different foods, and maintain separate histories and personality quirks. Egyptian humor is loud and boisterous; the Palestinian sense of humor is more urbane and sarcastic.

The fact that the roommates kept to themselves prevented arguments and fighting, as did the different schedules they maintained. The Egyptians worked during the day, and the Palestinians appeared to be very busy—as if they were on a mission. The mood and intensity of both Palestinians changed after Gazi Abu Mezer was issued a summons for jumping the turnstile at the Atlantic Avenue subway station.[3] Years ago, in the city run by mayors Abe Beame, Ed Koch, and David Dinkins, jumping a turnstile was a minor offense—part of doing business with the millions of straphangers who traveled underground daily—that police officers dealt with. A summons was issued and the individual had to appear before a judge to plead his case and, ultimately, pay the fine. Most turnstile jumpers never made it to court and the NYPD was too taxed with fighting violent crime to chase teenagers and homeless people who did not bother to pay their fare.

Under Mayor Rudolph Giuliani and his first swashbuckling police commissioner, Bill Bratton, scofflaws were no longer abandoned to the "system." The theory was that individuals responsible for minor offenses were *probably* responsible for perpetrating major offenses. One of the first directives issued by Bill Bratton when he became police commissioner in 1994 was that all individuals arrested for minor offenses—urinating in public, spray-painting graffiti, and turnstile jumping—be processed at a precinct: fingerprints would be taken and a case history of any police record examined. This close scrutiny of minor offenders reaped enormous dividends. Men arrested for sneaking into the subway station at Seventy-second Street and Broadway in Manhattan were later discovered to have been wanted for multiple homicides in the Bronx.

For the offense of not paying his dollar-fifty fare, Gazi Abu Mezer *should* have been taken to Transit District Thirty-two on Carroll Street in Brooklyn, been fingerprinted and processed, and had his identification run through a state and nationwide computer search. Abu Mezer's status as an illegal alien, as someone who never appeared at his final court process, should have come up. But Abu Mezer was the beneficiary—once again—of inefficient bureaucracy and good luck. On May 14, 1997, the entire New York City bus and subway system began accepting the MetroCard as payment for entrance through turnstiles; the MetroCards, thin plastic sheets with a magnetic strip indicating an amount of money the commuter had prepaid, were to replace subway tokens that had been used in one form or another since July 25, 1953. The MetroCards created confusion and disarray—New Yorkers didn't adapt to change without grunts and moans, and the MTA was determined to help make the transition from coin to the computer age as painless as possible. There were bound to be difficulties with the new payment system, and officials urged police officers to be understanding of any glitches with people having trouble paying their fares.

The introduction of the MetroCard saved Gazi Abu Mezer

from central booking and deportation, yet the confrontation with one of New York's Finest seemed to spark rage and fear within the arteries of the West Bank native. It appeared, on the surface at least, to motivate him to take decisive action.

Or, perhaps, the subway summons was simply an excuse.

The next two days were spent gathering bits and pieces from old television sets and radios lingering around the neighborhood, and talking on pay phones; according to reports, each of the Palestinians had pagers.[4] They shopped at a nearby hardware store and purchased six feet of electrical wire, electrical tape, and large batteries.[5] The two also bought handfuls of four-inch construction nails and lead piping.

July had virtually come to an end. Inside the squalor of the apartment, the four men coexisted in a silent Middle Eastern commune of sorts where day by miserable day they faced an inescapable routine. Take away the Central American neighbors and the wailing sirens of the Seventy-eighth Precinct, and the small three-room slice of lower Park Slope could have been anywhere in the Middle East.

The two Palestinians became quiet and introspective. They kept to themselves and made frequent trips carrying gear in cardboard boxes. They wrote letters and they spoke, for the first time, of jihad.

Anytime, Baby...

Captain Ralph Pascullo fastened his heavy Kevlar ballistic vest one last time as the elevator raced toward the observation deck. He fastened his helmet and, checking his right hip, made sure that the black leather holster for his Glock model 19 9mm semiautomatic pistol was unfastened. He wondered if his service weapon would be needed. Patrol officers and backup were already at the scene, but it wasn't every day that a major New York City landmark was a crime scene, and this one promised to be bloody. Shots had been fired and there were DOAs. Upstairs, officers armed with German-made Heckler & Koch MP5 9mm submachine guns were methodically securing the area while downstairs, chiefs with one, two, three, and four stars on their epaulets were arriving in droves.

As the elevator doors opened Pascullo popped open the flap on his holster and grabbed hold of his weapon. Old habits died hard. As a patrolman, as a sergeant, and even as a lieutenant, Pascullo spent much of his career working rooftops and confronting junkies, rapists, and the odd assortment of violent felons. He would usually peer ever so carefully through the crack of the door leading to the roof, and when convinced no one was on the other side, he'd slam it wide open—his weapon always drawn. It was a matter of pure survival.

One foot onto the observation deck and Pascullo realized he could holster his weapon; the shooting was over and the cleanup had begun. A determined winter's wind pushed harshly on the eighty-sixth floor, yet the dead were frozen where they were shot and where they fell. To Pascullo the carnage looked like a massacre. Blood was everywhere, as were spent shell casings. The efforts atop the observation deck were frenetic—it was the Webster's definition of a cluster fuck. EMTs were everywhere trying to revive the victims while officers ran around attempting to bring calm and order to the battlefield; bosses from nearby precincts and from the borough were interfering, asking questions and trying to figure out just what the hell happened. Terrorist gunfire wasn't supposed to happen on top of the Empire State Building.

Up until that afternoon Ralph Pascullo would have been the first person to admit that he didn't know the difference between a jihad and Jiminy Cricket. But at five fifteen p.m. on the cold sunny Sunday afternoon of February 23, 1997, gunshots rippled through the blue skies on the eighty-sixth floor of 350 Fifth Avenue—better known as the Empire State Building. The shooter, a sixty-nine-year-old Palestinian man named Ali Hassan Abu Kamal from the Gaza Strip, had apparently gone berserk and started shooting tourists looking at the Manhattan skyline from the observation deck before he put the .380 pistol to his head and blew a hole straight through it. Detectives would find a suicide note, a bullet-ridden statement of politically inspired hate and radical Palestinian nationalism that prompted the explosive Sunday afternoon carnage.

Pascullo breathed a sigh of anger and disbelief as he took the elevator down. He unfastened his body armor, removed his helmet, and summoned additional units to prepare an emergency response should this fusillade have been an opening salvo in what would turn out to be a much larger terrorist offensive in New York City. The city braced for the worst, as did Pascullo. He entered his unmarked maroon Chevy Caprice, avoiding the throng of reporters rushing to the crime scene, and headed to city hall. As he drove down the FDR Drive, darkness descended upon Manhattan; the

Twin Towers of the World Trade Center were basked in a towering stream of orange light. As he neared city hall, Pascullo approached a red light and began to think carefully about the long list of questions he knew Mayor Rudy Giuliani and Police Commissioner Howard Safir were bound to ask. Among them would be "Why did this happen?" and "Was the Emergency Service Unit response sufficient?"

Captain Ralph Pascullo was the executive officer, or second-in-command, of the department's elite Emergency Service Unit, or ESU—the NYPD's tactical and emergency rescue force summoned to respond to any major calamity or threat that the city might absorb. There is an old saying in the NYPD: "When a citizen needs help he calls a cop; when a cop needs help he calls ESU."

ESU traces its creation to 1925 and the formation of a reserve force of patrolmen who could be called upon to perform "extraordinary" rescue assignments; many of these volunteers were part-time carpenters, welders, riggers, and electricians. They rode around the city in modified fire trucks and soon carried larger and more specified emergency equipment; years later, lifesaving gear was added to the trucks and the cops were sent to emergency medical training. The unit was supposed to be a force of full-time jacks-of-all-trades capable of extraordinary work that no other city agency could claim the skill, tools, or resolve to perform—from rescuing workers trapped in subway tunnels to talking down a suicidal jumper about to leap off of the Brooklyn Bridge.

ESU was one of America's first special-weapons-and-tactics police units; known by such names as the Firearms Battalion and the Machine Gun Squad back in the old days, the unit's officers carried .45-caliber Thompson submachine guns and were New York City's last line of defense against full-fledged riots and large-scale political insurrections. Because of the firepower they carried and the tools at their disposal, the unit executed raids against the worst of the worst of New York City's organized crime—from Lower East Side gangs dealing in Prohibition liquor to actual pirates who used to terrorize the shipping lanes along the Hudson River. During the Second World War the unit patrolled underneath New York City's numerous bridges, searching for German and Italian midget submarines.

During the 1950s the unit would eventually develop into a force called the Mobile Security Unit, which was tasked with responding to emergencies such as airplane wrecks and building collapses, as well as incidents, such as hostage situations, that precinct cops were just not capable of handling. The unit's tactical and hostage rescue skills would become a focal point of city emergency management planning following the 1972 Munich Olympics massacre, when law enforcement agencies around the world redefined their capabilities to confront well-trained heavily armed terrorists.

ESU is a unique creation. Neither a SWAT team nor solely a rescue force, they have always prided themselves upon the fact that they are one of the few tactical police units in the world that also handle rescue work. ESU handles just about every type of job imaginable—from EDPs, the NYPD vernacular for "emotionally disturbed persons," to dangerous animals, and from building collapses to plane crashes. The unit responds to automobile accidents where injured motorists are pinned in the wreckage of what was once their spanking new cars, and they have entered the rivers donning scuba gear to pull people out of the polluted and choppy waters. And, with heavy weapons in hand and Kevlar vests, the unit executes high-risk warrants, or "hits," against the most violent and desperate criminals in the city. The unit also responds to "barricades," the generic term for a psycho, escaped felon, or just run-of-the-mill armed nut job with a murderous intent holed up inside a fortified location. ESU officers respond to all incidents involving hazardous material, and they assist detectives in the bomb squad when they suit up and deal with suspicious devices. Heavily armed

ESU counterassault teams help to protect the president of the United States and other high-threat world leaders when they visit New York City, and ESU countersnipers keep potential assassins within their crosshairs.

ESU officers call themselves E-men—policemen capable of meeting and defeating any and all threats and challenges.

Becoming an E-cop is one of the most prestigious accomplishments any member of the department can ever hope to achieve. At any given time there are over fifteen hundred names on a waiting list to be reviewed by a board of ESU commanders. In NYPD circles just getting the chance to earn a spot in the unit is akin to winning the lottery. In other departments around the United States, hopefuls seeking to join an elite unit tend to be judged solely on merit and experience. In the NYPD, which is as much a society of backroom politics and connections as one can find anywhere else in the world, merit and experience will get you only so far. Often, it is a "hook"—the NYPD slang term for a friend of a higher rank who will look after you—who makes a phone call on an applicant's behalf that can be the difference between a candidate from the list being reviewed or being ignored and passed over completely.

ESU traditionally looks for policemen and women who have additional skills and are adept with their hands and with tools—electricians, carpenters, divers, former servicemen, and even volunteer firemen have always topped the list. Candidates with the pedigree and a nudge from a hook or a "crane"—a very powerful hook—who pass the intense psychological and oral exams must endure the "interview." ESU does not look for people who know it all or, worse, think they know it all—they are looking for people who can think on their feet.

The ESU training class, called the Specialized Training School, or STS, lasts sixteen weeks and consists of a crash course of tactical instruction. Officers must master their Heckler & Koch MP5 9mm submachine guns and Ruger Mini-14 5.56mm assault rifles, as well as be able to deploy with weapons at the ready in a multitude of scenarios. The officers are introduced to specialized police apprehension and hostage rescue tactics. They learn how to deploy with heavy ballistic shields, or Body Bunkers, carried on most warrants.

The instruction also consists of training in a wide array of emergency rescue procedures, including rigging and line techniques; welding and burning; first aid as first responders; operation of power rescue tools; elevator and escalator emergencies and rescues; water rescue techniques; helicopter rescue, rappeling, and medevac; recognition of bombs and improvised explosive devices; transportation of bombs and explosive devices; recognition and rescue relative to hazardous material (HAZMAT); operation of specialized vehicles; dignitary protection and escorts; use of chemical agents; use of auxiliary electrical generators and lighting equipment; handling of electrical and gas emergencies; aircraft emergencies and rescues; forcible-entry techniques; Department of Corrections procedures inside detention facilities; crime scene investigations; and high-rise-structure rescues.

Additional specialized training comes in the package of a course in remote tactics with the unit's wheeled robots, instruction in less-than-lethal responses, a two-week scuba certification course, and a three-week emergency medical technician (EMT) certification course.

The unit bases itself in workstations and operating bases known as "Trucks," which resemble firehouses more than typical NYPD precincts. ESU is not an on-call force of emergency responders—the unit actively and aggressively patrols the city around the clock in three eight-hour shifts. The basic ESU patrol vehicle is anything but basic. Known as the REP, or Radio Emergency Patrol, the vehicle is a cabin of emergency gear loaded on a 4×4 pickup (see appendix). Each ESU Truck usually maintains three REPs, of which two are regularly on patrol through the Truck's area of responsibility. They are known as the "Adam," "Boy," and "Charley" cars; on rare occasions, during times of heightened terrorist awareness, there might even be a "David" car, as well. By performing roving patrols, REPs are in an excellent position to respond to situations requiring ESU expertise, such as "pin jobs," where an injured motorist is pinned in a wrecked car, and to provide tactical support for precinct officers responding to confirmed reports of shots fired or robberies in progress. The larger truck carries even more specialized gear.

With a little luck, and some pushing and shoving, six fully equipped ESU cops could fit inside the rear cabin of the big truck; the truck is often used to transport the ESU officers on high-risk warrants. Some of the ESU Trucks also field specialized vehicles for specific emergency response tasks. These include a bomb truck; a total-containment vessel; a truck for the two "Remote Mobile Investigators," or robots; mobile light generators (MLGs); construction accident response vehicles (CARV trucks); jumper response vehicles ("Air Bags"); a hazardous-material decontamination trailer; generator trucks; a photo observation vehicle; a temporary-headquarters vehicle; and two snowmobiles. ESU also fields two Peacekeeper armored cars and two counterassault, or CAT, cars, including one that is unmarked and not in the NYPD's blue-and-white paint scheme.

ESU is headquartered in a remote series of hangars at Floyd Bennett Field, on a desolate stretch of airstrip attached to a federal park at the southeast end of Brooklyn. Because of its citywide responsibilities, though, ESU is divided into ten Trucks or squads spread throughout the five boroughs. The Trucks interact and overlap, supporting each other in carrying the burden. They are ten separate and equal pieces of the complex puzzle known as the NYPD's Emergency Service Unit.

ESU maintains two squads in Manhattan. One-Truck, situated on East Twenty-first Street next door to the Thirteenth Precinct, is responsible for the lower half of Manhattan—from Fifty-ninth Street, river to river, all the way to the very bottom tip of the island at Wall Street and Battery Park. One-Truck is responsible for the hustle and bustle of Wall Street, the congestion and clamor of Chinatown and Little Italy, the trendy streets of Tribeca and SoHo, and the bizarreness of world-renowned Greenwich Village. One-Truck covers midtown, with offices and tourist sites, and areas like the East Village, the Lower East Side and Alphabet City, with their narcotics supermarkets, squatter-filled warehouses, and teeming housing projects. Because of its proximity to the federal courthouses at Foley Square, One-Truck gets a lot of security work for sensitive trials and arraignments of criminals (from terrorists and bombers to notorious drug dealers), and a lot of VIP and dignitary protection work safeguarding important guests to the city speaking at the United Nations or staying at the city's luxurious hotels—most of which are also in One-Truck's half of the island.

Two-Truck, located next to the Twenty-sixth Precinct in Harlem, is responsible for the northern half of Manhattan, from the border at Fifty-ninth Street all the way north to the Bronx border along the Harlem River Drive and Inwood. The range of Truck Two encompasses some of the most diverse socioeconomic groups in the city—from the wealthy Upper East and Upper West Sides to pockets of poverty in the heart of Harlem and Washington Heights.

Trucks Three and Four are based in the Bronx. Three-Truck, which covers the southeastern portion of the borough, includes the infamous Forty-first Precinct known once known as Fort Apache. Positioned amid a crisscross of networking roadways, Three-Truck is a busy rescue outfit called to countless pin jobs on the major arteries, such as the Cross Bronx Expressway and the Hutchinson River Parkway, and is also called to countless EDP jobs, as a result of being situated in the area of Bronx Psychiatric Center. Four-Truck, known in the ESU vernacular as "Ice Station Zebra" for being located in one of the northernmost edges of the city near the exclusive domain of Riverdale, covers some of the more desperate stretches of the Bronx, such as Marble Hill, University Heights, and East Tremont.

Nine- and Ten-Truck are based in the borough of Queens—the city's most diverse, with over two million residents speaking well over a hundred different languages. Nine-Truck, located behind the 113th Precinct in Jamaica, is responsible for the southern half of the borough, stretching from the Nassau County border to the Brooklyn line, from the southern half of the Queens shore along the East River to the Van Wyck Expressway and Hillside Avenue. Ten-Truck, responsible for Queens-North, is based behind the 109th Precinct in the heart of Flushing and covers all of northern Queens, from the riverfront housing projects in Long Island City and Astoria that overlook Manhattan, to the suburblike neighborhoods of Douglaston, Little Neck, and Bayside near the Nassau County line.

Five-Truck is based in Staten Island and has responsibility for all emergency incidents in the city's outermost borough.

Brooklyn is the only borough in New York City to field three ESU Trucks. Six-Truck covers Brooklyn South and is one of the most diverse Trucks in the entire division, operating in an area from the Brooklyn Bridge and the old Brooklyn Navy Yard to the boardwalk at Coney Island all the way to Bensonhurst, Red Hook, and Flatbush. Based next to the Sixty-eighth Precinct in Bay Ridge, Six-Truck covers some of the most dangerous precincts in New York City and some of the most beautiful—from the notorious Red Hook Housing Projects to the promenade near Fort Hamilton overlooking the Verrazano-Narrows Bridge and the vista of lower Manhattan. Seven-Truck, situated right behind the Seventy-fifth Precinct in East New York—one of the city's most crime-ridden—is responsible for southeastern Brooklyn and the neighborhoods of East New York, Flatlands and Canarsie, Cypress Hill and East Flatbush. It is positioned in an area where it can easily back up both Six-Truck and Eight-Truck in Brooklyn, as well as Nine-Truck in Queens-South. Eight-Truck, one of the busiest of all ESU squads, is based next to the Ninetieth Precinct near the elevated Broadway subway line in Williamsburg, a residential and commercial neighborhood consisting of factories, warehouses, one- and two-family private homes, as well as numerous apartment buildings and five major housing projects. The Eighty-fourth Precinct, which covers the Atlantic Avenue enclave, is within Eight-Truck's area of responsibility.

In addition to the ten citywide squads, ESU also fields an Apprehension Team, known in the unit's vernacular as the "A-Team," which on a rotating basis pulls officers out of patrol and places them on a purely tactical team that executes high-risk arrest warrants for precincts and borough commands throughout the city.

ESU worked seven days a week, twelve months a year, in three rotating shifts—the morning's eight-to-four, the evening's four-to-twelve, and the midnight crew's twelve-to-eight. The work was difficult and often dangerous, and overtime—the true bread and butter of a police officer's existence—was far less than in narcotics, or other investigative units. But the life of an E-cop was something all the pay in the world couldn't buy. On big jobs, when chiefs would terrorize inspectors, who in turn terrorized captains and lieutenants, who in turn made life miserable for sergeants and patrol officers, ESU officers were welcomed and greeted like visiting dignitaries. "We were the cops' 911," reflected a former officer in the unit. "They were *happy* to see us pull up on jobs because it meant that the job would get done and nobody would bust their balls later. We were citywide. While some cops couldn't even leave their precincts to grab a bite out to eat, we were citywide. We had the big guns, the big toys, and we were always the stars. On jobs when the chief of department would berate a duty captain for his handling of an incident, that same four-star chief would stop his verbal tirade in order to greet us with a pat on the back. Hell, he knew most of our first names. We were like center fielders in Yankee Stadium in the most important league there was anywhere—New York City."[1]

ESU was the department's elite. Life inside ESU was considered such a plum assignment that officers who had passed the sergeants' exam declined promotion and the bump up in rank and salary just to keep on being E-cops.

Early in his career, Ralph Pascullo would have done anything in this world to be in a unit like ESU or even in a force like the NYPD.

Up until 1995 there were three major* and very separate police departments operating inside New York City—the NYPD was responsible for the city aboveground, and the New York City Transit Police was responsible for crime and anticrime operations underneath the asphalt and skyscrapers, safeguarding the 659 miles of main-line subway track, 22 major subway lines, 3 shuttle lines, 6,350 cars, and 468 stations of the New York City subway system. In 1991, the Transit Police, under chief William Bratton, became one of the 175 police departments in the United States to receive national accreditation. With some forty-five hundred uniformed and civilian members, it was the sixth largest police department in the United States.

The New York City Housing Authority, an agency tasked with creating affordable housing for the city's lower-income families, was created in 1934; the Housing Authority Police Department was officially established in 1952. Initially, Housing cops weren't even regular policemen, but were instead considered "special patrolmen"

---

*In addition to the Transit and Housing Police Departments, other police agencies included the Sanitation Police, the New York City Hospital Police, the ASPCA Police, the New York City Parks Department Police, and the New York City Department of Environmental Police.

with limited police powers, including the authority to effect arrests and to carry firearms while on duty. With 252 public housing projects in New York City, with their six hundred thousand *legal* low-income residents, more people lived in subsidized housing in New York City than lived in most major cities around the world. Many of the residents were hardworking, but many were not. Crime was rampant in the projects, from murders to rapes, savage beatings to incest. A project had everything. Even though the Housing Police, with its twenty-seven hundred officers, was the seventh largest police department in the United States, the agency was always considered the lesser stepchild to the larger NYPD and Transit PD.

A young man or woman from Long Island, Westchester County, or the five boroughs hoping to be an NYPD officer had to take a civil service exam that assessed his or her eligibility. The lucky ones who passed were accepted into the ranks of the larger NYPD. In the days before the forces were consolidated, those whose stars weren't exactly shining upon them earned a spot in the Transit Police. And, based on the sentiments of many, the truly unlucky ones went on to become Housing Police officers.

On November 19, 1973, a young and wide-eyed Ralph Pascullo entered the New York City Housing Police Academy as a new recruit to the city's least-heralded law enforcement agency. In terms of technology, equipment and materiel, the Housing Police was light-years behind the city's other police agencies in everything from procedure to very basic equipment such as radios and squad cars. The projects were overcrowded, riddled with poverty and despair, and plagued by some of the city's most desperate criminals perpetrating despicably heinous crimes. Rapes, stabbings, and gunfights were commonplace inside the projects—especially during the high-crime decades of the 1970s and 1980s, when drug use and New York City budgetary woes crippled the inner city. Elevators inside many of the projects stank of urine and feces; in most cases it was a miracle if the elevators worked at all. Stairwells, often the only way a tenant could get to his high-rise apartment, were dark and had often become favorite shooting galleries for junkies. Kids walking up and down a project's staircase risked murder, robbery, and molestation; perverts, pedophiles, and some of the most evil psychopaths in the city preyed on victims inside the stairwells. Police officers witnessed some of the saddest cases of child abuse and cruelty that hopelessness and addiction could produce. In one of young Police Officer Ralph Pascullo's first arrests, he collared a father-and-son rapist team; the old man was eager to show his son "how it was done."

Rooftops were ideal for crime and drug use. Junkies shot up on rooftops and then turned the building tops into skyscraping toilets when, after shooting heroin and other substances, they would shit where they stood once their sphincter capacities diminished. Rapists violated their victims atop the tar roofs, and murderers often tossed their victims fifteen or twenty stories below to their deaths. Young punks eager to show their manhood in a project would often hurl heavy objects, such as bricks, bottles, or metal appliances, at the Housing policemen walking patrol below.

The drug trade inside the projects was always booming. Junkies, sellers, and traffickers all called the projects home. Turf wars were common and fought with heavy firepower. "There would often be gun battles waged between one project building and another," claimed a retired Housing Police sergeant. "The perps would fire AK-47s, Uzis, Mac-10s, and shotguns out their windows in battle with rival gangs across the way. They were terrible shots and most of the people they hit were innocent folks, sitting inside their living rooms or having dinner in the kitchen."[2]

Crime statistics were always higher inside the projects than they were outside in the real world in areas covered by the NYPD. As much as the Housing Authority wanted to portray their projects as affordable city-run housing for the economically underprivileged, the buildings were often twenty-story towers of fear and violence where the poor were warehoused.

The Housing Police did not have precincts but rather what were known as Police Service Areas, or PSAs; in all there were nine geographically based PSAs throughout the city. Much of the day-to-day operations inside the Housing Police centered on foot patrols—squads of officers were assigned to individual developments, or clusters of several adjoining developments, and they attempted to keep violence down and establish themselves as symbols of law and order. The patrol officers received little supervision. "Housing cops survived by their wits, their ability to mingle in with the communities, their courage," a former officer reflected, "and their ability to fight it out if necessary and to survive. In Housing, the saying went, if you weren't a good cop, you didn't survive."

Ralph Pascullo was determined to do more than survive. He wanted to make a difference.

Pascullo was the first Housing cop to routinely carry an NYPD radio alongside his Housing communication gear so that he could hear jobs being broadcast near where his PSA was, in order to be able to respond and lend his assistance. He aggressively patrolled his sectors and began making more arrests than others in his watch. Commendations and medals soon followed and he developed a reputation as a go-getter cop who had balls and brains. When, in the early 1980s, the Housing Police toyed with the idea of creating an ESU of its own, Pascullo was the officer selected to undergo the arduous STS training course.

Throughout the years Pascullo rose through the ranks inside the Housing Police, becoming a detective, then a sergeant, and finally making lieutenant; he worked in a variety of narcotics and crime suppression units with officers like him who enjoyed a good laugh, worked hard, and would never be satisfied with a day on the job unless they were making arrests and closing cases.

NYPD cops always considered their brothers and sisters in the Housing Police to be nothing more than second-rate security guards; Housing cops had to process suspects in NYPD precincts and often rely upon the larger department's specialized units, like ESU, for emergency equipment and tactical support.

In 1992, however, Housing's Emergency Rescue Unit was born. Two Housing Police detectives pursuing a suspect were shot and critically wounded and then taken hostage. Housing dispatchers summoned the NYPD's Emergency Service Unit, but ESU refused to respond to the initial reports until the job was confirmed by other units. Housing Police chief of department Deforest Taylor was outraged by the lack of support from the NYPD and he tasked the Patrol Division commander, Inspector Doug Zeigler, with making the department self-reliant in its emergency rescue and tactical capabilities.

When the decision was made to revive the onetime notion of creating an indigenous Housing emergency unit, Pascullo, then a lieutenant and commander of the Brooklyn Robbery Unit, lobbied for the job of commander. "At the time the idea being kicked around at headquarters was to create a purely rescue-oriented emergency unit," Pascullo later remembered, "but I truly felt that we needed a tactical response so that we could handle hostage and barricaded situations and that we could make sure that we had the tools and the skills to back up the officers in the field."[3]

For years, in Brooklyn, the Bronx, Queens, and Manhattan, Pascullo had led anticrime and narcotics teams that routinely raided crack dens, heroin labs, arms caches, and barricaded apartments where psychos and killers lived. He developed tactical plans, led the raids, and was often the first through the door with his Smith & Wesson .38 snub nose. Pascullo developed a reputation throughout the department and, indeed, throughout the city. NYPD cops in the precincts around the PSAs where he worked knew him to be a balls-to-the-wall cop who was relentless in his hunt for perps. He became the most decorated police officer ever to wear the Housing Police Department patch.

The NYPD hierarchy was angry that the upstart agency would

dare start its own elite unit; Police Commissioner Ray Kelly was against the idea, but Chief of Department Taylor, a barrel-chested African-American who had Mayor David Dinkins's ear, was determined to create his own elite rescue and tactical unit. The NYPD's Emergency Service Unit had seen its monopoly of work in New York City slowly being chiseled away for years. The unit was always at war with the Fire Department of New York over rescue assignments—ESU officers and FDNY personnel battled, sometimes literally with fists, at pin jobs, building collapses, water rescues, and air crashes. Eventually the fire department became the primary agency tasked with rescuing motorists in highway accidents. Then the Transit Police created its own emergency unit and took work away from ESU underground in the subway system. And now Housing was doing the same. Units were only as good as their workload, and ESU was determined not to help this fledgling new force ever see the light of day. When the Housing Police requested that ESU help train them, the answer was a flat-out no.

Undaunted, Pascullo turned to the city of Yonkers—the fourth largest city in New York State, situated directly north of the Bronx in Westchester County—for help. The Yonkers Police Department Emergency Service Unit was built around the same tactical and rescue principle as its counterpart to the south in New York City; the unit's commander, Lieutenant Gary Hanley, and one of his most senior trainers, Officer John Rinciari, were nationally recognized tactical instructors. Both men agreed to help Pascullo out without reservation. The Housing Police Department's Emergency Rescue Unit, or ERU, was born.

After nearly nine months of extensive tactical, rescue, and emergency training, the Emergency Rescue Unit graduated its first class on October 7, 1993. The unit was forty-five strong, including Pascullo and his cocommander and one of the guiding forces behind the unit's creation, Lieutenant Charlie Rubin, as well as four sergeants and thirty-nine police officers, four of whom were female. From 1993 until 1994 Housing ERU was *the* elite unit within the department's order of battle. But on January 1, 1994, Rudolph Giuliani was sworn in as mayor of New York City. As part of his mayoral campaign, candidate Giuliani pledged to end the long unresolved discussion and merge all three of New York City's major police departments into a single, coordinated force. Under the guidance of incoming police commissioner William Bratton, a former commander of the Transit Police, the first seeds of the merger were planted when specialized units from Transit and Housing amalgamated with NYPD ESU. The officers still wore their indigenous patches but were part of the overall ESU command structure spread out to the unit's ten citywide Trucks. By April 1995 the three agencies formally merged into one. The NYPD was now the only game in town.

The newcomers to ESU were all given a three-month crash course in STS basics—as far as the NYPD was concerned, it was just to make sure they knew what they were doing when they hit the streets. The ESU instructors made their sentiments about the merger plainly known to the Housing and Transit cops proudly sporting the new patches and machinery.

The merger increased the size and strength of ESU to four hundred officers, but the transition was not an easy one. Both the Housing and Transit newcomers were not welcomed with open arms by the officers in the various Trucks they were assigned to; in many cases the reception was downright hostile. Many in ESU, especially officers with fifteen or twenty years in the unit, felt slighted that Housing and Transit cops without the same experience and knowledge, and without having endured the rigors of STS, were now their equals. "Initially the NYPD ESU cops didn't respect us as worthy enough to hold their jockstraps," a former Housing ERU officer said. "They were the heroes, the E-cops, the men with the big trucks and the cool toys. We were nothing. But to get to where they were, many of the cops started off working in places like the fashionable Nineteenth Precinct on the Upper East Side of Manhattan, where they took complaints from millionaires upset that a homeless man had taken a shit on their steps, or in Bayside, Queens, where the lawns were manicured and crime was relatively minor. We all worked in dangerous confines in pure shit holes. We worked in the ghetto. We all had to be brave and bad and never show any fear, even though often we patrolled drug-infested buildings alone."[4]

Yet the disdain that some ESU old-timers expressed was quickly overcome by performance and enthusiasm. The Housing cops in particular viewed the merger as the greatest thing in the world. They had gone from anonymous war zones like the Ravenswood Projects in Queens and the Brownsville Projects, where a young Mike Tyson beat the faces of little old ladies to a bloody pulp in order to steal their welfare checks, to standing guard, with the NYPD patch on their sleeve, outside the Waldorf-Astoria Hotel assisting the U.S. Secret Service in protecting the president of the United States. The Housing cops new to ESU were grateful and gracious for the opportunity the merger had offered their careers.

Pascullo couldn't believe his good fortune. As a Housing cop rooftops were always important to him, yet now he was on the rooftop of the United Nations protecting world leaders assembling for the organization's fiftieth anniversary, and he was inside Saint Patrick's Cathedral leading the security package for Pope John Paul II. He responded to jumpers on bridges and ledges, and led tactical operations against armed felons and drug dealers.

Yet bosses like Pascullo were under great scrutiny. The higher the rank, the more political the game became, and many ESU supervisors were wary of the new competition inside the supervisors' meetings and on the streets. Pascullo in particular, because he was the highest-ranking Housing cop in the unit, had to work twice as hard for half the credit. Yet Pascullo persevered beyond the comments made behind his back about "those Housing cops" to endear himself in the hearts of his men and in the minds of high-ranking police commanders who valued his tenacity, determination, and the fact that he was always a reliable supervisor on hand at the darkest of moments. Because he lived in the city, Pascullo was often the first high-ranking ESU officer to be summoned out of bed or on weekends to be the "white shirt," the vernacular for a boss, on the scene at a major job—whether it be a hostage situation or a major water main break at four a.m. A family man, Pascullo begrudgingly endured the absences from his son's Little League games and his daughter's recitals.

Pascullo wore the embracing personality that matched his Mediterranean complexion like a suit of armor; his salt-and-pepper mustache was always wrapped around a smile. Pascullo would never let the others know that the backstabbing, jealousy, and snide comments got to him. He was, after all, grateful. He was out of the projects and thrust into the limelight of center stage.

In ESU Pascullo was one of the architects of what would become known as Operation Archangel, a tactical-response plan meant to deal with a major terrorist attack against the city or an assassination attempt on the life of the president. Archangel was created in preparation for what was to be the most hectic two weeks in NYPD and ESU history—the massive security operation surrounding Pope John Paul II's October 1995 visit to New York City, followed by the arrival of 152 world leaders, from Castro to Arafat to Clinton, converging on New York City for the fiftieth anniversary of the United Nations. The threat level was unlike anything the city had ever experienced before and ESU was taking no chances.

The premise of Archangel was simple. While ESU assets were busy responding to one incident, a separate force, consisting of dozens of cops and several vehicles crammed with equipment, would be on standby status at a strategic location, ready to respond at a moment's notice to any developing contingency. Operation Archangel was a plan to initiate a rapid and disciplined response to the site of a deliberate disaster or other appropriate incident and to quickly establish specialized emergency operations, including the creation of conditions providing for the maximum security and safety of all rescue personnel. Archangel packages were designed to meet any potential threat—from car bombs to weapons of mass destruction. The E-cops had the tools, the trucks, and the knowledge to cope with anything.

When Ali Hassan Abu Kamal began firing his .380 automatic atop the eighty-sixth-floor observatory of the Empire State Building that blustery February afternoon in 1997, Pascullo, the on-duty ESU patrol captain, immediately put Archangel into motion. The order to put the emergency plan into full-steam-ahead mode came from Chief of Department Louis Anemone, the swashbuckling four-star-general-like commander of the NYPD; Howard Safir might have been the politically appointed commissioner, but the NYPD was Anemone's. Louis Anemone was a dynamic and authoritarian leader whose trademark was decisive action. Whether it was directing units to the site of the World Trade Center bombing in 1993 or patrolling stretches of the city while serving as the department's highest-ranking officer, Anemone was all about action. To Anemone, the shooting atop the Empire State Building had the potential for being the first shot in a terrorist fusillade; any member of the NYPD that witnessed the destruction underneath the Vista Hotel at the World Trade Center knew that the "bad guys" were capable of just about anything. Anemone wasn't about to take any chances here. He ordered Pascullo to assemble units from around the city at a central location and to make sure that they were positioned and ready for an immediate tactical and rescue response. But as night fell over Manhattan and the detectives were picking through the bloodstained personal effects of the shooter, it became clear that the attack was not a coordinated terrorist strike but merely the deranged act of a madman.

As he walked into the mayor's office at city hall, past the security detail along a carpeted corridor, Pascullo knew that Mayor Giuliani and Police Commissioner Safir would want answers about the carnage that resulted in the death of a Danish tourist and critical injuries to half a dozen others. Pascullo couldn't answer questions as to the Palestinian's motives or means of acquiring a semiautomatic handgun in the city. All Pascullo could do was speak for the unit.

Giuliani appeared calm—much calmer than Pascullo had seen him after previous homicides in the city—as the ESU captain entered the mayor's office, removing his baseball cap with the unit patch in the process. Pascullo was nervous to be inside the halls of power, but he knew that the one answer he needed to give would placate a concerned city. Whether it was a madman or a terrorist, ESU was ready to respond to any sort of attack.

Morning After Jerusalem

Lieutenant Owen McCaffrey piloted his black unmarked Chevy Caprice on the Cross Bronx Expressway, pulling into the toll plaza as he returned from a job in Three-Truck's section of the borough. Another summer night was coming to an end, greeted by the first glimpse of a warm July sun that began to blanket the Throgs Neck Bridge with a rainbow of color. As he crossed the western part of Long Island Sound from the Bronx into Queens, McCaffrey fiddled with the divisional radio frequencies, switching from one borough to the other, monitoring jobs and precinct runs; he also checked his own radio, zeroed in on the Special Operations Division (SOD) frequency, but it was silent. New York City was pretty quiet at 5:50 A.M.

McCaffrey was the ESU midnight lieutenant. His job, like those of all the other bosses on the midnight shift, began at ten p.m. and ended at six a.m., bridging the shifts. He was the citywide supervisor who, without exaggeration, covered the most difficult and life-threatening incidents in New York City from ten p.m. to six a.m. During the day and evening shifts, each of the ESU Trucks always had a sergeant at the helm; the sergeant ran the Truck, he was in charge of the jobs, and he controlled the responses until lieutenants and captains could come and run interference and keep the big bosses out of the mix so that the cops could do their jobs. On midnights, though, with a depleted work force, most of the Trucks were left with skeleton crews, often no more than four officers. Two of the sergeants from the midnight shift would act as regional supervisors. One sergeant would get the north, which consisted of the Bronx and Manhattan; his ESU call sign was U-4. The other sergeant would cover the south, which consisted of Queens, Brooklyn, and Staten Island; his call sign was U-5. The overall ESU commander during the midnight shift, the citywide supervisor, was known on the radio as U-6; he could drive around in any of the five boroughs, patrolling or visiting the Trucks, responding to jobs everywhere in the Big Apple.

McCaffrey loved being U-6.

Larger-than-life, boisterous, and as unemotional as they came, McCaffrey was so stereotypically NYPD Irish that a colleague once said, "His picture appeared next to the words 'Irish cop' in Webster's Dictionary." Put a white fisherman's sweater on his large frame and hand him a pint of Guinness, and he could have easily been a poster child for tourism to the Emerald Isle. He would be the first to admit that he lived life to its fullest and enjoyed every bit of it. But as aloof as McCaffrey could appear to someone who didn't know him well, he was a careful and deliberate tactician who thrived on the most valuable asset any police officer could have—knowledge.

The ESU midnight commander began his career as a Housing cop. Police Officer Owen McCaffrey was sworn in as a new member of the city's Housing Police in October of 1983 and thrust into the world of the projects, violence and despair. He had learned, through generations of McCaffreys in the civil service, that careers were made or broken by politics. Often it didn't matter what you knew or how good a cop you were. Who you knew meant everything. It was the currency of advancement and easy living inside the bureaucratic and nepotistic world of New York City civil service—especially a police agency. The old boys' network, especially among the politically influential and Irish, was priceless. A desire to move from one PSA to another, or from one shift to another, was always solved by a phone call to one's "rabbi"—a higher-ranking police officer who was a cop's guiding force in the department. And if that same cop had a problem with a boss, a call from a hook, that all-important high-ranking connection, could make reprimands and personal squabbles disappear forever. A cop with a lot of hooks was a superman in a department. He was invulnerable.

To flourish in this you-scratch-my-back-I'll-scratch-yours world of New York City policing, McCaffrey became a political beast—running the Housing Patrolmen's Benevolent Association and in the process, according to the words of one cop, "acquiring more juice than Tropicana." Because of his political connections in the union and in such organizations as the Police Emerald Society, McCaffrey knew, throughout most of his career, that he was made of Teflon; as a volunteer fireman in his Long Island suburb, Mc-Caffrey knew more chiefs, inspectors, and political higher-ups in his time off from the NYPD than he could ever have met on The Job. Because he knew just about everyone worth knowing, Mc-Caffrey was as relaxed on The Job as a cop could be; it was almost as if he knew, somehow, that he would never experience the "Oh, shit" when one fateful mistake or encounter could end up jeopardizing his career and, most importantly, his pension.

McCaffrey was smart. He was also lucky and he knew it. He wore his good fortune like a badge of honor.

On the street, or inside the projects, he was as gutsy as they came. According to cops who worked with him in Brooklyn, Mc-Caffrey would never shy away from a confrontation or a fight. Criminals in the projects knew better than to mess around when McCaffrey was in charge. If a cop he worked with was hurt on the job by "air mail," the Housing term for junk thrown out a window to hurt someone below, then McCaffrey was the first to make sure justice was done. When he was a sergeant, McCaffrey made sure everyone—on both sides of the holding-cell bars—knew that he was boss. Yet still, in scuffles with perps or when dealing with inspectors or even chiefs, McCaffrey was McCaffrey—he called everyone "dude."

Sergeant Owen McCaffrey had worked with Ralph Pascullo in several PSAs and on anticrime details. The two had become friends. The men were absolute opposites in nature and demeanor and, naturally, they worked well together. Pascullo took McCaffrey with him to Housing Rescue, and when the merger came down, the two went to ESU.

In ESU, then-sergeant McCaffrey was assigned as a squad supervisor in Harlem's Two-Truck. Two-Truck, which covered the northern half of Manhattan, was one of the busiest Trucks in the city where the volume of serious jobs—gun runs, barricades, warrants, rescues, and emergencies—was numbing. Two-Truck, covering the very high-crime areas of Harlem, Spanish Harlem, and Washington Heights, was as hard a place to learn on the job as could be found in ESU. Manhattan-North was a challenging stretch of New York City that proved to be a treacherous place for an E-cop—physically and politically—from the crack wars in the notorious Thirty-fourth Precinct to the whiny Upper West Side liberals who hated cops. Two-Truck was the kind of pressure cooker that made or broke a career. Yet McCaffrey earned a reputation as a good boss and someone the cops in his squad could count on. For a newcomer to the unit, that was quite the accomplishment. He was determined and as cool under fire as they came. One of the Housing cops who came into ESU knew that McCaffrey was the type of boss who would back them up no matter how ugly it got and wasn't afraid to say it to whoever crossed his path. On big jobs, when patrol sergeants, lieutenants, and captains would get into this cop's face, his simple response was always, "Don't fuck with me. I carry a gun and work for a fat guy named Owen."

In the real world of law enforcement—whether it be the NYPD or the LAPD—a sergeant promoted to lieutenant is immediately taken out of the command where he serves. It's a traditional practice designed to provide the freshly promoted police officer with new on-the-job experience in a different command with expanded responsibilities and broadened horizons. The promoted officer can always request to transfer back into the unit he left, but he usually has to wait until a slot opens up in that rank. The wait can last for as little as six months and as long as ten years. That was the real world, and then there was McCaffrey's world. When Owen McCaffrey was promoted to lieutenant he managed to be out of ESU for all of a minute. He never went to another precinct, or a borough-wide unit or command. One day he was a Truck sergeant; the next day he was a boss.

But being a boss, McCaffrey was taken out of the Truck, where he enjoyed the camaraderie of the cops and their unique esprit de corps, and thrust into the world of the ESU lieutenants—bosses competing for special assignments, recognition, and, in the words of one former captain, "childish bullshit." Even with all the juice he had and all his connections, McCaffrey was still the Housing sergeant to most of the lieutenants. McCaffrey wanted none of the nonsense. He wanted to work and to be left alone, so he moved to steady midnights, where, running the depleted midnight shift as a patrol lieutenant, he'd be the only ESU boss working throughout the entire city.

McCaffrey enjoyed the midnights. They provided him with freedom and independence. The city was literally at his beck and call. On an emergency, he could—driving at the typical McCaffrey near-NASCAR clip of 120 miles per hour—travel from Brooklyn to the Bronx in fifteen minutes. He ran all major jobs. As the senior ESU boss on the midnights, he could wield tactical command and tell captains and inspectors what to do. He was the king of New York.

Driving back to Queens from the job in the Bronx—across the Throgs Neck Bridge to Fort Totten, a sliver of prime real estate on the northern tip of Bayside off of Little Neck Bay, overlooking the Sound—took all of two minutes. The seafront fort was used as a reservist post for the U.S. Army, as well as by the Coast Guard and the fire department; Little League teams and youth soccer clubs also called the fort home. ESU had received a small cottage on the base where supervisors turned out from.

It was just before dawn when McCaffrey walked through the door, holding a clipboard and his gear pack, and sporting the typical Owen McCaffrey smile. "Hey, dude," he greeted the day tour supervisors sitting around the Formica table that was covered with magazines, paperwork, the remnants of the night's doughtnut supply, and more half-filled cups of coffee than the sink of an all-night diner. "Man, it was a quiet night."

McCaffrey sat down and removed his navy blue shirt and the sweat-encrusted PBA bulletproof vest that was worn underneath. He grabbed a cup of coffee, scoured the Dunkin' Donuts box for something that looked edible, and grabbed paperwork from his box to take care of some last-minute administrative business; to a street cop, a "worker" who could spot a crime in progress a mile away and respond accordingly, paperwork was like kryptonite. McCaffrey did not like the bureaucracy, but administrative work was endless. As he sat and jotted down reports and signed forms, the SOD radio began to hum with activity. The city was waking up, and the jobs were flowing in like a regular day: an unconfirmed pin job in the 112th Precinct in Forest Hills, Queens, and reports of shots fired in the confines of the Forty-eighth Precinct in the East Tremont section of the Bronx. McCaffrey knew that the jobs were bullshit. He headed to the lockers and changed out of his uniform into jeans and a T-shirt. He hoped that traffic wouldn't be too bad on the way back to the Island.

As he was about to walk out the door he glanced at the twenty-one-inch color TV that was *always* on inside the small room. It was tuned to CNN and there was a "Breaking News" flash coming across the scene. "We are going to take you live to Jerusalem now," the anchorwoman said in a hesitant voice, "where we have just learned that there has been a suicide bombing at a crowded market."

The first live-via-satellite scenes from Jerusalem were ghastly. McCaffrey stood frozen by the carnage and the indiscriminate evil and simply shook his head in absolute abandon. "We aren't ready for this shit," he told the day tour lieutenant as he shook his head. "This better not come here."

It was Wednesday, July 30, 1997.

At one fifteen p.m. on the afternoon of July 30, 1997, hell came to the center of Jerusalem by the special delivery of two Palestinian suicide bombers.

The Mahane Yehuda market, Jerusalem's principal open-air food market, has always been a place where religion and politics were overshadowed by the day-to-day quest of bringing produce to market and undercutting the competition. Israeli and Palestinian suppliers sold their crops, meats, fish, and wares to Israeli and Palestinian stall owners. Sellers in the market sang songs of praise over their tomatoes, cucumbers, and radishes, and shoppers were careful to find the stall where quality and price were unbeatable.

Israelis in the market were as blue-collar as they came in Israel. Most of the people who worked in the market were Sephardic or Middle Eastern Jews whose families had been forced to flee their native lands of Morocco, Libya, Egypt, Syria, Iraq, and Yemen when the State of Israel was created in 1948. They were almost exclusively right-wingers. They voted for the Likud Party. Posters of Israeli prime minister—*their* prime minister—Benjamin "Bibi" Netanyahu adorned virtually every pole in the market.

Security was always tight in the market—as far as targets in Jerusalem went, the Mahane Yehuda market was at the top of the list. At any given time one could find thousands of shoppers carrying nylon baskets full of fruit and vegetables. On some days, locals knew, fresh fish from the Sea of Galilee arrived in the early-morning hours. On some days market regulars waited patiently for shipments of freshly slaughtered meat from Golan Heights farms. The market thrived on active foot traffic. Corrugated-tin patches covered areas of the market to shield shoppers from the merciless Jerusalem sun; in July or August the temperature could easily reach one hundred degrees in the shade. The air was stifling. The odors of leftovers and rotting garbage always mingled with the smells of the fresh meats, fruits, and vegetables.

Policemen and Border Guard officers, wearing heavy Kevlar vests and carrying M16 assault rifles, maintained perimeters in and around the market; exits and entrances were marked and manned by heavily armed law enforcement officials. The Israeli police profiled every shopper, and any Palestinian acting suspiciously or carrying a large satchel or bag was always stopped, ID'd, and searched. Ambulances were always at the ready outside the bustling marketplace.

The Israeli philosophy of security centered on the analogy of an onion—the more layers a potential target was wrapped in, the safer it was. It was impossible to stop all attacks, the Israelis knew, but if the security services could layer a target with so many obstacles and trip wires, terrorists would be inhibited from even attempting to strike; this philosophy was the cornerstone of how the Israelis protected their diplomatic facilities overseas and, of course, El Al, Israel's national airline. The first layer of security hinged on intelligence. "Knowing what the enemy was up to," a former Israeli intelligence officer once explained, "was always more valuable than a thousand cops standing around with their thumbs up their ass."[1] A determined physical security effort followed good intelligence, as did a determined police presence. Each layer was designed to complement the other. Layering hardened targets made the terrorists think twice about initiating an attack.

When the system of layers worked, intelligence reports would prompt the issuing of a "credible-threat warning" that would prompt a massive security operation around a particular target or even area. There were no warnings in the summer of 1997, however. Hamas and the other Palestinian terrorist groups had been relatively inactive for nearly a year as they and the Palestinian Authority maneuvered cautiously around the hard-line government of Prime Minister Netanyahu; the Palestinians feared the potential Israeli retaliatory response to any major act of terrorism. Yet throughout the West Bank, Hamas cells were incredibly active, preparing for military operations against Israel's cities. Hamas founder Sheikh Yassin was still languishing inside an Israeli jail cell, serving multiple life sentences since 1991, after all, and his organization had vowed to do anything and everything in its power to torpedo the U.S.-sponsored peace process.

One of the most active Hamas cells was centered in the village of Assirah Ash-Shamaliya near the city of Nablus. Even Palestinian policemen working for Arafat's Palestinian Authority feared to set foot inside the village, because the masked men from Hamas accepted no rule other than the message of the Koran and the word of the cell commanders. Some of the best "engineers," or bomb makers, lived in the village, as well, and produced loads of TATP, or triacetone triperoxide, a highly explosive composition made with acetone and hydrogen peroxide that was known as a "bathtub explosive" because it could be made in any room where there was a sink and running water. Given the difficulty in acquiring military-grade explosives or gunpowder, Hamas favored the combustible substance because it could be produced from hardware-store-bought material and crafted, with other components, to produce very effective bombs worn or carried by suicide bombers. TATP was incredibly unstable. It was volatile and could be set off by a number of factors, including friction, but that was what made it so cost-effective a substance—all that was needed to set it off was a spark, and that meant that the initiators and detonators only needed to be primitive at best.

On the night of July 29, 1997, twenty-three-year-old Mouai'a Mahmoud Ahmad Jarar'a and twenty-four-year-old Bashar Mahmoud Asad Zoualha, two childhood friends, left Assirah Ash-Shamaliya as they evaded Israeli police patrols and checkpoints on a circuitous path toward Jerusalem. At a safe house in Palestinian East Jerusalem they prayed and meditated, with two twenty-pound Hamas-built TATP devices fitted in saddlebag cases at their sides. Each man was given a brand-new dark gray business suit and white shirt; their measurements had been taken earlier.

A car, driven by an East Jerusalem resident who carried full-fledged Israeli identification cards, drove the two to the entrance of the market; the car, clean but not new, had its lights functioning properly and its license plates in order; the last thing Hamas wanted was for the vehicle to be stopped for a minor traffic infraction. Both men from Assirah Ash-Shamaliya were light-skinned—they needed fair complexions if they were going to pass for Israelis. Their hair had been cropped in short, yet modern, cuts. The gray suits and white shirts made them look like the hundreds of lawyers, government officials, and businessmen who flocked to the dozens of restaurants that dotted the side streets around the market; the eateries, Jerusalem staples that specialized in mixed grilled meats, were favorites among city residents. The policemen manning the entrance points to the market, the final layer of physical security, were unable to physically check each and every person coming in and out of the thriving bazaar. Hundreds of cops would have to be permanently stationed outside the market in order to check every man, woman, and child who walked into the narrow streets. The two men in the business grays seemed remarkably unremarkable; they were smartly dressed and they appeared to be modern Orthodox yuppies. Their acting skills were impressive. They walked straight past the Border Guard policeman searching for Palestinians attempting to enter the market; because they looked so Jewish, so very Israeli, the two didn't even slow down when approaching the policeman in order to open their

bags or show ID cards. The two men walked slowly, almost deliberately, into the Mahane Yehuda market. They walked together, yet
did not speak or interact. The masquerade was ingenious. Dark
sunglasses covered their eyes.

Their bags were heavy, yet the two acted as though the cases
were light, perhaps filled with nothing more than legal briefs, contracts, or even a copy of the day's *Maariv* newspaper. They walked
up to separate stalls and grabbed the tomatoes, peppers, and okra on
sale as if they were shopping. At a point in the center of the
sprawling market, the two walked to positions some twenty-five
yards apart. Witnesses of the two men later remembered something
very bizarre. At precisely one fifteen p.m. the two men stood still,
almost at attention, and then smiled at one another. Mouai'a Mahmoud Ahmad Jarar'a clutched his satchel close to his chest and then
pulled a cord nestled into the lining of his jacket, igniting a spark
that set off fifteen pounds of TATP; the device was packed with
nails and bolts to serve as shrapnel.[2]

The blast, a bright orange fireball of destruction followed by a
black plume of choking acrid smoke, was massive and earsplitting.
The force of the blast eviscerated virtually everyone and everything in its path; Jarar'a's body, like those of other bombers who
carried their devices in bags, was torn in two (bombers who wore
their devices strapped to their chests tended to lose their heads).
Anyone standing near the Palestinian was killed by the ferocious
force of heat, fire, and shrapnel. Metal shards, vegetables, and
wooden splinters from the shredded stalls flew everywhere. Car
alarms five blocks away were ringing in the afternoon sun, tripped
by the concussion of the horrific explosion. After the initial shock
passed, the cries of the wounded, begging for help, soon joined the
chorus of vehicle alarms. The wailing siren of arriving ambulances
would complete the wall of noise.

The destruction inside the market was absolute. Jerusalemites
knew right away that the blast had been the work of a suicide

bomber—it was the fourth suicide bombing in the city, and the fifteenth overall, since Hamas and the Islamic Jihad introduced suicide bombings to Israel's cities.

Seconds after the blast, those not killed or critically maimed slowly picked themselves up off the ground, scanned the devastation around them, and raced for daylight; the air in the market turned black after the blast, as the cloud of smoke, dust, and debris lingered in a haze of death. As those who could walk fled to the nearest exit, those tasked with protecting and serving the people of Jerusalem rushed toward the market. Police officers, EMTs, and fire officers permanently posted outside the market rushed in. At that critical moment, when those fleeing collided with those rushing in, Bashar Mahmoud Asad Zoualha detonated his larger, twenty-pound payload of TATP wrapped in nails, bolts, and screws. The blast erupted roughly three minutes after the first explosion.

The Mahane Yehuda market had been double-tapped.

The double-tap suicide bombing was as insidious a terrorist tactic as they came—not only were innocents targeted, but first responders, individuals trained and equipped to save lives, were placed inside the indiscriminate crosshairs of two large improvised explosive devices.

The carnage inside the Mahane Yehuda market was horrific. The twin fireballs created a shower of flying shrapnel, flesh, limbs, fruit, fish, wood, metal, and concrete. The dead, and their extremities, were thrown as far as one hundred feet away from the center of the blast, while the wounded were hurled inside walls and across alleyways. The twin bombings made even the most battle-hardened first responders hesitant to enter the kill zone. The delays would prove deadly. Much of the shrapnel that surrounded the Hamas bombs had been dipped in tubs of rat poison; not only did the toxic elements in the rat poison exacerbate infections caused by the blast and shrapnel, but rat poison is an anticoagulant and it accelerated the bleeding process in those cut to pieces by the bomb.

Police quickly cordoned off the area around the two smoldering stumps of the bombers, and rescue personnel risked a third bombing to evacuate those who could be saved; some rescue workers used plastic roof panels as litters to carry out the dead and wounded.[3] Jerusalem District police bomb squad officers rushed to the market to make sure that there were no more explosive devices there; in all suicide bombings, the police bomb disposal experts maintain tactical command until the crime scene is secured. Heavily armed Border Guard and police tactical units, some arriving on motorcycle, provided additional security to the area in anticipation of the politicians and international media that were rushing in. Detectives from the Crime Scene Unit reached the market for the grisly task of not only identifying the bombers for the Shin Bet and police investigation* but also of identifying the victims; in Israel, because of conscription, virtually every citizen is fingerprinted. Orthodox Jewish volunteers from an agency called Zaka (Disaster Victim Identifications) carefully picked up slivers of flesh and bone from the crime scene in order for the body parts to receive a proper Jewish burial. Shopkeepers wept as their small slice of heaven, of coexistence between Arab and Jew, lay in ruins awash in blood.

Seventeen men, women, and children were killed in the double-tap bombing. An astounding 168 more were rushed to Jerusalem hospitals with critical wounds. It was one of the bloodiest days in Jerusalem ever.

News of the attack reached Brooklyn with the first CNN breaking-news feeds from Jerusalem. For the many inside the immigrant underworld who didn't subscribe to cable, the first hint that there had been a historic attack in Jerusalem came at 6:40 A.M.,

---

* It took several months for the Shin Bet to identify the bombers because they weren't on record and had never been fingerprinted, and quite uncustomarily for Hamas, the organization *had not* produced a video living will of the two bombers showing the men, dressed in military gear, explaining why they were becoming *shahids,* or "martyrs."

when following the now legendary galloping music, the announcer on the 1010 AM WINS news station announced, "Give us twenty-two minutes and we'll give you the world." The first reports from Jerusalem broadcast eyewitness reports of the devastation. Soon the local network affiliates—CBS's channel 2, NBC's channel 4, and ABC's channel 7—began showing live-via-satellite broadcasts of the carnage in the market. Reporters wiped sweat from their brows as they walked along the outside perimeter of what had become a kill zone for so many. News spread to the Atlantic Avenue enclave courtesy of satellite television and stations like al-Jazeera, the Arab world's equivalent of CNN, that broadcast the Hamas claim of responsibility as well as music videos glorifying jihad and the war against Israel.

The videos were pure propaganda produced with MTV style and bite while sending a message of destruction and hatred. Images of Israeli soldiers rounding up Palestinian men were followed by images of suicide bombers preparing their lethal devices and then the aftermath of the numerous suicide attacks. Many of the top Hamas leaders, especially in the political wing of the organization, lived in and raised funds in the United States and they understood the Western—and primarily American—mass media approach to advertising a political message.* The United States, according to a federal agent whose desk dealt with Hamas, was a primary source of funds for all facets of Hamas operations worldwide; every time a suicide bomber blew himself or herself up on a bus or inside a market, the donation buckets swelled with cool hard cash donated by locals wanting to help the cause back home.[4]

---

* On May 5, 1997, the U.S. deported Musa Abu Marzouk, the political head of Hamas, to Jordan. Abu Marzouk, a *legal* resident of the United States since 1982—he lived in Falls Church, Virginia—used the freedoms of American due process to work, prosper, and travel throughout the Middle East, molding Hamas into one of the most vibrant and lethal political and military entities in the region. In July 1995 Abu Marzouk was apprehended at New York's Kennedy International Airport, on an Israeli arrest warrant, as he attempted to reenter the United States after a Hamas political junket and fund-raising venture in the Persian Gulf region.

It isn't known exactly when on the morning of July 30 Abu Mezer and Khalil learned of what happened in Jerusalem. It is known that later that afternoon the two men went out of their home to a delicatessen down the street that they frequented, and asked the store owner to turn to CNN. When the Cable News Network was covering some of the other events of the day, the two, primarily Abu Mezer, became agitated. "No, that's not what I want," he said, referring to a CNN business update, and then he left angrily.[5] They were hungry for more information. The two Palestinians knew that this was an opportunity. News of the Jerusalem attack brought them back to Jerusalem. There could be no turning back now.

To a homesick pair of West Bank natives, especially when one had a dominant personality of rage and the other seemed content to follow the leader, a double-tap suicide bombing in Jerusalem was a powerful and motivating statement. Hamas was achieving something tangible in Israel—it was producing victims and sowing fear and sorrow. While Arafat was having his photo plastered in the international press and getting rich out of his peace with Israel, Hamas was out in the trenches sacrificing its young for the holy war against the Jews. To the two West Bank natives on the fringes of Park Slope, the suicide bombers were heroes. They weren't just sitting on their asses working menial jobs and getting summonses at train stations; they were *doing* something about their predicament. They were fighting back. Whether by diabolical design or pure unfortunate luck, the bombings in Jerusalem lit a fuse inside the collective soul of the two Palestinians lying on their soiled mattresses in Brooklyn. If it could happen in Jerusalem, the two Palestinians decided, it could very well happen on the streets of America.

The two Palestinians were determined to follow in the footsteps of the martyrs of Jerusalem. They would try to achieve the one thing that had eluded—and would always elude—them in

America: significance. The two men vowed to become suicide bombers.

For two young men who swore and would later swear that they never had any connection to Palestinian terrorist groups, both Gazi Abu Mezer and Lafi Khalil were remarkably skilled in the basics of Bomb Making 101. It is unclear today where the two men learned this explosive ability; Abu Mezer, the brains of the operation, left the West Bank seven months before the first Hamas suicide bomber struck in northern Israel in April 1994. Perhaps when the two spent their endless hours on the public telephones talking in Arabic, they had phoned contacts in the West Bank to get the latest and most reliable recipe for the combustible concoction. Perhaps someone at the al-Farooq Mosque had explained the dos and don'ts of building an improvised explosive device at home; there were those who worshipped in the mosque who had combat experience fighting with Osama bin Laden's "Arab Volunteer" army in Afghanistan. PhDs weren't required to build a bomb, after all—anyone with rudimentary knowledge of force, energy, chemistry, and mechanics, along with a homicidal will, could build a delivery system that could kill or maim. It was the skilled hands of a terrorist, though, that built devices that were powerful and easy to use, able to be detonated with the simple flip of a switch.

By 1997 the basics of building a suicide device had become a matter of public knowledge in the West Bank and Gaza Strip. Hamas had mastered the simplistic and high-yield suicide bomb courtesy of the ingenious practicality of its most infamous engineer—a West Bank son named Yehiya Ayyash. Ayyash was born in 1966 in a small West Bank town and, after Israel forbade the university-trained electrical engineer from pursuing his master's degree in Amman, joined Hamas and put his tinkering skills to insidious use. Ayyash possessed special qualities desperately needed by Hamas in its fledgling years—electronic skills, a technical imagination, and a murderous spirit. It is said of people who concoct TATP that if they can make the deadly brew once and survive, they can make it a million times. Yet mixing the store-bought chemicals was one thing—the explosives chefs got used to the stinging burns of the acids and peroxides that singed layers of skin off hands and arms; the bomb builders, hoping to avoid the prospects of fatal static electricity, often worked in the nude and their torsos and genitals also suffered the painful burns of the spilled chemicals. Packaging the volatile mixture in a functioning explosive device that was lethal and safe to carry was another matter.

Traditionally, Palestinians in the territories had built an improvised explosive device by cramming a pipe with hundreds of match heads, supported by specially treated cotton, fitted to a 9-volt battery or something larger. Once an electronic circuit was completed, the electrical charge would ignite and initiate the detonator and cause the match heads to explode in a fireball of destruction. The blasts these homemade devices produced were not large, and as a result, the shrapnel from the exploding plumber's pipe traveled a very short distance at slow speeds. But if you were unfortunate enough to be anywhere near the device when it exploded, chances were you would end up dead.

With Ayyash's design, a pipe would be filled with TATP and then sealed and attached to a battery and a switch connected to a heating element; the battery powered the element, which created the spark needed to ignite the explosive mixture. To make the device all the more potent, nails, screws, and other bits and pieces of metal shrapnel that could be molded around the pipe or metal casing would ensure that the bomb killed as well as maimed. Ayyash's design was a destructive piece of frugal genius; anyone with twenty shekels in his pocket—roughly five dollars—could buy the materials needed to build a device that, on a crowded bus, would kill dozens.

The Shin Bet, the Israel Defense Forces, and the police hunted Ayyash for nearly two years; he never slept in the same bed twice and found safe haven within a Palestinian population eager and determined to shield him from Israeli vengeance. His stature as a Palestinian folk hero grew with each passing day that the Israelis didn't catch or kill him; Prime Minister Rabin, in fact, during a cabinet meeting, coined the term "the Engineer" when talking of the need for the security services to terminate him. Ayyash dressed as a woman, an Orthodox Jew, and an old man to evade Israeli patrols and checkpoints. Eventually, he was offered shelter and protection inside the confines of Gaza courtesy of Yasir Arafat's Palestinian Authority and its intelligence services. When Prime Minister Rabin was assassinated on November 4, 1995, and the Shin Bet, the agency responsible for the protection of the Israeli leader, was disgraced, a spectacular mission to reinstate the agency's stature in the eyes of the Israeli public was desperately needed. On January 6, 1996, the Shin Bet managed to find Ayyash—he was assassinated with a cell phone fitted with fifty grams of RDX explosives that blew the right side of his head clear off.

The Israelis had hoped that by killing Ayyash, they would end the career of a master bomb builder. But Ayyash, fearing his own death, had trained legions of new Hamas engineers—many of whom were more imaginative and daring than their martyred instructor. There were dozens of men inside the West Bank and Gaza who possessed advanced bomb-building skills, and they trained hundreds more. Any one of a number of Abu Mezer's contacts in Hebron or elsewhere in the West Bank could have provided him with the expertise needed to construct the deadly bombs that would be used in the planned attack. Abu Mezer wrote down the instructions for building a device in Arabic, on a crumpled piece of paper.[6] The list included the materials that would be required: gunpowder, toggle switches, drills, and nails. The list also included a heating coil from a hair dryer.

Throughout the day on July 30, 1997, Gazi Abu Mezer and Lafi Khalil built what was going to be their explosive statement against Israel, the Jews, and the United States. The bombs consisted of four nine-inch slices of galvanized-steel pipe crammed with high-velocity gunpowder. There are two types of gunpowder—the old-fashioned black powder, which is a highly explosive substance, and smokeless powder, which is used in most handgun ammunition. Smokeless powder is commercially available in any store that sells bullets and shotgun shells, as well as, in some parts of the country, sporting goods and even department stores. Abu Mezer had been able to buy smokeless powder in North Carolina.

Smokeless powder consists of almost pure nitrocellulose, often mixed with some nitroglycerin, that burns only on the surfaces of the granules. In devices such as pipe bombs, smokeless powder regulates the burn rate of the material so that constant pressure is exerted on whatever is propelled, forcing the blast—and shrapnel—out in a path of high-velocity destruction.

Throughout the day the two Palestinians labored hard on the four devices. Each of the pipes could serve as a bomb unto itself, or they could be wrapped together to produce one large device with two or three pipes attached to one another, and one smaller one; the basic element of any double-tap suicide attack is that the smaller bomb is always followed by a much larger explosion. There were two Hamas signatures in the devices that the two Palestinians were building in Park Slope: the first was the dozens of four-inch nails taped around the pipes; the second was that the devices had no timer. Each pipe was attached to a battery by an electrical wire connected to a bank of four toggle switches and a hair dryer heating element. The device was to explode the moment enough juice circulated through the coil to ignite the smokeless gunpowder. As with all Hamas suicide devices, whoever tripped the toggle switches was going to kill himself.

If Abu Mezer did, indeed, learn the A to Z of how to build a suicide device from contacts back in the Middle East, then they would have also told the West Bank native when and how to deploy when perpetrating an attack. Up until the Mahane Yehuda bombing, the most effective suicide bomb attacks had been perpetrated against buses and primarily in the summer and the winter; closed confines maximized the devastating effects of an explosion, and bus windows were closed in the summers due to the air-conditioning and shut in the winter to keep the cold out. Train travel wasn't very popular in Israel, but for a target in New York City, a subway train was ideal. The cars, enclosed with windows shut, would be ideal kill zones; the pressure of the blast would have no place to vent beyond reaping a destructive toll inside the crowded path of straphangers.

The New York City subway system was a perfect target to strike in a city considered the business and commerce capital of the United States. The subway system, one of the largest in the world (behind only those of Tokyo, Moscow, Seoul, and Mexico City in terms of number of riders), operates twenty-four hours a day, seven days a week, 365 days a year, unique among the world's great subway systems. An astonishing 4.5 million people a day use the system; 1.4 billion riders use the system annually. The New York City subway system is the definition of egalitarian. There are no first-class cars, no special services for the privileged. Blue bloods on the Upper East Side heading from their ten-million-dollar town houses to work on Wall Street stand, crowded like sardines, with blue-collar workers from 125th Street and high school students from the Bronx. The subway is an artery of New York City existence, pumping people through the heart of the local economy.

Targeting the subway system would be an attempt to strike at the lifeblood of America's economic engine and the soul of a city defined by letting nothing ever get in its way.

Abu Mezer and Khalil intended to target the Atlantic Avenue station, a bustling subterranean transit hub that served as a commuting nexus to ten subway lines as well as a Long Island Rail Road commuter terminal. The Atlantic Avenue complex, complete with a grand, yet crumbling, kiosk of vintage Beaux Arts stonework built between 1908 and 1910, was one of the central transit points for Brooklyn's two-million-plus residents to travel to and from Manhattan; the lines served by the station brought straphangers to lower Manhattan's financial district, midtown, and both the Upper West and East Sides. Significantly for the two Palestinians plotting and mapping out their destructive designs, the Atlantic Avenue station served the B train, which was a popular line for the Orthodox Jews in Borough Park commuting to their jobs in the Diamond District on Forty-seventh Street in midtown. Both Abu Mezer and Khalil were determined to strike a Jewish target. Interestingly enough, the Atlantic Avenue station was also connected by an underground passageway to the Pacific Street subway station in which Abu Mezer was cited for jumping the turnstile.

To two native sons of the West Bank, the Atlantic Avenue subway and Long Island Rail Road station was a *soft* target. Police officers stationed at the complex centered their attention on fare-beaters, pickpockets, and vagrants, whom the cops called "skels." The police weren't looking for terrorists. As long as they paid their fare, there was no stopping Abu Mezer and Khalil for boarding a train.

The two Palestinians planned to double-tap the B Train. In order to perpetrate maximum destruction and loss of life, the ideal spot for the first bomber to flip the four toggle switches would have been underneath the East River, as the B Train raced inside the narrow tunnel carved under the riverbed toward the first stop in Manhattan at Grand Street on the Lower East Side. The Palestinians had not given much thought to just how many people could be killed by the load of smokeless gunpowder and nails, but they estimated that the shrapnel would be lethal to anyone in the car; the Arabic instructions suggested that they try out their bomb to see how effective it would be, but test runs were a luxury the Palestinians just couldn't afford.

In keeping with the double-tap formula, the Palestinian carry-ing the larger device would have to blow himself up in another car of the same train minutes later.

The impulses for the two men to commit a tandem suicide bombing must have been compelling. Being so far from home and living on the edge of poverty and deportation generated great anger and insecurity in the two. Becoming suicide bombers—*achieving something*—did have immediate appeal. Hamas, in particular, had been able to recruit legions of men, and later women, willing to kill themselves by luring them into the fold with the promise of post-martyrdom glory and paradise. The glory of death was a key moti-vational factor for two men bordering on absolute insignificance to take their own lives. The *shahid*s were rock stars in the West Bank and Gaza. The faces of those who sacrificed their lives were proudly displayed in every alley of every refugee camp throughout the ter-ritories. Their faces even adorned posters displayed along Atlantic Avenue. Those who sacrificed themselves were seen, in never-ending video loops, on CNN and al-Jazeera. "Fifteen minutes of fame" for a Palestinian meant an eternity of celebration and glory.

The talk of paradise, too, was so attractive when the American dream had turned into a putrid room, two soiled mattresses, and Marlboro cigarettes. Hamas recruiters in the territories, especially those headhunting in the West Bank universities, pitched in-depth song-and-dance routines about paradise to anyone fitting the job description (light-skinned, intelligent, pious, and poor) for a suicide bomber. According to material captured by the Israel Defense Forces in Nablus,

> Allah builds good and pleasant dwellings in heaven. The in-habitants receive rooms, under which flow rivers. There are also tents in heaven, each one made of pearl sixty miles high and sixty miles wide. Each mile contains a special corner for family members of the believer, hidden from others.

"In paradise," the explanations continued, "Allah provides the inhabitants of heaven with rivers of water, milk, honey, and wine." Perhaps most important for sex-starved young men,

> the women of heaven are pure. They have no monthly period or bleeding after birth and no other secretions. The women of heaven sing beautifully in anticipation of good husbands. The *shahid* for Allah receives immediate atonement of all his sins, with the first drop of his blood being shed. He is exempt from the suffering of the grave, a crown of honor is placed on his head, and he weds seventy-two virgins. The *shahid* receives the potency of seventy men.[7]

In the two days before the July 30 turning point, the other roommates noticed that the two Palestinians had become alarmingly more religious. They prayed with greater intensity on a rug in their room littered with empty pizza boxes, soda bottles, and cigarette butts. They spoke of jihad.

Afternoon bled effortlessly into evening on the last Wednesday in July. As the sun set over the Hudson into Jersey, a crimson glow was cast over Brooklyn. The temperature hovered near ninety degrees and the humidity—sometimes a lethal affliction of New York in the summer—was barely noticeable. Brooklyn was uncharacteristically quiet; crime tended to rise slightly during the heat-inspired season of short tempers, romances, sweat, and violence. Precinct radios in both Brooklyn-South and Brooklyn-North were buzzing with jobs but not hopping.

As darkness fell, Captain Ralph Pascullo continued his patrol tour of the city. As the unit's second-in-command, its executive officer, much of the day-to-day operation of the four-hundred-plus cops, detectives, sergeants, and lieutenants in the unit was Pascullo's responsibility. In addition to attending endless meetings with officials from the city's Office of Emergency Management, the FDNY, the Federal Emergency Management Agency (FEMA), and other federal agencies, as well as with police higher-ups, Pascullo also patrolled and responded to individual jobs. The role of a boss of Pascullo's rank in an incident was to stand as a white-shirted shield protecting his men from the ranting and raving of precinct and borough commanders whose knowledge of what ESU did was nonexistent. Pascullo's job was to be a buffer—he was to make sure the E-cops had everything they needed to get the job done, and the bosses, the chiefs, had everything they needed to keep them happy.

During his afternoon shift, Pascullo had visited the two ESU Trucks in Manhattan and he had responded to jobs in Queens and Brooklyn. He cruised back toward Fort Totten in his maroon Chevy Caprice, one eye always scanning the surrounding streets for anything out of the ordinary and one ear glued to the SOD frequency. The beauty of a city in the transition between day and night was inescapable. The view of lower Manhattan from the Brooklyn-Queens Expressway was inspirational. The glow from the Twin Towers, the MetLife Building, and the hundreds of skyscrapers in between basking in beads and rivers of multicolored light was just remarkable to behold. Pascullo remembered his early days on the job inside the projects when he walked a lone foot post inside a hallway illuminated by nothing more than the dying flickers of a fluorescent bulb.

If the silent SOD radio was any indication of what the mood in the five boroughs was like that splendid summer night, New York City was at peace with itself.

The apartment was a far cry from the American dream. The one window, near the kitchen sink, kept fresh air out for some unexplained reason. The heat was stifling and the stench unbearable; the decaying rice containers and grease-stained pizza boxes attracted flies and roaches. The sink dripped in a mind-altering cadence. Hollywood had always portrayed America's streets as lined with gold—the splendor, the opulence, the decadence, and the money were all there, at least the pipe dream said, for the taking. Yet the dream inside the back house of 248 Fourth Avenue was anything but gold coated. It was a malaise of exhaustion and despair punctuated by the inescapable trappings of the bare necessities—a toilet, a sink, a shower, and a mattress.

The two Egyptians found the apartment to be a temporary refuge whose stark realities only made them all the more homesick. Mosabbah, in particular, after a full day of washing dishes, would close his eyes on the bare mattress, using rumpled clothes for a pillow, and close his eyes to remember his village, Cairo, and his bride and family back in Egypt. The exhaustion from the sunup-sundown below-minimum-wage labor numbed the pain of homesickness. Who had time to think of home some six thousand miles away when bones ached, fingers were stiff, and eyes could barely be kept open? Abdel Rahman Mosabbah was in the capital of the world, New York City, and there wasn't the time, the strength, or the money to see the Empire State Building, marvel at the Twin Towers, or, God forbid, take in a Broadway show. That was the New York City of tourists and Donald Trump. His New York City was a bare sixty-watt bulb casting a sense-dulling yellow bath over a heartbroken soul.

In the apartment, the two nationalities kept to themselves. Egyptians viewed themselves as the keepers of Arab civilization; Egypt, the largest Arab country with over sixty million people, was home to the pharaohs, the pyramids, the Nile, and the largest Arab army in the world. Egyptians, at least on the streets of Cairo and inside the halls of their security services, viewed Palestinians as stuck-up, elitist troublemakers, and greedy ones at that.

Palestinians, on the other hand, viewed Egyptians as primitive, cultureless, and sadistic; the Egyptian occupation of the Gaza Strip from 1948 to 1967 was characterized by cruelty, corruption, and complete lack of respect for the indigenous Palestinian population. West Bank Palestinians, who considered themselves to be smarter and more cultured than their brothers and sisters in Gaza, saw Egyptians as common peasants—impoverished and unenlightened. Talk of a unified Arab nation was nothing more than a myth propagated at Third World summits and on al-Jazeera.

Abdel Rahman Mosabbah didn't think much of the two moody and aloof Palestinians he was rooming with. They were pieces of background scenery to him, like the crud-covered sink and the smelly walkway leading toward the shacklike structure. All that Mosabbah was interested in was working, saving, and seeing his family walk through the gates of the International Arrivals Building at John F. Kennedy International Airport, where he hoped to greet them in a brand-new set of clothes and drive them to their new house in a brand-new big American car.

Lying on his mattress fantasizing about his family's arrival in the United States was about the only form of entertainment Mosabbah had. Anything that cost money siphoned off the savings the Egyptian figured might be needed to rent a small, nice apartment in Brooklyn, not to mention get a car and buy airline tickets for his wife and extended family. So Mosabbah was resigned to his fate of stretching his aching muscles, clenching his hands behind his head, and closing his eyes. When he thought of home, and he thought of his wife, suddenly the stench inside the apartment seemed bearable. His stay at 248 Fourth Avenue was only temporary. He'd be out of there soon enough, he calculated. He could survive a few more months of the close-quarters living with anonymous travelers. He was determined to make the most of his one-in-a-million luck of getting a green card, no matter how hard it was at night when he felt the loneliest.

An ambulance or a fire truck drove by on Fourth Avenue, its sirens wailing at an eardrum-piercing pitch, prompting Mosabbah to close his eyes tighter to attempt to keep the noise from interrupting his train of thought. Yet there was noise coming from Abu Mezer in the adjacent room. Suddenly, his Palestinian roommates opened the door and asked Mosabbah if he wanted to see something. It was roughly ten thirty p.m.

"Did you hear what happened in Jerusalem today?" Abu Mezer asked the Egyptian with a transparently eager smile. "Well, come see this."

Mosabbah tried not to engage the Palestinians—particularly Abu Mezer—in political discussions. Abu Mezer was angry— volatile. He made a point of expressing his hatred for Israel and the Jews to the roommates. The loathing in his heart was like pressure leaking from a valve—no matter how tightly it was capped, the spill off was unavoidable. Mosabbah couldn't have imagined, for the life of him, what the Palestinians wanted to show him. Their room was filled with literature from the local mosque about Sheikh Rahman and those *unjustly* convicted in the World Trade Center bombing trial, and other fundamentalist Islamic propaganda.

Mosabbah thought that Abu Mezer would hand him just another piece of mimeographed tripe with an inflammatory speech on it and a photo of Sheikh this or Mullah that. Yet as the Egyptian righted himself on his mattress to go to the doorway separating his corner from the Palestinians' room, he saw Abu Mezer standing there holding a satchel with what looked to be pipes inside. Mosabbah was an educated man, yet his knowledge was not acquired inside the alleyways of the West Bank where the Popular Front held classes, or inside the damp corners of an Israeli interrogation center. At first Mosabbah didn't understand what the Palestinian was showing him, but then he analyzed the pipes, nails, wires, and batteries and figured it out. The Egyptian took a step back. His heart began to race. Bombs weren't meant to impress— they were designed to explode and kill, and one look into the Palestinian's eyes and Mosabbah knew that Abu Mezer's intentions were genuine. There was nothing bombastic in Abu Mezer's tone of voice or his demeanor. *His* eyes were fixated, his expression the one worn by a man possessed by a mission and hatred. Abu Mezer told his Egyptian roommate that he was going to blow up a subway train the next day. "Did you see what happened in Jerusalem?" the Palestinian asked again, his eyes growing larger with each word uttered from his lips. Mosabbah noticed that Abu Mezer's mouth, draped by a neatly trimmed goatee, opened wider with each passing sentence. His body language, at first constricted by rage and then flailing with animated theatrics, became threatening. "Well," Abu Mezer concluded, "tomorrow it will happen here."

Just to prove his point, Abu Mezer grabbed a pinch of gunpowder from a bag he had used to fill the plumber's pipes, and sprinkled it gingerly on the floor and then set the line of grayish black granules afire. "This is how the Jews will burn," Abu Mezer promised as the gunpowder sizzled in a bright, light blue fire that filled the room with a distinctive acrid smell.[1]

Mosabbah stood in dumbstruck silence as he was shown the

mini-bomb-factory inside the small room; he wiped his sweaty hands on his tan trousers and opened a button on his blouse. Mosabbah suddenly felt pressure squeezing at his insides. He found it hard to breathe. He felt fear the likes of which he never encountered before. In the instant of a roommate's madness, Mosabbah saw the promise of his American dream—his fantasies of family and riches— disappear into the cloud of tomorrow's planned destruction.

Mosabbah did not want to see Jerusalem recreated inside the bowels of the New York City subway system, regardless of his feelings toward the Jews or his opinions on the rights and wrongs of either side in the Arab-Israeli dispute. His thoughts transcended the question of Palestine, for Palestine had nothing to do with his earning money to bring his wife and extended family over, and buying a car, a house, and everything that the Americans took for granted. Mosabbah feared that once the investigators sifted through the rubble of what had been a subway car filled with people to find the fingers, toes, and head of Abu Mezer, law enforcement would be able to put two and two together and come up with him as a co-conspirator. Guilt or innocence mattered little in Mosabbah's native Egypt. Luck was always so much more important. If you could stay below the radar of the police and the intelligence services in Egypt, you could survive and build a life.

Abdel Rahman Mossabah knew nothing of how the police, or the FBI, operated in the United States—he didn't know if the NYPD was a brutal, corrupt, law-unto-itself type of organization or if it was, like the letters "CPR" on the police cars promised, a force dedicated to "Courtesy, Professionalism, and Respect". For Mosabbah, doing the right thing, informing the authorities about the Palestinians and their plot, wasn't only a matter of preventing lives from being destroyed in the fireball of Abu Mezer's bomb. Informing the police was his sole path of self-preservation.

Abu Mezer wasn't worried about Mosabbah knowing too much;

informants were looked at like dogs inside the Arab world, and the Palestinian was convinced that his Egyptian roommate didn't have the guts, wherewithal, or resolve to be a traitor to his fellow Arabs. Still, before returning to his room, Abu Mezer told Mosabbah that it didn't matter if he went to the authorities. If the police tried to intervene, the Egyptian was warned, Abu Mezer promised to blow himself up along with anyone who tried to stop him.

The thirty-one-year-old Egyptian green card lottery winner who had been in the United States fewer than two weeks had his good fortune come to a screeching halt at a crossroads of right versus wrong. The safer bet would have been to disappear for the next twenty-four hours: wander the streets, go to a hooker, or find an all-night movie theater and just hope and pray that the Palestinian was full of shit. But that would have been a gamble with enormous stakes, and Mosabbah knew that the repercussions of doing nothing would be hell for him, so he decided to do what his conscience—and his fear—urged him to do.

Mosabbah told Abu Mezer that he was going out for a while. There were no good-byes. No "see you in paradise's" exchanged. Mosabbah just wanted to get out of the bomb factory as quickly as he could. He grabbed his shoes, made sure he had his key, and then proceeded out the door. He walked nervously through the alley into the building on Fourth Avenue, and then quickly onto the street. Walking past the Middle Eastern and Hispanic men outside the livery cabstand, Mosabbah searched for some way that he could contact the police. He wasn't schooled in the nuances of counter-surveillance. What if the Palestinians had followed him? Informants in the Middle East, whether they were in Cairo or Ramallah, were rewarded for their treachery with a knife in the back. Mosabbah wondered who would come from behind the shadows and stick him in the back. Would it be Khalil? Would it be someone from the mosque? Was he being followed? Mosabbah walked onto

Fourth Avenue a man without friends in a strange city. It was a terrifying exercise in loneliness and despair.

There wasn't an Egyptian who didn't understand the fear
caused by the terrorists and those who spied on them. He did not
want to be in the middle of this cat-and-mouse game. He didn't
want to be anywhere near the Palestinians or their bombs. The
stakes of this deadly game were simply too high.

Standing on Fourth Avenue, Mosabbah realized that he had no
clue how to contact the police. There was no *What to Do When Your
Illegal-Alien Roommates Are Suicide Bombers* pamphlet handed out at
JFK upon his arrival into the United States; 911 wasn't the emergency phone number in Egypt. Turning around as he walked in the
middle of the street, Mosabbah was a man with a terrible secret
pressing against his heart.

A block away, Mosabbah found a pay phone. He looked around
to see if he was followed and then attempted to read the graffiti-
covered instruction insert. He pressed zero and received an operator. Almost hyperventilating out of fear, the Egyptian could barely
get a word out, and when that word emerged across his lips, it was
an unintelligible *"bomba,"* the Arabic slang for bomb. The operator
was unsure what the heavily accented voice on the other end of the
line was talking about, so she simply hung up. Frustrated, Mosabbah
headed north, toward Flatbush Avenue, where the sounds of traffic
and life seemed vibrant. Mosabbah walked at a hurried pace, not
sure whom to let in on the terrible secret he now had to share.
Could he trust a pedestrian walking past him? Should he stop inside
one of the all-night bodegas? Who would believe him?

Mosabbah headed toward the Atlantic Avenue train station.
There were always people there—commuters, merchants, musi-
cians with their hats on the floor looking for spare change. If he
couldn't find a police officer, Mosabbah thought, at least it was a
well-lit area with lots of witnesses where a man with a knife might

think twice before sticking an informant in the back. Outside the train station, though, Mosabbah came across a white Chevy Caprice, with a light bar on the roof, whose doors were adorned with the word POLICE.

It was ten forty-five p.m.

John Kowalchuk and Eric Huber were relative newcomers to police work—both men had less than two years each on the job. The two men were police officers from the Long Island Rail Road Police Department, a force consisting of two hundred-plus officers who patrolled the 124 stations of the busiest commuter railroad network in North America; the LIRR carried some 275,000 commuters a day (84,000,000 a year) on 730 daily trains in and out of the large suburban tracts east of New York City. The system stretched from its main terminus, Manhattan's Penn Station at Seventh Avenue and Thirty-second Street, through Queens, Nassau, and Suffolk Counties to Montauk, the farthest tip of eastern Long Island, some 120 miles away. A spur line served Brooklyn, its western terminal at the intersection of Atlantic, Fourth, and Flatbush Avenues, feeding into the complex interchange in Jamaica, Queens. It was the job of the Long Island Rail Road Police to keep this massive electric- and diesel-rail infrastructure safe from vandalism and theft and the typical property-related crimes that afflicted most rails, as well as the homeless, pickpockets, scam artists, and other petty thieves who preyed on tired commuters. There was little serious crime on board the railroad, although on December 7, 1993, a thirty-five-year-old Jamaican-born psychopath by the name of Colin Ferguson marched up the aisle of a crowded rush hour train heading east from New York City and began to indiscriminately shoot passengers just as it pulled into the Merillon Avenue station near Garden City, some twenty miles east of Manhattan. Before he was subdued, Ferguson killed six commuters and wounded nineteen others. The case of Colin Ferguson was unique in the lengthy history of the rail system.

Kowalchuk and Huber were working the midnights at the Atlantic Avenue station on foot patrol. They had recently come on duty and had just finished checking the nearby tunnel. They had come up to the street level by the station's entrance at Hanson Place to breathe a bit; the tunnels in summer were like pizza ovens—absolutely suffocating. The two officers stood and watched people move in and out of the station, and then Kowalchuk noticed a pair of nervous eyes across the street. "Watch, here comes a question," Kowalchuk remarked to his partner. One look at Mosabbah and the rookie cop knew that he was going to come across Fulton Street to ask something; railroad cops were walking information booths and always had to answer questions ranging from "When is the next train to Farmingdale?" to "Why aren't the seats comfortable on the Hempstead line?"

Mosabbah was agitated, extremely scared. The Egyptian locked eyes with Kowalchuk. "How can I help you, sir?" In very broken English, Mosabbah attempted to say he would like to report an explosion. "Just where did this explosion take place?" Kowalchuk pressed. Mosabbah was finding it harder and harder to form words. He was trembling. Once again Mosabbah tried to speak. "I would like to report a bomb," he uttered, in a series of words that both officers had to drag out of him. He illustrated the nature of his worry by saying *"bomba"* and mimicking explosion sounds.

On any given night, the two LIRR policemen could have *easily* dismissed Mosabbah as an emotionally disturbed person who went off of his medication or was in desperate need of the drunk tank or detox. There was no shortage of the mentally ill in Brooklyn, and indeed, there was a long list of mental patients who liked hanging around the vicinity of train stations. Yet the two newcomers to the force both saw something genuine in the Egyptian's body language and heard it in his tone of voice. If he wasn't insane, he was one hell of a convincing actor. If he was truly out of his mind, then he was absolutely convinced that there was some sort of impending peril about to befall him. He was close to panic. "The man was sweating profusely. It was warm but not that hot. My partner and I had our uniforms on, our vests, and all our gear and we weren't sweating like this guy. He was serious. Anyone who looked into his eyes that night would have known just how serious he was."[2]

The two LIRR cops couldn't understand Mosabbah's frenetic attempts to articulate the nature of the Palestinians' plot. Police officers are faced with similar scenarios throughout their careers—incoherent individuals, insane ramblings, and the inability of someone who is agitated to speak and explain his position. The two Long Island Rail Road cops could have easily blown the Egyptian off, telling him, "Yeah, yeah, pal, bomba all night, just sleep it off somewhere else"; they could have easily locked him up for disorderly conduct and blocking traffic near the train station. Kowalchuk and Huber could have done a million and one things wrong that night, but they followed their gut instincts. They believed Mosabbah had something to say. They called their headquarters, who in turn contacted the Eighty-eighth Precinct; the Long Island Rail Road Police didn't have the resources to handle bomb jobs on their own.

The officers asked Mosabbah if he had any identification. He seemed confused. Kowalchuk even removed his own driver's license from his wallet and showed the Egyptian. "ID!" the rookie officer said. "Are you sure that you don't have anything that could identify who you are?" Mosabbah smiled and removed a tattered piece of paper from his pocket with a hand-scribbled number; the number began with the letter *A* and was a lengthy government-type number. It wasn't a social security number, nor was it an address. Kowalchuk and Huber were confused. "Can you write down your name for us?" they asked of the Egyptian. He proceeded to write down "Abdel Rahman Mosabbah" in Arabic. It was going to be a long night.

The two LIRR policemen told Mosabbah that a car from the Eighty-eighth Precinct would be there momentarily and that he just needed to relax and sit tight. Mosabbah became even more panic-stricken. "If they see me talking to the police, they will kill me!" he replied. Now Kowalchuk knew that the young Arab was serious. To keep him from view, the two Long Island Rail Road cops took the Egyptian to a staircase that was buttressed by metal planks on both sides—Huber stood at the bottom of the stairs and Kowalchuk protected Mosabbah from the top flight.

Both Long Island Rail Road officers accompanied the Egyptian back to the Eighty-eighth Precinct. Two forty-eight Fourth Avenue was *not* in the Eighty-eighth Precinct—but the LIRR Police HQ had contacted the Eighty-eighth and this was where the ball was rolling. Two forty-eight Fourth Avenue was actually in the Seventy-eighth Precinct, which covered the Park Slope section of Brooklyn-South. The Eighty-eighth Precinct house at 249 Classon Avenue was a three-story brick building with a spiraling minaret-like structure that looked like it could have been found in the Middle East. The precinct headquarters was a busy house—the area covered a swath of the Borough of Kings with enough industrial and residential pockets to keep patrol sectors hopping.

Mosabbah was reluctant to walk into the Eighty-eighth Precinct house. Two green lanterns marked the station—monuments to the "Rattle Watchmen" who patrolled New Amsterdam in the 1650s and carried lanterns with green glass sides at night as a means of identification; when the Watchmen returned to the watch house after patrol, they hung their lantern on a hook by the front door to show people seeking them that they had returned. In Egypt, when one walked inside a police station or a security service substation, the muffled cries of men being tortured were heard; seats, by the front desk, had ankle locks and arm restraints. Mosabbah walked slowly into the Eighty-eighth Precinct house expecting his worst nightmares. Instead, the only screams he heard were the loud debates exchanged between officers as to who was better, the Mets or the Yankees.

The hustle and bustle of police officers, detectives, suspects, and victims being shuffled through the door and lobby was dizzying. People, some with bruises, were waiting to speak to a detective about making a complaint. A prisoner was brought before the desk, his hands restrained by a shiny pair of handcuffs keeping his arms securely behind his back; the man was disheveled and shouting profanities. The inside of the police station was like nothing the newcomer from Egypt had ever seen before. The bluish apple green paint that adorned the wall, chipping in some spots, deteriorated in others thanks to a pipe leaking, was designed to make the distraught and fearful calm and subdued. The effect was lost on Mosabbah. He seemed more agitated once inside than he had on Flatbush Avenue with the Long Island Rail Road police officers.

The desk sergeant greeted the two LIRR cops with a brief nod of acknowledgment. Standing before an American flag and NYPD-supplied photographs of Commissioner Howard Safir, First Deputy Commissioner Patrick Kelleher, and Chief of Department Louis Anemone, he didn't have the time to react to the Egyptian. Barely looking at Mosabbah from behind a battered oak desk, the desk sergeant directed Mosabbah, Huber, and Kowalchuk upstairs to the detective squad.

Mosabbah's head was moving in all directions, like a father searching for his lost children; his hands were fluid as he walked up to the squad room.

Anytime anyone walked through the doors of an NYPD detective squad room, he was greeted by banners proclaiming the men and women in the room to be the GREATEST DETECTIVES IN THE WORLD. The fifteen thousand detectives in the NYPD were truly unique—

their demeanor, their presence, and their ability to make cases were world renowned. But the true-life successes, such as cracking the "Son of Sam" serial murders that gripped New York City in the late 1970s, as well as the fiction of Hollywood, from *Kojak* to *NYPD Blue,* were lost on Mosabbah.

When Mosabbah walked into the squad room, his eyes took in the men, some older and very overweight, laboring in front of Smith-Corona electric typewriters and cursing at the top of their lungs with each *a* they typed instead of an *s.* He saw women, one wearing a white tank top under a blue Kevlar bulletproof vest, flaunting her rear end in the face of a colleague as they exchanged the equal-opportunity-employment-forbidden sexually charged squad room banter that was all so typical. He saw detectives who looked like fashion models straight out of a *GQ* photo shoot, with thick black hair, slicked back tightly, and wearing Armani suits. These detectives were always suntanned; their manicured fingers were adorned with specially made detective shield rings. Mosabbah saw other detectives, who cared little for their appearance. They wore off-the-rack slacks from Sears, flannel shirts with missing buttons, and ties so insanely colorful suspects were often blinded by the bright glow. The clothes didn't make them detectives, after all.

Detectives had phenomenal memories related to the job. A detective with twenty-plus years in a squad might have trouble remembering his wedding anniversary, or what his wife wanted him to bring home from Waldbaums after finishing a tour, but he could remember any and all details about cases—he remembered where arrests were made, who was with him, what he wore, and what the Mets' score was that particular afternoon. The war stories were endless and memories could be tapped at a moment's notice. Beyond their computerlike memories, detectives had Mark Twain–like abilities to tell their anecdotes over a few beers (especially if they were "on the arm," or free). Detectives loved to think of themselves as human lie detectors that could, just by hearing someone speak and gauging his or her body language, judge if someone was on the up-and-up or telling a lie. The skills the detectives employed inside the interview room, where suspects were tricked into slipping up with one infinitesimal inaccuracy, were often inherent. You either had it or you didn't. Careers and endless files of cases were made by that instinct. And as the clock ticked on the last seconds of July 30, those skills were fixed on a newcomer to the United States from Egypt.

Sitting by a desk cluttered with manila folders, cups of stale coffee, and a half-eaten sandwich, Mosabbah once again retold his story. He looked nervous as he spoke, twisting his head around and staring at the Wanted posters on the walls. The telephones rang incessantly. Across the room, a crime victim, one eye swollen completely shut, flipped through a huge book of mug shots looking for someone who fitted the description of the person responsible for administering the beating. Mosabbah wiped beads of sweat dripping in an almost deliberate rhythm from his forehead. He clasped his hands to prevent them from shaking.

The detective who caught the case called in colleagues and supervisors to determine if the Egyptian was a nut or someone privy to impending doom. There was a major language barrier to be overcome. They made a few phone calls to try to find an Arabic-speaking detective and came up with a third-generation Levantine who spoke a dialect that didn't jibe with the very distinctive Egyptian dialect, especially the heavily accented version spoken in the southern part of the country. The Arabic-speaking detective was concerned that, perhaps, Mosabbah hadn't even understood his roommates when the threats were made.

Mosabbah was placed inside an interview room—the same room where suspects were dealt with and confessions extracted—while the detectives talked. Each of the men and women in the squad wearing their gold shield on their belt knew that the story Mosabbah was telling—because of the language factor—was far from complete. But they had a dilemma on their hands. Did they ignore the tale only to be driving back to their home on Long Island or Staten Island and hear a breaking-news flash on WINS that there had been an explosion inside a subway train, or did they start the ball rolling to mobilize the department's resources and take the risk that this would turn out to be nothing more than a bullshit job? After all, the detectives knew, in the political undercurrent of the NYPD, careers were sometimes destroyed over bullshit jobs and pulling the wrong chiefs out of bed on the wrong night.

But the detectives had all heard of what had happened in Jerusalem eighteen hours earlier. No one wanted that on his or her conscience. Mosabbah was told to sit tight and wait inside the stifling heat of the interview room while the detectives summoned the Operations Center at One Police Plaza in lower Manhattan.

This was now officially a job.

The Bomb Job

In the NYPD, "procedure" is one of the department's holiest of words—there are protocols listed in patrol and emergency guidebooks that specify, in overkill detail, who is to be notified, when, and how in case of a major incident. In emergencies, when gunfire erupts on a city street, for example, and citizens dial 911, that call is routed to a divisional emergency dispatcher responsible for a section of precincts in a particular borough, who routes the job to a divisional precinct and sector car; on large jobs, several sector cars and precinct response cars also take action, as do units from nearby precincts. The Special Operations Division frequency carries jobs to which the Aviation, Harbor, or Emergency Service Unit would respond.

On sensitive jobs that are developing and ongoing, especially those on the midnights, the borough-wide duty captain will be informed as will the citywide duty inspector; the duty-wide are bosses who, several times a month, have to work midnights and a weekend in order to be the on-call senior supervisor. Duty captains have to do a lot of things—they respond on major jobs and provide status reports to bosses summoned from home on major incidents. They respond to routine gun runs, perp searches, and other standard assignments. They sometimes help sweep messes under the rug, like cops who are stopped for driving under the influence or calls to a police officer's home after a domestic dispute.

Duty captains sometimes take an officer's gun and shield away from him, and they sometimes have to lock up fellow cops. Midnights could be treacherous. It was not a great assignment, but all captains—from precinct commanders to ESU patrol bosses—have to do it.

And, always, the citywide duty chief is notified.

On the night of July 30, the citywide duty chief was the commander of Bronx detectives, Assistant Chief Charles Kammerdener. Kammerdener was known as a topflight detective and a highly skilled investigator. He earned his stripes, and a few scars along the way, inside the ranks of the Housing Police Department. Kammerdener joined the NYCHPD in 1973, along with Ralph Pascullo, in a class that would produce scores of captains, inspectors, and chiefs; Pascullo and Kammerdener were not only good friends, but highly decorated former partners who fought crime in some of the roughest projects in Brooklyn and closed multiple homicide, robbery, rape, and assault cases that squad lieutenants thought simply unsolvable. Kammerdener, like Pascullo, hated to sit by and do nothing. They were workers, determined, brave more often than smart, and resolute to always do the right thing.

Housing cops earned respect by their size or by their actions. Kammerdener wasn't a behemoth of a man—wiry and muscular, he succeeded in wielding an iconic presence that men a foot taller could never hope to achieve. Kammerdener was all about respect—he was, after all, a former marine. In the projects, those who mistook his size or broad smile shielded by his blond-and-gray mustache as a sign of weakness were always sadly mistaken. As a boss, Kammerdener could be difficult to work for. He learned to hate excuses while a Housing cop and demanded that the men and women in his command be serious, energetic, and dedicated. He was as sharp as a razor, knowing what answers he wanted when posing a question to someone, and always pushed his people to the envelope because he knew that the city's streets were dangerous; mistakes cost people their lives.

Three times a month Kammerdener, like all one-star chiefs, pulled the midnight duty; he had to give two weekends a month for citywide duty, as well. The midnight citywide duty went from eleven p.m. to seven a.m. and covered all major jobs in all five boroughs. As the CO, or commanding officer, of Bronx detectives, Kammerdener worked in a gray suit and tie—the uniform of the bureau. But the duty chiefs had to be in uniform, and Kammerdener put on his navy blue trousers, white shirt, and blue blazer before calling the operations desk at shortly before eleven p.m. to sign on as the city's top cop for the night. Rows of medals bristled above his gold assistant chief's shield worn over his left breast pocket. One gold star was worn on each shoulder and on the collar tabs of his white shirt. The eight-point hat, which has been in use since 1928 as a symbolic salute to the eight original members of the first watch in Dutch colonial New Amsterdam, completed Kammerdener's uniform for the night.

Kammerdener always checked which supervisors were working throughout the city on the midnight roll call; in Housing, where backup was sometimes spotty, habit always prompted one to know whom he was working with. Kammerdener also checked the log to see which task forces were working and if there were any planned mobilizations for the night tour. When he had the duty, Kammerdener made it a point to visit at least one or two precincts in each of the five boroughs. It was his way of showing the flag and making sure that those in charge of the precincts knew who was out there.

Kammerdener was heading into Queens to start his tour, crossing the Triborough Bridge in his black Crown Victoria. He was heading east on the Grand Central Parkway, just over the East River crossing where Manhattan, the Bronx, and Queens are connected by the spanning bridge, when he received a call on his cellular phone. It was from operations. There were reports about bombs in a building in Park Slope and he was requested to the Eighty-eighth Precinct.

It was just before midnight.

For the Emergency Service Unit the midnight tour began with the changing of the guard—one boss ending his evening tour and, in an overlapping fashion, handing the baton to the midnight commander.

Captain Ralph Pascullo made it back to Fort Totten shortly after ten p.m. on the night of July 30. Pascullo liked being out on the streets on patrol more than anything, but he always had administrative work to do. There were phone calls to be made, the ESU desk needed to be checked in with, and he had some memos concerning upcoming FEMA meetings with the fire department—the unit's dreaded rivals in the rescue business—for review. It was, after all, a quiet night. It was the perfect time for some paperwork. Lieutenant Owen McCaffrey was already suited up in his dark blue ESU fatigues and blue baseball cap with the ESU patch with the gold lieutenant's bars pinned on the center, worn tightly around his close-cropped hair. The two former Housing cops exchanged a few words, the customary gripes, and a few old war stories from the good old days in Brooklyn's PSA 3; reminiscing was good for the soul—it brought out good memories and always a bellyful of laughs. It was typical for the two to see one another on the odd ends of a tour change. Both men genuinely liked one another. McCaffrey, for all his laid-back never-frazzled demeanor, knew that bosses like Pascullo, who would do virtually anything for the men in their command, were part of what made him so invulnerable. Pascullo, a stickler for detail, admired McCaffrey's don't-give-a-shit attitude and his uncanny ability never to let anything get him nervous or upset.

With his paperwork complete and his bullshitting with Mc-Caffrey done, Pascullo changed from his white captain's blouse and uniform into jeans and a T-shirt, hopped into his car, and headed home. As he left Fort Totten, Pascullo gazed to his right to take in the splendor of the Throgs Neck Bridge. It was a beautiful summer night and the view, one of the New York vistas that were unavailable anywhere else, made Pascullo glad to still live in the city.

Pascullo arrived home on a sleepy street determined not to make too much noise when coming inside the house. His two children were already asleep and Pascullo removed his shoes and headed upstairs just to check in on them; evening tours were a burden during the summer months when it would have been so nice to go out with the family on a drive through the neighborhood, stopping off for ice cream, but work was work, and always reflecting back on his early days of walking a post up the urine-covered stairways inside a project at PSA 3, Pascullo was grateful for his rank and his assignment. He smiled with relief as he checked on his wife, Lorraine, eight months pregnant, who was fast asleep. No point waking her up, Pascullo thought.

It was hard to wash eight and a half hours of police work off one's mind, and Pascullo ran the cold water in the bathroom sink for nearly ten minutes trying to recuperate from another night in the city. He splashed the cold and refreshing water across his cheeks and felt uneasy; he had shaved off his trademark salt-and-pepper mustache a few days earlier and his face just didn't seem right. He looked inside the refrigerator, eager for a snack, and brought a tall glass of soda to the living room, where he put on the late-night news broadcasts and fired away with his remote control in search of anything that wasn't a commercial or a bad repeat. Flipping through the channels, Pascullo found CNN and scenes of police officers removing the dead and wounded from the Mahane Yehuda market in Jerusalem. Pascullo rubbed his eyes. He was thankful to be in New York City and not in the Middle East. Pascullo knew what crime scenes were like and he knew the sights and smells that accompanied horrible accidents and multiple homicides where people were shot, butchered, or burned—one got to see everything inside the projects. Crime scenes were gory and they stank. Pascullo couldn't imagine, though, a crime scene with dozens of DOAs, nor could he imagine the fear that would grip the city if such carnage came to New York. It had been four years since the bombing of the World Trade Center, but the pictures released from the epicenter of the blast showed property destruction—not mangled and eviscerated limbs. Mayor Giuliani, Pascullo knew, would not be happy responding to a crime scene with twenty dead New Yorkers.

It was late, though, and the images from Jerusalem weren't the ideal going-to-bed entertainment needed to unwind following a long day. Pascullo turned off the TV. Tomorrow was another day.

Lieutenant Owen McCaffrey checked the midnight roll call, checked in with the ESU desk back at Floyd Bennett Field, and then hopped into his Chevy Caprice for yet another tour. He had hoped to visit one of the Trucks in Queens that night as well as head over to Four-Truck, at the uppermost tip of the Bronx in Riverdale; administratively, McCaffrey was the Four-Truck lieutenant, and picking up the paperwork and making sure that all his cops were happy campers was part of his job. As always, the SOD radio had other plans for the ESU lieutenant. There was a barricade job in lower Manhattan requiring ESU's tools and services, and McCaffrey radioed the central dispatcher that he was responding.

McCaffrey liked midnights because when most of the bosses had headed home upstate or all the way to the eastern fringes of Long Island, jobs were finished a lot quicker—no bullshit, no hour-long dissertations or waiting for the higher-ups to arrive, no endless nonsense. When McCaffrey worked, the cops did what they *had* to do—period. If a door had to be taken down, the cops broke it down. If a suspect had to be handled a *certain* way because he posed a risk to the cops or civilians, then he was "handled." More bosses on a job meant more cooks in the kitchen, and McCaffrey liked to be the only chef working. "There was no playing around when Owen worked," one of the midnight crew would comment. "He made sure that the jobs were taken care of right."[1]

A barricade job was an elongated affair, though, and usually involved someone who was mentally ill, violent, drunk, strung out, or a combination of all four, who had barricaded himself inside a house, an apartment, a basement, or even an elevator, and threatened to kill himself, anyone with him, and anyone who tried to make it through the door. Barricades were delicate jobs—often the people who fortified themselves inside a location to make a final stand were armed or they had booby-trapped the place with gasoline, lye, or another combustible and dangerous agent. Often people who barricaded themselves inside a location wanted to commit suicide by cop; they were looking for that confrontation, with the media looking on, where they could commit suicide by forcing a police officer to employ lethal force. Whenever there was a barricade job in the city, ESU always got the call—the Trucks had the tools and equipment to gain entry, and the officers had the experience and training to overcome any possible scenario.

McCaffrey arrived at the perimeter for the barricade job and saw the crew suiting up in their Kevlar vests and helmets to deal with the incident. ESU always maintained control of the inner perimeter and they always tied off the door so that no one could surprise them; the only people moving in and out of the location would be the E-cops. During a day tour, or in the evening, the job would have lasted hours; perhaps even HNT, the NYPD's famed Hostage Negotiations Team, would have been summoned. But this was the midnights and McCaffrey didn't like wasting time on jobs that needn't be dragged out. Within moments, McCaffrey was suited up, in line with the other officers from the Manhattan Trucks, and gaining entry into the location to apprehend the suspect.

At just around midnight McCaffrey was in his Caprice heading back to Queens. He'd passed through the Midtown Tunnel and was on the Long Island Expressway when the SOD radio summoned him. "U-6 on the air?" the dispatcher asked. "Please 10-1 the ESU desk forthwith." McCaffrey attempted to figure out just what the hell was going on that the desk wanted him to phone them—which is what the 10-1 meant—and hadn't conveyed the message over the radio. The Trucks sometimes used 10-1s when they wanted to invite a patrol boss to dinner, but it was too early to eat. McCaffrey knew it had to be serious.

The words "Palestinians" and "bombs" had set off rows of red flags a mile long at the NYPD Operations Center—especially fewer than twenty-four hours after the bombings in Israel. It was feared that if Mosabbah had uncovered a major—and professional—terrorist cell, one with electronic surveillance equipment, all NYPD radio communications would be compromised. After all, anyone with a hundred dollars could walk into a Radio Shack and buy an emergency response frequency scanner that covered just about every law enforcement and emergency response agency in the New York metropolitan area. These days, even criminals had become masters of eavesdropping on cellular phone communications. Everything would have to be done via landline.

A stellar crew of ESU officers works the midnights. Some who work the midnight tour do so because they have family commitments that require their presence at home during waking hours; others are getting their degrees during the day, and others have separate day jobs in order to make ends meet. Patrolling at midnight is different from working an eight-to-four or a four-to-twelve. The midnight hours are a perp's best friend. The cover of darkness and the solitude of many city streets make the time ripe for crime. It is also the hour when many businesses, following a successful night, are full of cash and void of customers and employees. It is a time when potential EDPs, unable to sleep or make love, decide that it is time for a standoff with family and the cops. It is the time when precinct holding cells swell with drunks, drug addicts, and perps, and when a select few behind bars, en route to central booking, decide to go psycho. After four a.m., when all bars in the city close, the midnight tour is also the time to be very busy, with pin jobs. Eight beers and a few shots of tequila are the perfect recipe for a man behind the wheel to end up a twisted ball of steel and bleeding organs.

ESU cops throughout the city who work the midnight tour are always a bit more cognizant, a bit more aware in the inner reaches of their sixth sense, concerning radio calls for a signal 10-13 when it is late and dark. After all, midnights are also the time when perps get stupid and decide that they can actually shoot it out with a New York City police officer and win. Late nights in the city are when police work becomes more dangerous.

After checking in with the ESU desk, McCaffrey's first phone call was to Eight-Truck in Brooklyn-North, which covered, among many others, the Eighty-eighth Precinct. Police Officer Mario Zorovic, one of the more experienced men on the midnights, with twenty-one years on the job—thirteen on midnights with ESU— was walking into the squad's kitchen when he heard the phone ringing in quarters. "Eight-Truck, Officer Zorovic," the veteran E-cop answered; he was expecting the call to be from one of the wives or girlfriends who tended to check on their mates at the start of the midnight tour, or a narcotics squad seeking ESU's help with a last-minute warrant. McCaffrey didn't have the time—or the knowledge—to go into the full details about the job. He told Zorovic that the Truck and the Adam car should head to the Eighty-eighth Precinct for "a possible warrant involving explosives or hand grenades." ESU patrolled their sector in REPs that were designated Adam, Boy, and Charley cars. If a Truck had four officers who could fill two REPs, then the Truck fielded an Adam and a Boy car; the Eight-Truck Adam car would respond on the SOD radio with the call sign "Adam-Eight." On midnights the Trucks were lucky to have a sergeant and a police officer for the Truck, and four additional officers for both the Adam and Boy cars; mostly, the squads were either "Truck only" or Truck and Adam car.

Zorovic had a sinking feeling that this was a serious job. "There were no bullshit jobs on the midnights," Zorovic reflected. "Most of the jobs were confirmed. They were all real. In Eight-Truck the jobs on the midnights were mostly gun work, perp searches, shots fired, violent EDPs, hostage barricades, and the occasional pin job, and a few minor jobs thrown in, from aided cases to the mundane."[2]

Zorovic and his partner, Police Officer John Reardon, took the Truck toward the Eighty-eighth Precinct. The other officers working at Eight-Truck brought the TCV, or total-containment vessel bomb truck, used to transport explosive material safely for disposal. Zorovic and his partner headed out of quarters in the hulking big blue emergency response truck, lights and sirens on. Eight-Truck was *always* busy. *Here we go again,* Zorovic thought. *Here we go again.*

By the time McCaffrey reached the Eighty-eighth Precinct at approximately twelve thirty a.m. dozens of police vehicles had assembled outside the station house. Parking was always at a premium around a police station; unmarked Caprice and Crown Victoria sedans from the Detective Bureau were outside the station house, as were vehicles from the borough command.

The bomb squad was also there.

The squad, part of the Detective Bureau's Forensic Investigations Division, was formed in 1903 as a force of specialists tasked with dealing with the Sicilian "Black Hand" and its use of explosives to extort money. From the world's fair bombing in 1940 to the mid-1970s bombings of LaGuardia Airport and Grand Central Station by Croat terrorists, the bomb squad responded to hundreds of actual devices and thousands of false alarms; six members of the bomb squad were killed in the line of duty throughout the years.

The year 1997 started as one of the busiest ever for the unit. On the morning of January 13, two letter bombs were discovered in the ultrabusy and ultrachaotic United Nations mail room, which processed over thirty thousand pieces of mail every day. The letters arrived eleven days after the Washington, D.C., office of *al-Hayat*, a Saudi-owned Arabic-language newspaper based in London, received five packages, each with an Alexandria, Egypt, postmark, a computer-generated label, and a number written on the envelope, and each containing an ample supply of grade-A Czech–produced Semtex plastic explosives, needles, wiring, and electrical contacts. That same day, two similar packages were also received at the federal penitentiary in Fort Leavenworth, Kansas, and a third was intercepted at the Fort Leavenworth post office.

At the UN the bomb squad responded, along with ESU units, to safely remove the intricately produced devices; two more devices were found later that day, each successfully removed and rendered safe by bomb squad detectives. It was an absolutely hectic day of frazzled nerves and fear, yet the job got done.

There isn't a cop in the NYPD who would honestly say that working with the bomb squad was easy; the technicians were temperamental and abrupt, and lived in their own peculiar universe, though, according to one former ESU cop, "if you handled material that could disintegrate you and force your eyeballs to fly out of your head at three thousand feet per second, you'd have a quirky personality."[3] Even ESU cops had a hard time working with the detectives in the unit, which was especially indicative of explosive-ordnance disposal work, since many in the unit were former E-cops. The bravado and sometimes hard-to-take personalities were accepted by most in the department—the bomb squad was one of the finest in the nation and one of the busiest.

ESU sergeant John English was at the unit's headquarters at Floyd Bennett Field when he received a call to report to the Eighty-eighth

Precinct. The third-squad sergeant from Seven-Truck, English worked regular morning and evening shifts, yet the regular midnight sergeant had asked English to switch tours with him as a favor; the patrol sergeants often helped one another out when family needs or second jobs necessitated a day off. Sergeant English, known universally throughout the unit as "good people" (the NYPD vernacular for someone who could be counted on, trusted, and followed into harm's way), enjoyed the work. Covering some of the most dangerous streets in the borough, Seven-Truck wasn't the place where a cop went if he didn't like to work. The projects, tenements, squalid single-family homes, high-crime areas, and numerous avenues and highways made it one of the busiest squads in all of ESU.

English had picked up the U-5 Citywide-South patrol car at headquarters when he was summoned on the phone to report to the Eighty-eighth Precinct. English was certain that the call involved a warrant or some sort of barricade incident. English, with piercing blue eyes and a mustache, was an optimist by nature. He was sure that the job would be routine.

Sergeant English walked into the Eighty-eighth Precinct house and found the activity worrisome. "Bodies" (the slang for cops) were moving at a hurried pace. The duty chief was present. There was a Long Island Rail Road Police car parked in front. McCaffrey came out to greet English with a huge smile on his face. "Dude," McCaffrey said, "this is the big one."[4]

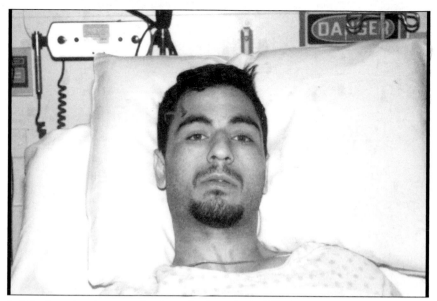

Gazi Abu Mezer, less than twenty-four hours after being shot by NYPD Emergency Service Unit members, recovers in his hospital bed. (Author's Collection)

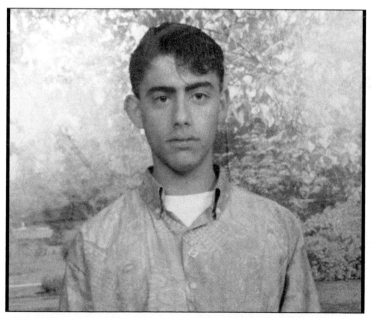

Lafi Khalil, in an undated West Bank photograph (AP/Wide World Photos)

July 30, 1997: Israeli crime scene investigators look at the body of one of the two Hamas suicide bombers in the bloody wreckage of Jerusalem's Mahane Yehuda Market. (Israel Government Press Office)

Gazi Abu Mezer, in a photo from his bomb-building material days in North Carolina, clutches a twelve-gauge shotgun. (Gerald Herbert/New York Daily News)

The outer facade of the bombers' home—248 Fourth Avenue, Park Slope, Brooklyn (Samuel M. Katz)

Fourth Avenue, Park Slope, and the path the bombers would have taken to the Atlantic Avenue subway and Long Island Rail Road hub (Samuel M. Katz)

An FBI mock-up of the suicide bombs (Gerald Herbert/New York Daily News)

NYPD assistant chief Charles Kammerdener, the commanding officer of the Special Operations Division at the time of this book's writing—and the duty chief working the night of July 30–31, 1997 (Samuel M. Katz)

Emergency Service Unit captain Ralph Pascullo, seen here shortly after the Housing police, Transit police, and NYPD merged, monitors a perp search from atop a project rooftop in lower Manhattan. (Samuel M. Katz)

Several of the NYPD Emergency Service Unit officers who answered the call to respond to the two Palestinian bombers' attempt to blow themselves up on a Manhattan-bound subway train. From left to right: Police Officer Mario Zorovic, Lieutenant Owen McCaffrey, Deputy Inspector Ralph Pascullo, Sergeant John English, and Police Officer Dave Martinez. (Samuel M. Katz)

U.S. State Department Diplomatic Security Service special agent Jeremy Yamin, a member of the NYPD-FBI JTTF in 1997, seen here during a protective detail for PLO Chairman Yasir Arafat in New York City (Courtesy of Jeremy Yamin)

An NYPD ESU countersniper peers through the scope of his Remington M24 precision rifle during a job in Brooklyn. (Samuel M. Katz)

Captain Ralph Pascullo assists in the execution of a high-risk warrant in Brooklyn shortly before the suicide bomber "job."
(Samuel M.Katz)

An ESU entry team storms a high-risk location during a job in Harlem. (Samuel M. Katz)

Inside the projects: ESU officers prepare their ballistic Body Bunker during a "barricade" job of an EDP—emotionally disturbed person—holding hostages. (Samuel M. Katz)

NO ACCESS! NO ACCESS! NO ACCESS! NO ACC
Y VEST & HELMET WITHOUT HEAVY DUTY VEST & HELMET WITHOUT H

An ESU "Truck" with all its equipment on display (Courtesy of NYPD ESU)

National Association of Police Organizations
TOP COPS AWARDS

New York City mayor Rudy Giuliani, with the officers involved in the incident, addresses a press conference two days after Gazi Abu Mezer and Lafi Khalil were shot hours before their plan to detonate their bombs in the subway. (NYC Mayor's Office/Courtesy of Ralph Pascullo)

The 1998 Top Cops recipients meet President Bill Clinton and Attorney General Janet Reno in the oval office. From left to right: Sergeant John English, Lieutenant Owen McCaffrey, Deputy Inspector J. McDermott, U.S. Attorney General Janet Reno, President Bill Clinton, Police Officer Joe Dolan, Police Officer Dave Martinez, Police Officer Mike Keenan, and Police Officer Mario Zorovic. Absent from the photo is Captain Ralph Pascullo, who was exiled by One Police Plaza to a mission in the Dominican Republic. (White House Photo/Courtesy of Owen McCaffrey)

The Tac Plan

The U-5, or City-South, ESU supervisor, on the second shift of a double, and Chief Kammerdener at the Eighty-eighth Precinct were taken immediately to a small interview room upstairs where Mosabbah sat nursing a Coke. Detectives spoke with him, as did the first members of the bomb squad to arrive; if, indeed, there were explosive devices at 248 Fourth Avenue, then getting information on their detonating mechanism was crucial. McCaffrey peeked into the room and saw the Egyptian and everyone trying to communicate with him. *This is what they are basing this job on?* McCaffrey wondered. "He was super excited," McCaffrey remembered. "You could tell he was concerned. He was shitting in his pants."[1] The detective who spoke Arabic could translate only a couple of words for English, McCaffrey, and Kammerdener, but right away McCaffrey believed Mosabbah to be genuine. McCaffrey felt the Egyptian to be credible, even though he didn't understand a single word of the Arabic he was spraying at the detective. Anyone that scared, McCaffrey thought, just had to be telling the truth.

When operations was notified about the possibility of a bomb job in Brooklyn involving Middle Eastern individuals, the operations officers immediately scanned the computer records to see who was working who had Arabic as a second language. The computer search came up with a rookie officer, someone in his early twenties, who worked at the Thirteenth Precinct on Twenty-first

Street in midtown Manhattan; because he had less than two years on the job he was still on probation. The rookie cop working the Thirteenth Precinct had come into the house hours earlier hoping for a quick and uneventful midnight tour. Midnights in the Thirteenth were routine and ordinary: drunks in Union Square Park, disturbances in the illegal drinking clubs on Seventh Avenue, and details targeting hookers and johns working the gentrified corridors of Fourteenth Street. The Rookie* liked the Thirteenth Precinct because it was relatively quiet. Not many chances of a cop getting killed in that part of Manhattan.

The Rookie's family came from North Africa and his colloquial Arabic was different from Mosabbah's, but this was the best the NYPD had. The Rookie was rushed to the Eighty-eighth Precinct so that he could act as interpreter. The clock was ticking. It was nearing one a.m.

The Rookie walked into the Eighty-eighth Precinct very concerned—for newcomers to the force, being summoned from patrol to the mysterious reaches of Brooklyn-North in the middle of the night was not something that happened every day. The Rookie was ushered upstairs as if he were a VIP, taken by the arm, and escorted toward the side room where Mosabbah was waiting. The detectives in the squad room looked at the rookie officer as if he were the great expert they were waiting for. The Rookie wasn't used to the attention. It made him extremely uncomfortable. Chief Kammerdener, Lieutenant McCaffrey, and Sergeant English watched as the Rookie entered the room and was introduced to Mosabbah. The greeting was brief and serious. The two began to talk.

After an exchange in Arabic, the Rookie raised his hand to pause the Egyptian and then translated the gist of the exchange for the ESU bosses and Chief Kammerdener. "Did you see what happened to the Jews today in Israel?" the Rookie relayed, attempting

---

*Due to security concerns, the rookie officer's identity has been withheld.

to follow Mosabbah's statement word for word. "Well, that's what is going to happen to the subways tomorrow in Brooklyn." McCaffrey stared at Mosabbah in initial disbelief, and then he looked at the quivering Egyptian and felt uneasy. He then looked at the Rookie and saw the fear resonating from the officer's face.

The Rookie had the most reason for concern, of course. He knew, more than anyone in the room with the exception of Mosabbah, that this was, indeed, a *real* job. Growing up in a home full of Middle Eastern immigrants, the Rookie was well versed in the nuances of Arabic speech and exaggeration. He had been raised by Arabic-speaking relatives who were masters at the Middle Eastern penchant for drama and embellishment—when his relatives gossiped with one another, a story about a hangnail could take on the seriousness of terminal brain cancer; accounts of an argument in the marketplace with a fish vendor were often replayed as an epic conflagration bloodier than the Battle of Stalingrad. The Rookie had been well schooled in the inflection of bombastic speech. He knew that Arabic storytelling was a choreography of vocabulary and flailing hands. But when Mosabbah spoke, the Rookie found the Egyptian newcomer void of any language of grandiose claims. The informant's tone was subdued, almost desperate. He didn't say that the bombs in the apartment were gargantuan. He gave the Rookie the exact dimensions of the devices. There was no embellishment. His account was genuine.

McCaffrey placed his hands on his utility belt, wedging his fingers across his holster. "Ask him why he's giving the two Palestinians up," McCaffrey told the Rookie, expecting to hear something about a money dispute or even an argument over a woman as the reason why Mosabbah was coming forward.

"I am just renting this place out and they're there," Mosabbah responded, this time looking straight at McCaffrey. "I just want to be an American and live the American dream. I don't want any part of this and I know if they do this, I am going to get blamed."

McCaffrey now folded his arms across his large frame, raised his eyebrows, and glanced at Sergeant English. He was convinced. Mosabbah was the genuine article. This was going to be a long night.

The more Mosabbah spoke, the more the story became the basis for a large-scale investigation. Chief Kammerdener ordered the Seventy-eighth Precinct's anticrime detail into action. The anticrime unit was a precinct's plainclothes force of officers, primarily young ones, who patrolled in unmarked vehicles and in raggedy civilian clothing to saturate areas of high crime or suspicious activity with a nonuniformed presence. Dressed as hip-hop wannabes in loose-fitting urban apparel (convenient when hiding a bulletproof vest and a sidearm), or in oversized Notre Dame football jerseys, the anticrime cops could patrol and stop crimes in progress. Anticrime work was dangerous—very dangerous; all plainclothes details were, because the perpetrators could, mistakenly, not properly identify the responding officer as a policeman, and a uniformed officer might very well mistake the armed individual as a perpetrator and not a fellow officer; the risk of friendly-fire incidents was very real. To help reduce the risk of such tragic and potentially lethal mistakes, each officer wore a color-of-the-day armband; officers also removed their tin shields from behind their clothing once they identified themselves as police officers. But in the dark, inside an alley while chasing a robbery suspect, the dangers existed at every corner.

Anticrime cops were very good in knowing virtually every back alley, side street, after-hours club, gambling joint, and drug location in their precinct—that was their job. Kammerdener ordered the Seventy-eighth's anticrime detail to place 248 Fourth Avenue under surveillance from a distance; the details rode around in beat-up vehicles that were difficult to identify as NYPD. If anyone left 248 Fourth Avenue, Kammerdener ordered, anticrime cops were to stop and question him at least two blocks from the building—just in case the Palestinians were employing lookouts and countersurveillance support. It was important that the growing law enforcement operation not tip off the bombers.

Kammerdener and the detectives also began a quick and extremely pressurized investigation into both Mosabbah and the address in question. Was Mosabbah a plant? Did he have a criminal record? Was he on a terrorist or narcotics watch list? Under Kammerdener's directive, Eighty-eighth squad detectives contacted the DEA NY HIDTA (High Intensity Drug Trafficking Area) Task Force to access the city, state, and federal computer systems that were unavailable to the NYPD. Operators of the HIDTA computer, just by typing in "248 Fourth Avenue," could locate drug dealers, informants, or other federal criminals living in and around any particular address; the HIDTA system could also tap INS and customs checks, which were used to see when and where Mosabbah entered the United States. For some unknown reason, which was causing some doubt of the Egyptian's story, there was no record of Mosabbah *ever* entering the United States.

The two Long Island Rail Road police officers remained behind at the Eighty-eighth Precinct throughout the mobilization—the job had started with them and they were going to be there to the end. John Kowalchuk just happened to be walking past the squad room when he heard that the detectives were having a hard time finding out when exactly Mosabbah had come into the country. "Maybe this'll help?" Kowalchuk asked as he removed the piece of paper from his pocket that Mosabbah had handed him when the whole ordeal began. It was invaluable. Mosabbah had written down his INS number. When the detectives ran the number through the INS system, Mosabbah's entire file came up on screen.

Lieutenant Owen McCaffrey understood that Mosabbah's story was going to end, one way or another, with ESU making entry into the apartment to deal with the situation, and he needed his troops. McCaffrey ordered every Adam car operating in the city—nearly twenty police officers in total—to respond "forthwith" to the Eighty-eighth Precinct; all notifications were made on landline phones and without McCaffrey explaining anything more than this was a bomb job. McCaffrey ordered that several pieces of specialized ESU equipment be brought along, as well, including the TCV, at Two-Truck, and the unmarked CAT car from Three-Truck in the Bronx.

McCaffrey also summoned several members of the ESU countersniper team to the Eighty-eighth Precinct. The snipers were used during dignitary protection details, often in conjunction with the U.S. Secret Service and the U.S. State Department Diplomatic Security Service, as a high-powered sharpshooting force tooled and trained in removing threats from hundreds of yards away. Using Remington M24 7.62mm precision rifles, the ESU snipers were teamed with observers armed with Ruger Mini-14 5.56mm assault rifles, who not only could shoot a threat between the eyes at four hundred yards, but whose high-powered scopes were invaluable observation and intelligence-gathering tools. McCaffrey didn't know how many Palestinians were involved in the plot or what sort of tactical fight his men would end up waging. He wanted to be ready for any and all contingencies.

McCaffrey also had to notify his bosses. The first call went to Pascullo. It was just after one thirty a.m.

Ralph Pascullo was half asleep on his couch, eyes closing gently and the remote on his lap, when his home telephone rang. The ringing startled him, and he leaped up off the couch hurriedly to grab the call before anyone else was woken up. "Yo, dude, there is a big bomb job in the Eighty-eighth Precinct involving terrorists," McCaffrey said, not having to identify himself because he was the only one, Pascullo knew, who began and ended each sentence with the word "dude." "You don't even want to come to this. We are going to end up getting killed. You have a wife and kids and you don't want to be here. This is a suicide mission."[2] Pascullo paused for a second, attempting to wake up fast enough in order to discern if this was, indeed, Owen or some sort of sick crank call. But there was no mistaking McCaffrey's voice and demeanor. While he pleaded with Pascullo not to show up, McCaffrey's real message was all subliminal; he wanted his friend, and his boss, there with him. Pascullo knew McCaffrey well enough to know that he had to be there. "I'll be there in ten minutes," Pascullo replied. "I'll get there as fast as I can."

Pascullo hung up the phone, rubbed his eyes, and suddenly felt a shudder of concern. McCaffrey *never* called about anything; police-involved shootings, major incidents, and even the juiciest of rumors were never considered important enough for McCaffrey to call. This had to be beyond major, Pascullo thought. This was the big one.

Grabbing his keys and his off-duty revolver, Pascullo gave his wife a gentle kiss on the forehead, hoping not to wake her up, but the call had sparked alarm; being a police officer's wife was never easy, especially one whose husband went straight from the projects to the most dire emergencies in New York City. He smiled before he left and said he'd be home soon, and then he checked on his children one last time before walking out the door.

Driving toward Fort Totten in his own maroon Ford Taurus station wagon to pick up his captain's car, Pascullo ran several red lights on Northern Boulevard rushing through northeastern Queens before he spotted a patrol car from the 109th Precinct in front of a Dunkin' Donuts. *At last,* Pascullo thought, *an escort;* racing through the boulevard at eighty miles an hour in his own car without lights and sirens was going to get someone killed. Two older officers sat in the car, monitoring the radio and enjoying the quiet night in the borough. Pascullo honked his horn and flashed his captain's shield at the patrol car and yelled, "I need to get to Fort Totten now. Can you guys give me an escort?" Pascullo was a man who loved to drive fast and his high-speed skills were impressive; as a hobby, he restored vintage vehicles and displayed them at car shows. Yet the escort was a slower journey than it would have been had he just leaned on his horn and blazed through intersections. At the entrance to Fort Totten, the patrol car banked a sharp left and the officers' logbook, the leather memo folder with their summonses inside, came flying out of the driver's window; the summonses, tickets already issued, and other personal papers went flying all over Bell Boulevard. Pascullo felt bad that his need for speed caused the unfortunate memo book chaos, but he didn't have time to help pick up the pages tossed into the wind. He headed to the ESU building, quickly changed back into uniform, and raced out again—past the officers on their knees picking up their papers—en route to Brooklyn. *Those guys will be cursing me all night*, Pascullo chuckled to himself as he headed toward the Borough of Kings at a clip of nearly a hundred miles per hour. He didn't even want to think of the two poor old-timers sifting through the grass looking for the parking tickets they'd have to submit at the end of their shift. He wanted to focus his mind on Owen's phone call and the prospects of some sort of bomb job before dawn.

By the time Captain Ralph Pascullo reached the Eighty-eighth Precinct shortly before two thirty a.m., the station house looked like a Pentagon command center. Officers from a multitude of commands had assembled and were crowding the front desk. ESU officers, mostly just biding their time until given a job to do, sat around on the staircases and upstairs, by the detective squad, seeing their friends in the unit whom they only got to see on the very big jobs. The E-cops greeted Pascullo with the typical "What's going on, boss?" Pascullo had no answer. He maneuvered his way up the stairs toward a back room where he saw McCaffrey, English, and his old partner from PSA 3, Chief Kammerdener.

Each time another detective, another ESU cop, or another member of the bomb squad needed to get the story about the

location, the Rookie was pressed into action to translate Mosabbah's tale. Everyone wanted different bits of information from
Mosabbah, who became light-headed and overwhelmed by the
fusillade of questions from so many new faces. The detectives, primarily from the Intelligence Division, which investigated terrorist
threats to the city, pressed Mosabbah for information on the identities of the two Palestinians. Bomb squad detectives grilled the
Egyptian on the type of batteries that were hooked up to the device, as well as questions about other bombs. "Were there booby
traps in the apartment?" detectives asked, already wearing their
faded navy blue coveralls with the words NYPD BOMB SQUAD on the
back. "Were there any trip wires in the room? What did the explosive agent look like? What type of smell did the agent give off?"

English told the detectives that he needed time to speak to
Mosabbah alone. The tactical element of the operation was all-
important and English wanted to get a feel for the informant's description. Perhaps most interesting to English was the mind-set of the
two Palestinians. "Do you think that the two would blow themselves
up when we came through the door?" English asked Mosabbah
through their interpreter. "Absolutely," Mosabbah replied through
the Rookie. "If they can't get to the subway, they would love to take
you guys out instead."[3] English was floored by the response.

McCaffrey, English, and now Pascullo sat with Mosabbah and were
most concerned with the apartment's layout. The three ESU bosses
would have to formulate the safest and most effective tactical
plan—which Kammerdener would have to sign off on—for
storming the Palestinians' apartment. Even though Mosabbah had
sketched out a complete diagram of the apartment, including
where the doors were, where the Palestinians slept, and where any
possible obstacles in the flat lay, there were items about his description that just seemed off. "The informant said that there was a
bicycle leaning against the front of the building and that there was

The ESU sketch of the targeted apartment in the back building at 248 Fourth Avenue (Courtesy of Owen McCaffrey) a small stoop of a few steps to get to the front of the building," McCaffrey explained, "but when the detectives drove by the address it didn't look like anything he had described. It looked like a five- or six-story basic Brooklyn railroad-flat building that you walked into with no stoop in front of the building. We knew this didn't match. He said that it was a two-story building. We had our question marks and they were serious. I believed the guy, but the information just didn't fit."[4]

Adding to the inconsistencies was the fact that Mosabbah claimed that a street—President Street—was visible from the one window in the apartment, but the ESU officers looking at their detailed precinct maps couldn't see how the street was visible from the Fourth Avenue building. Mosabbah also didn't know about whether or not the Palestinians had firearms or any other potentially lethal surprises at their disposal.

"The more we go to the actual layout and tactical planning," McCaffrey remembered, "the more the story seemed to be pieces from different puzzles. Yet I still believed him. He was petrified when he told us that the bombs were on the floor in between the two mattresses the Palestinians slept on. And the informant added that the two Palestinians would either be sleeping or praying around the bomb. That got my attention."

Usually before ESU raids a location on a high-risk warrant, in what is known in the unit vernacular as a hit, the homicide, robbery, or narcotics detectives who have gathered all the intelligence on the suspect's house or apartment will lay out a highly detailed diagram clearly marking where a sofa is, how many windows are in the location, and where lay fire escapes or other exit points a suspect could use as an escape route. The intelligence is crucial for the ESU assault team when planning where to go inside an apartment.

"On a hit you just didn't break down a door and run wildly," claimed a former ESU cop now working for a federal law enforcement agency. "You had to know where to go, where to peel off into, who was in the apartment, and how was the furniture set up. Were there children in the apartment? Were there dogs? Drug dealers often used pit bulls and Rottweilers, sometimes with their voice boxes surgically removed, as guard dogs. To make these dogs cruel, the dealers often fed the dogs a steady diet of cocaine and kittens. What else could be in the location to trip you up? The last thing you wanted to do was trip over some wires or a table. Often when we went into a location, the place was dark. We had to know what to expect."[5]

Knowing what to expect inside the location was especially important in light of a job that ESU had handled months earlier, also in Brooklyn, against a radical cult from the 1960s. The cult members, wanted on a child health warrant for alleged reports of abuse, lived in a series of structures that were connected to each other by underground catacombs; the apartments and catacombs were fortified and booby-trapped, but the intelligence ESU received prior to the warrant mentioned nothing of the subterranean escape network. Officers could have easily been ambushed by booby traps that the cult had laid out for them in the darkened tunnels. Officers could have been killed by gunfire while chasing escaping cult members in uncharted territory.

Pascullo was determined that the intelligence available be as accurate as humanly possible.

Kammerdener, Pascullo, McCaffrey, and English sat down inside the squad room and reviewed their tactical options. Three possible assault scenarios were envisioned. The first was that ESU would surround the location and then, using a loudspeaker, summon the Palestinians to come out with their hands on top of their heads. The option was a safe, remote tactic, but since Mosabbah had hinted that the Palestinians wanted to emulate the suicide bombing in Jerusalem a day earlier, this plan was dismissed because if one of the two men inside the apartment flipped the switches and detonated the bombs, then everyone in the building could be killed.

McCaffrey once again asked Mosabbah if the Palestinians would blow themselves up if the cops raided their home, and the Egyptian responded immediately and forcefully. "Killing cops doing a raid is just as good as blowing themselves up in the subway," Mosabbah replied. He was adamant. McCaffrey and Pascullo looked at each other with grave concern. The bomb squad confirmed that, according to the Egyptian's description and their technical assumptions, the Palestinians' device could very well take down the entire structure.

The second option was to quietly evacuate everyone from the building and then, when the risk of casualties to innocent civilians was minimized, utilize the loudspeaker approach, but even this was seen as an unlikely possibility. Evacuating several apartment buildings' worth of sleepy men, women, and children was not seen as something that the ESU cops, and their borough-wide support, could have done without sparking some sort of noise and warning to the Palestinians. Kammerdener, in fact, had ordered something known as a COLES check of the building, which listed everyone who had a registered phone in the location, and many of the surnames came back as Middle Eastern in origin. The concern that the Palestinians might have accomplices in the building could not be overlooked.

A third option was to wait, covertly, in front of the building until the two Palestinians walked out of the door en route to the subway station, and to apprehend them on the street; the ESU snipers, who would nestle themselves atop the roofs of the buildings across the street, would make sure that the two young West Bank natives were unable to trip any wires. But, Pascullo thought, what if the bombs had dead-men switches, which would activate the devices the moment pressure was released from a trigger mechanism? Even if the snipers noticed the Palestinians about to detonate their devices and fired first—hitting both men with head shots—a dead-man feature could still detonate the bombs.

The final option available—and the riskiest—was entering the apartment covertly and apprehending the suspects with stealth, speed, and hopefully no firepower before they were able to access the devices. The one grave concern about this plan was that the officers would be walking into a trap and that the Palestinians would detonate the bombs and blow themselves up, killing the cops and, in the process, everyone who lived in the building. The one plus— and it was a huge plus—of this option was the fact that Mosabbah had the key to the front door. ESU wouldn't have to knock down the door with a sledgehammer, as they often did on hits, nor would they have to resort to a "rabbit tool," which was a hydraulically powered spreader that wedged an opening between a locked door and the frame. The E-cops could simply—and silently—turn the standard hardware-store-cut key and enter the apartment without anyone knowing. After all, the Palestinians were expecting Mosabbah to return sometime that night and the noise of a key jingling in the door wouldn't cause alarm.

The key also removed one always present obstacle to any law enforcement endeavor—the warrant. This was a textbook emergency situation where entering the apartment was vital in saving the lives of the people in the building. And, most importantly, because Mosabbah handed the detectives the key to the apartment, he was inviting them into his home. No warrant was necessary. The district attorney's office didn't require notification.

Kammerdener realized that time was of the essence. When Mosabbah mentioned that the Palestinians would attack in the morning, Kammerdener thought he meant dawn, when Muslims embark on their morning prayers. It was crucial, the chief thought, to get the job done before morning's first light.

Pascullo, McCaffrey, and English sat down to fine-tune the tactics and to select the entry team.

Because the apartment was so small, McCaffrey and English didn't want to employ the typical nine-man ESU entry team. This consisted of the lead officer with a Body Bunker, or protective shield, who was carrying a 9mm semiautomatic pistol, followed by an officer with a Heckler & Koch MP5 9mm submachine gun, followed by another Body Bunker, again armed with a Glock, followed by an officer with an MP5, followed by a boss (a sergeant or lieutenant) and two officers with handcuffs to secure the suspects. Two breachers, the officers who would be first to line up outside an apartment with a sledgehammer or other entry tools, followed the line of officers at the end. McCaffrey was concerned about not flooding the apartment with too many bodies, especially around something as volatile as a bomb. "I just wanted to keep the carnage down," McCaffrey recalled. "I'd rather have seen five or six guys get killed than nine."[6]

Further discussion, sometimes heated, erupted over what the team would take with them into the apartment. McCaffrey wanted to have the officers coming in hot and fast without the heavy and cumbersome ballistic shields impeding their path. Kammerdener was adamant that the officers bring their shields. "What if the other roommate has a gun?" he asked. "What if when you guys go into the apartment you start getting hit with bullets? Then I'm in trouble. Won't gunfire slow down the assault on the room with the two bombers?" The exchange went back and forth. The ESU supervisors knew that the ballistic shields, while effective against handgun rounds, could not stop shrapnel launched at thousands of feet per second by the force of a powerful bomb.

In the end Chief Kammerdener and the ESU bosses compromised. There'd be one Body Bunker taken along on the hit.

Green Light

The tactical end of the operation was the centerpiece of stopping the Palestinians, but there were so many other elements involved. ESU would control the inner perimeter around 248 Fourth Avenue, but the predetermined outer perimeter, covering several blocks of the neighborhood, had to be completely cordoned off. Kammerdener summoned the Brooklyn-South Task Force, a group of officers who patrolled borough-wide sectors and were always on call to respond to any major incidents, to be mobilized and presented with a list of assignments; their mission would be to cordon off all the junctions and streets around the targeted building to make sure that the police operated in a completely sterile area. Pascullo and McCaffrey also had to prepare for a building collapse contingency, in case the assault was unsuccessful, the Palestinians detonated their devices, and the structure came crashing down. ESU has special vehicles, tools, and training to deal with such nightmarish scenarios, and ESU personnel had displayed their second-to-none skills bringing out survivors and corpses in the aftermath of both the 1993 World Trade Center bombing and the 1995 bombing of the Murrah Federal Building in Oklahoma City, Oklahoma; ESU officers, because of their rescue expertise, had been assigned, along with members of the FDNY, to a regional FEMA task force.

A mobilized FDNY presence was also needed now. If the bombs were detonated and the resulting fireball caused several of the surrounding buildings to go up like a torch, a massive firefighting effort would be required to complement the rescue and recovery operation.

All notifications, *everything,* was done over secure landlines, which could not be intercepted like police and fire radio frequencies. McCaffrey called the fire marshal hotline. "Listen, this isn't a crank call, my name is Lieutenant Owen McCaffrey from ESU, I'm at the Eighty-eighth Precinct, here's the phone number, call the desk downstairs, and they'll kick the call back to me, just so that you know that this is an official job." McCaffrey knew of the poison blood that existed between ESU and the FDNY; ESU and the fire department were bitter rivals in rescue work, and ESU cops called firemen a virtual thesaurus of derogatory names. There were pranks in the past lobbed by one agency to the other, and sometimes things got stupid, including fistfights on jobs where both ESU and the FDNY responded. McCaffrey wanted to make sure that the fire marshal knew that this was no joke. "I need three fire trucks. You cannot put it over your radio—you have to call from your location to their firehouses and have the responding units *not* use their radios. We are hitting a terrorist bomb factory. Our frequencies might be monitored."[1]

A series of phone calls back and forth between the FDNY hierarchy and McCaffrey secured the vehicles. McCaffrey also had to contact EMS to get a small convoy of ambulances ready, and the Metropolitan Transportation Authority also had to be mobilized and placed in emergency mode because it was discovered that the Fourth Avenue subway, the N and R Lines, ran practically underneath the suspected building. If the Palestinians did, indeed, blow up the ESU entry team and the building subsequently collapsed, the chances were extremely high that the weight of the rubble could force a collapse deeper into the subway tunnel; or, it was feared, the vibrations of subway trains hitting the tracks at speeds in excess of forty miles per hour could cause a tenuous foundation to buckle under and give way—possibly on top of a passing train. "MTA officials went ape shit," one of the ESU officers would later reflect, "because nearly three hundred thousand people used those lines each morning during rush hour. But this was not a matter open to negotiation."

In addition to shutting the subways down, Kammerdener also requisitioned two city buses that would be used to ferry the inhabitants of the building, once evacuated, back to the Eighty-eighth Precinct for a debrief by detectives to make sure that accomplices and other cells weren't living nearby.

Con Edison had to be contacted to restore electricity should an explosion knock out wires and underground cables; so, too, did Kings County Hospital, to let them know that they might be flooded with wounded come dawn. The city's Office of Emergency Management also had to be notified, as did the Department of Sanitation to pick up debris from a possible blast. "People think that the city shuts down after midnight," Chief Kammerdener reflected, "but there is a whole force of police officers, firemen, and other emergency workers who work around the clock making sure that what needs to get done actually does get done."[2]

The final bit of planning that needed to be finalized was the actual makeup of the six-man entry team. Selecting the assault team was tricky. Some twenty-plus ESU cops had assembled inside the Eighty-eighth Precinct. Some smoked cigarettes; some munched on snacks from the vending machine. Others just took the opportunity to bullshit and talk with friends from the unit or inside the precinct. "SWAT" might stand for Special Weapons and Tactics, but in reality it meant Sit, Wait, and Talk. "Tactical work," one veteran would comment, "was mostly foreplay with a very quick, sometimes never realized, climax. You responded to a job, suited up, waited, watched, waited some more, and more often than not, the entire ordeal was resolved without requiring the men in the heavy vests and helmets."

Yet it was nearly three a.m. The window of planning was closing.

Pascullo, McCaffrey, and English summoned the ESU cops into the squad room to end the endless rumors with the ugly truth about what lay ahead. "Listen, fellas, we're going on a raid here—we have to hit these guys. These guys are suicide bombers, they have a pretty big bomb, and if they get to the bomb before we get to them, the entry team, according to the bomb squad, isn't going to make it. The building is going to come down." ESU cops had a lethal wealth of gallows humor and could laugh in the light of the direst dangers, but the assembled were absolutely silent when Mc-Caffrey spoke. McCaffrey never dramatized danger. His tone was daunting. "I need some volunteers to go in on this," McCaffrey continued, "and I am going to pick you by who's married and who has kids, and I am going to put you on the side, and I am going to pick guys that don't have kids because this is half a suicide mission. I give us less than a fifty-fifty chance of coming out of this one alive."[3]

The E-cops absorbed McCaffrey's premonitions. They were used to dangerous circumstances, and each had executed his fair share of "hits" on violent felons where firepower was needed, but in the words of one of the officers, "this wasn't like a shooting where one or two guys might be hit and everyone else is coming out okay. Here, either the entire team got killed or everyone lived to fight another day." Each man in the room understood the dangers, and every police officer assembled that night wearing the ESU uniform had joined the department's flagship force so that it could, indeed, be him that the city turned to on the big job. Many E-cops spent their entire careers waiting for that one monumental job when the eyes of the department, the city, and even the world would be upon them. They lived for the challenge. It defined who they were as police officers and collectively as a unit with a rich and proud tradition. They all wanted to be selected for the entry team.

Police Officer Joe Dolan, from Six-Truck in Brooklyn-South, told McCaffrey that the thinking behind his selection process was pure unadulterated bullshit. "This is a Six-Truck job," Dolan told McCaffrey. "We are going to do it." The sentiments were echoed by Police Officers Dave Martinez and Mike Keenan, also from Six-Truck. They were going to be the first ones through the door. Police Officer Mario Zorovic, the first man to get the call from McCaffrey about the incident, put himself in the team, as well. McCaffrey had his volunteers. "I looked at the guys who volunteered and I had one hundred percent confidence in their experience and their ability to do the right thing," McCaffrey explained.[4] The six-man entry team would be rounded off by Sergeant English and McCaffrey himself.

Zorovic looked at the crew volunteering for the team and smiled to himself. "If I go," he said under his breath, "I go in good company. If I die tonight, I'll die with a good group of cops."[5]

McCaffrey knew the men in the entry team well—the midnight crews were his. The veteran officers were confident and capable, and when running into an apartment on a hit, described by the supervising lieutenant as a suicide mission, confidence was worth its weight in gold.

The rest of the officers would support the operation. They would follow the entry team, secure the outer perimeter, and assist the bomb squad. A sniper position was set up on the building across the street. In case the entry team found itself in trouble, or engaged in a hellacious shoot-out, the sniper was ordered to select targets and fire away. McCaffrey was determined to keep collateral damage—especially among his own men—down to an absolute minimum.

"I was very proud of the guys," English would later reflect. "Everyone came forward and wanted to be on the entry team. And those not selected didn't bitch and moan or complain. Everyone accepted their assignment properly and went about their business in true ESU fashion."[6]

With his entry team now selected, McCaffrey summoned the five men into a side room for the kind of conversation police officers have among themselves with no witnesses. "Listen, this is the deal," McCaffrey explained. "We have to go in and these dudes are going to blow themselves up, according to our informant. If our informant is lying to us and he's a nut and this is a little old Jewish lady inside the apartment and we go shooting up the place killing everybody, we are going to end up going to the grand jury. We'll have to tell the grand jury that this is the information we got from the informant and that's why we killed these innocent people. If this guy is telling us the truth and we go in and shoot these guys, we are going to be heroes, and we'll come out alive and everything will be good. If, however, you go in there and hold back a little, and you wait to see who and what they are, and they get to that bomb, we are dead!"[7]

The ESU supervisors, studying the layout of the apartment that Mosabbah had drawn for them as if it were a battle map of some enemy coastline about to be hit by the marines, fine-tuned their tactical plan, maneuvering ideas and possibilities like pieces on a chessboard. Police Officers Dolan and Martinez volunteered to be the first two through the door—the tandem responsible for handling the two Palestinians and the bombs. "We're doing it, boss, and that's the end of that," Martinez and Dolan both told McCaffrey. "We know exactly what you're saying, we'll do the right thing, and we'll take care of business."[8] The Seventy-eighth Precinct, where the Fourth Avenue home was located, was in Six-Truck's territory, and to the two veterans of the unit, this just had to be a job led by officers from Brooklyn-South.

Martinez would be the first through the door. He'd have the ballistic shield and the 9mm semiautomatic Glock; Dolan, instead of taking a submachine gun, opted for the Ruger Mini-14 5.56mm assault rifle. Both Zorovic and Keenan would follow, armed with the MP5 submachine guns. "I wanted to go in there with a firearm, a weapon, so that if I see a threat I'm going to take it out as quickly as I can," Zorovic recalled, "so that if I see as much as a cigarette being lit and I think that this guy is thinking of igniting something, I'll take him out."[9] Zorovic was confident taking the Heckler & Koch MP5 with him—capable of firing eight hundred rounds per minute and fitted with a thirty-round magazine, the MP5 was considered the Rolls-Royce of the world's submachine guns.

English and McCaffrey would be the last in, armed with hand-guns and flashlights. "I told Martinez that once that door opens in the apartment, there'll be a guy sleeping right there in the kitchen," McCaffrey explained. "I want you to put your Body Bunker up to the right so that if he's a lookout and he's armed, your Bunker will absorb the rounds. Even if you incur fire from the guy in the kitchen, you run right past him, let your Body Bunker do its job, and you get inside and stop the guys with the bomb. I told Zorovic and Keenan that your jobs are not to go into the room but go right to the guy in the kitchen and take him down."[10]

Kammerdener liked the plan, as did Pascullo. It was quick, safe, and prudent.

It was just after three a.m. and there was one more detail that McCaffrey had to work out. The entry team needed *permission* to shoot one or both of the Palestinians if they were lunging for the satchels with the "alleged" devices inside. "We needed permission to shoot someone who didn't have a gun or a knife," McCaffrey remembered, "because just making a move toward a package is not in the police department's policy for shooting people."

On any other night Chief of Department Louis Anemone would have been running the show. The highest-ranking uniformed officer, a veteran and highly decorated cop who was dynamic, forceful, insightful, and always and undeniably completely in command, Anemone would normally have been in the precinct house, his body armor already on, ready to lead his troops into battle; Anemone led by example. That was his style. When he wasn't at his office or in high-level meetings, Anemone rode in the chief of department's car, "Car-Three," patrolling and even responding to jobs. If Car-Three happened to be in the vicinity of where officers were responding to a call, Chief of Department Anemone would be outside a door, or outside a store being robbed, his sidearm in hand, ready to do police work. The mobilization in the Eighty-eighth Precinct was the type of situation that Anemone would have run like a military operation, but Anemone was away in Mexico on vacation. In addition, the two-star chief in charge of the Special Operations Division was also unavailable. It was also extremely doubtful that Police Commissioner Howard Safir—the "PC," as Safir was known—would have shown up for a job that, at this stage, was still considered unfounded. Perhaps it was better he wasn't there. The commotion, the chiefs and deputy commissioners who would have followed in the entourage, would have made decision making an arduous process. The rank-and-file cops didn't care much for Safir. Safir, whose law enforcement credentials included a lengthy stint inside the U.S. Marshals Service, had replaced William Bratton as NYPD commissioner when Giuliani, many felt, was outraged by the media attention the charismatic and well-spoken Bratton received for his crime-fighting efforts. It is believed that it was a photo of Bratton on the cover of *Time* magazine that eventually sealed his fate, along with the careers of the brain trust that he'd brought with him to One Police Plaza. Stiff and uncomfortable before the cameras, Safir could never compete with Bratton's polished charm, media savvy, and CEO skills. The cops on the street were always wary of Safir because he was perceived as such a Giuliani "yes-man," and perhaps most importantly, his previous job for the mayor was as fire commissioner. The cops never trusted the firemen.

The suits from city hall were nowhere to be found this hot July night. This was Kammerdener's show. He was in charge.

"Do we have the green light?" McCaffrey asked Chief Kammerdener as the ESU entry team was finalizing its assault plan, in a veiled search for some sort of career-saving authorization to shoot the Palestinians if they posed a threat to his men. Kammerdener looked at the ESU lieutenant and didn't even have to utter a word. McCaffrey had known Kammerdener from Housing; Kammerdener had earned a reputation as a stand-up guy and a terrific boss. McCaffrey knew that the chief's word was as good as a contract reviewed by a hundred lawyers. But still, this night was developing into something of an aberration. McCaffrey stared straight into the chief's eyes, pleading with his own blue eyes. Kammerdener sighed, an expression that all but vocalized the authorization that the ESU lieutenant was seeking. Kammerdener moved closer to McCaffrey, smiled, and said, in unequivocal terms, that he would testify in court that he had, indeed, authorized the use of deadly force because of the unique and mitigating circumstances and because of the word of the informant—which was deemed absolutely credible—concerning an impending terrorist incident that could have resulted in a considerable loss of life.

McCaffrey was satisfied. ESU had the green light.

CAT Car

Lord, I ask for courage—
Courage to face and conquer my own fears,
Courage to take me where others will not go.
I ask for strength—
Strength of body to protect others,
And strength of spirit to lead others.
I ask for dedication—
Dedication to my job, to do it well,
Dedication to my community, to keep it safe.
Give me, Lord, concern for those who trust me,
And compassion for those who need me,
And, please, Lord, through it all, be at my side.

"A POLICEMAN'S PRAYER"

The two Palestinians were in their room, talking just above a whisper. The traffic on President Street was quiet—even in Brooklyn the pace of cars zooming by slowed to a crawl in the hours just before dawn. The snoring from the other room didn't bother them. They were used to the sounds of their roommates. Living in such close quarters, where everyone smelled each other's farts, was something the two had gotten used to. And anyway, the inconvenience and discomfort didn't matter much anymore. Their feelings of worthlessness and fear were about to come to an end. They were planning, and armed, for a journey to paradise. They would receive the adulation of Islamic warriors and be rewarded with over seventy virgins. They would, perhaps most importantly, kill Jews and show the Americans—the people stupid enough to let them linger inside the United States—that it took only two warriors with a few dollars' worth of goods conveniently packaged into a device to bring the West Bank to the underground arteries of New York City.

The Palestinians prayed on a tattered prayer rug placed in between the two mattresses in their small room. The black satchel was between them. The bag was open and available. Just in case.

Both men immersed themselves in prayer and then returned to their mattresses. The talk was reserved and low-key. Both men weren't in the mood to sleep. They were hours away from becoming martyrs—they were only hours away from Jerusalem.

Captain Ralph Pascullo left Mosabbah, the Rookie, and a dozen other bosses and ESU personnel in the interview room to grab some air. It was hot, "Africa hot," as the cops used to like saying, and the combination of angst and exhaustion was now becoming an issue he had to deal with. He walked toward the staircase and found a window that he could open partially through iron gates and mesh wire screens. Brief gusts of air, enough to refresh his perspiring face, came in through the open window. Pascullo was the senior ESU boss on scene that night in Brooklyn, and although he wasn't going to be the first one through the door in a few hours, the weight of the risk was squarely on his shoulders. Talk of this being a suicide mission didn't sit well with him. He just couldn't sign off on something in which he knew that his cops were going to get hurt. He knew all the senior officers in the division personally. They were married, they were fathers, and they had friends and loved ones who counted on them returning home after every tour. There were six wives and who knew how many kids at home, sleeping soundly in their air-conditioned rooms, waiting to see their fathers in the morning. He had seen cops shot and killed; he had stood in the processions of thousands of police officers, some who traveled from as far as Maine and Miami, to pay their respects at the funerals of those killed in the line of duty. He didn't want anything to happen to the men on his watch.

But Pascullo also knew that there would be countless eyes on him, Monday-morning quarterbacking his every move should the job go bad. Having a former Housing cop serve as the second-in-command of the city's elite force—and the largest special-operations police unit in the country—did not sit well with many ESU veterans. Pascullo knew the laser beams of the unit would be square inside the crosshairs on this job—if it went well, then perhaps the "Housing" nonsense would forever disappear; if the job went terribly wrong, then it would be forever reaffirmed.

Pascullo looked outside the window and saw a sea of blue-and-white police cars—there must have been fifty ESU vehicles, borough command cars, patrol cars, bomb squad trucks, and other response vehicles in all shapes and sizes. It was reassuring. At least the six-man entry team would have all the backup in the world. As he wiped his brow again, battling the Brooklyn humidity and the stifling corners of the station house that weren't air-conditioned, Pascullo thought of backup and how, as a Housing cop, he would often be alone, never knowing when the proper support—and rescue—would arrive. As he saw yet another unmarked Caprice pull up to the Eighty-eighth, Pascullo's mind wandered even more.

He remembered that day, in Housing, when he was patrolling the Van Dyke Housing Project in Brownsville, Brooklyn, along with his partner. A call came over the radio for the two officers to respond to complaints about a very loud party on the tenth floor of one of the complex's buildings. In by-the-book fashion, the two men walked up the ten flights of stairs; the elevators *always* got stuck in the projects. After climbing up the darkened staircase, stepping on needles, crack vials, and discarded condoms, the two young

cops walked down the dimly lit hall, toward the end of the corridor to the apartment in question. Suddenly, from behind, some
fifty people emptied from an apartment into the hall. "What do
you white boys want up here?" a large man asked as he cracked his
knuckles in his fist with thunderous impact. "Ten-thirteen Central," Pascullo uttered into his radio, "officers need assistance on the
tenth floor of the Van Dyke houses, 10-13, 10-13. . . ."[1] There was
no acknowledgment of the officers' plea for help, and, of course,
no help at all. The two young Housing cops beat their way out of
the mob, punching and clawing all the way, realizing that if they removed their service revolvers, it would be a massacre.

A cool breeze returned Pascullo to 1997 and Park Slope. That
night in Brownsville, a police career ago, sparked sudden rage. He
was determined not to send the ESU team into the location unless
everything that could be done to ensure their maximum safety was
done. And there was one inconsistency in Mosabbah's tale that
was causing him grave concern. A claw was still gnawing at his
insides. Worry was now joining the heat and exhaustion.

Time and time again the detective and then Pascullo, McCaffrey,
and English returned to the diagram of the location that Mosabbah
had drawn and the description of the building and the surroundings. Detectives dispatched to look at the area came back with an
image that looked *nothing* like the Egyptian's version. Where was
the stoop? Where were the bicycles and the trash? Kammerdener, in
particular, was concerned about Mosabbah's claim that he could see
a street from the window. The cops checked maps, precinct guides,
and even a copy of Hagstrom's *New York City 5 Borough Atlas,* which
most patrol supervisors carried in their cars.

Pascullo didn't want to send the entry team into harm's way
without personally seeing the target. He wanted to get a feel for the
street that his cops would be hitting. He wanted to have the blueprint of that small speck of Fourth Avenue seared into his mind before he could truly and grudgingly sign off on the raid itself.

The drive-by of the address on Fourth Avenue had to be done discreetly—if the Palestinians were, indeed, part of a professional terrorist cell, with support and countersurveillance, then the sight of ESU commanders driving by and scouting the location would prompt alarm and, perhaps, even immediate action.

It was vital that Lieutenant McCaffrey and Sergeant English both look at the building with their own eyes. Pascullo wanted to see the targeted location, too, as did Chief Kammerdener; Deputy Inspector Ray McDermott, the executive officer of the Special Operations Division, who had by this time responded to the Eighty-eighth Precinct as a representative of his chief, also wanted to come along. It would have been hard to fit five men inside a Caprice without warranting just a little bit of suspicion on the streets of Brooklyn, so it was decided to take the CAT car—the vehicle McCaffrey had earmarked to transport the entry team to the Fourth Avenue address.

The CAT car was as good a war wagon as could be found for the mission at hand. The armor-plated Ford Econoline 350 van, designed to follow presidential motorcades and absorb the brunt of an assassination attempt, had been a faithful tool in the ESU's war on crime. Unmarked, the van could be used on late-night warrants in high-crime areas, where drug lookouts, often posted on street corners, could pick up the blue and white colors of a police van from blocks away. The CAT car provided ESU with stealth, even if marginally; it was enough stealth to get sufficiently close to the bad guys without ringing alarms that the cavalry was on its way. The van usually carried ballistic shields, sledgehammers, hydraulic spreading tools, emergency medical and communications gear, and whatever weaponry, ammunition, and pyrotechnics were needed for a prolonged firefight. On some jobs, the cops even dragged body bags with them—just in case. Stripped clean, according to its factory specs, the van had room inside for eight people—but that never took into account how many overweight cops, wearing bulky protective gear, could actually squeeze inside the upholstered interior already filled to capacity with equipment.

A stealth approach was needed because Mosabbah had mentioned, in his numerous statements, that there was a car service stand in front of the building where Middle Eastern men, *perhaps* in cahoots with the Palestinians, could always be found. The closer the time came to the actual raid, the more disturbing the possibility of lookouts became.

The drive from the Eighty-eighth Precinct to 248 Fourth Avenue took less than ten minutes. Sergeant English was behind the wheel and drove cautiously, careful not to run through red lights or get into any fender benders, which might spark undue attention to the vehicle. Between President and Carroll Streets, the CAT car slowed ever so slightly. It didn't stop. There was no stoop leading to an apartment, and there were no bicycles chained outside. Mosabbah's description was off. Concern turned to worry. But the intelligence on the cabstand in front of the location was dead-on. The five men inside the CAT car stared at the five men in front of the Family Car Service, playing cards and laughing. They looked Middle Eastern from the quick view afforded through the tinted windows of the unmarked van, but they could have been Mexicans or Italians. Music, emanating from a radio, filled the street with tunes that were hard for the cops to decipher.

Do we go or do we not go? Pascullo was not happy that Mosabbah's description of the building differed from his personal observation. Something there just didn't feel right. As a boss, Pascullo knew that ESU had responded on warrants where the information was one hundred percent wrong. A snitch had deliberately misguided a detective, or a detective had inadvertently jotted down a wrong apartment number, and when ESU entered a location hot and heavy hurling a diversionary device on a hit, they ended up surprising an elderly couple having a bowl of Cheerios at the kitchen table and, in the process, giving them fatal coronaries. At least this was a bomb job, the cops thought, and it made no tactical sense to toss a diversionary device, or flash-bang grenade, into the room, because one spark could detonate the explosive payload.

Yet Mosabbah's sincerity once again became an issue as the cops wondered if they were being set up for a hit of their own. Would they hit the apartment and find innocent people asleep? Could the cops, primed for a lethal encounter, mistakenly shoot a civilian they perceived to be a threat because of the Egyptian's acting skills?

Every cop in the unit knew the sad tale of the E-cops hung out to dry in 1984 by the Bronx district attorney over the shooting death of Eleanor Bumpers, a deranged three-hundred-pound grandmother who, armed with a steak knife, lunged at ESU officers serving a mental-health warrant. The cops poised to enter the apartment were told by a neighbor that Mrs. Bumpers was cooking lye to use against anyone foolish enough to evict her from her home. When the ESU cops punched a hole through the door to see what was going on inside the apartment, they saw a hazy cloud of mist hanging over the living room and they smelled a strong acrid odor. When the officers stormed the apartment, Mrs. Bumpers attacked with an eight-inch knife in her hands. It took two blasts from a 12-gauge shotgun to knock the old woman down. The officers feared for their own lives and were justified in blowing the woman away, but Eleanor Bumpers was black and the officers were white.

The ESU cops were vilified by the press, the black community, and their own department. When they were in front of the grand jury, it took the miraculous work of defense attorneys and a police department on the verge of rebellion for the cops to be cleared of manslaughter charges and reinstated on the job. But the officers' lives were never the same after that fateful morning in the Bronx.

"If it embarrasses the city, you're not going to get any backing," Zorovic would later reflect. "That's the way it is. If it's something that you've done and you can't justify yourself, and it doesn't come under their guidelines, then they wash their hands of you and you are on your own."[2]

If Mosabbah's tale had involved anything other than Palestinians and a suicide bomb threat, the entire momentum toward a go might have been postponed after the drive-by. Any other scenario—a drug deal, a man with a gun, an imminent robbery—would have warranted closer scrutiny before cops were thrown into the fire on a half-translated account and a bad diagram of the target. But there was really no room for second-guessing at this stage. Dawn was only a couple of hours away, and Kammerdener realized that this was going to be ESU's only window. If, indeed, there was a threat, now was the only time in which preventative action would succeed.

It was roughly four a.m. when the bosses returned from the drive-by. The mood inside the Eighty-eighth Precinct house was becoming anxious. The moment ESU had begun to arrive in droves, the natural infusion of adrenaline filtered through the veins of every cop, sergeant, lieutenant, and captain involved in the operation. But as the hours dragged on, and the minute details of planning, notifying, double-checking, making more phone calls, and pulling cops off of duty assignments turned into lengthy ordeals, the initial buzz of adrenaline-charged fear and excitement turned into melancholy angst. If it was going to get done, the cops thought, let's get it over with.

McCaffrey returned from the drive-by more concerned than ever. He still believed Mosabbah's story and could not fathom that the Egyptian was fabricating his story out of some psychotic delusion or, worse, setting up the cops for a hit of their own. But the inconsistencies illustrated from the view of the target from inside the CAT car proved to McCaffrey that some additional contingencies had to be anticipated and prepared for. McCaffrey selected a second six-man team that would wait in the wings outside the target and be the extraction force to lay down cover fire should Martinez, Dolan,

Zorovic, Keenan, English, and he find themselves cut down by gunfire in an ambush; if the Palestinians were to blow themselves up
and take the building and the cops with them, then the extraction
team would secure the kill zone and attempt to pull as many survivors out of the debris as they could. A rescue team, with stretchers and building collapse material, would follow the extraction force
inside the CARV, or collapse truck, that ESU fielded. Every ESU
cop at the Eighty-eighth Precinct had a job to do. Every worst-case
scenario was envisioned and a response prepared, but all the planning and stomach acid in the world weren't going to neutralize the
threat of the Palestinians. It was time to get the whole operation in
motion, or as McCaffrey told the cops back at the Eighty-eighth,
"Let's bust a move."

After Pascullo and Kammerdener made their last series of
phone calls and last marks off their mental checklists of things that
had to be finalized, the ESU contingent made its way out of the
"house," as precincts were called, and downstairs toward where the
vehicles had assembled. The E-cops brought down Mosabbah and
the Rookie, as well. They would be embedded in the entry team
until McCaffrey was satisfied that the information was genuine.
Mosabbah was led down like a delinquent child about to be walked
into the principal's office. He almost had to be dragged down as
the Rookie explained to him why he had to come on the raid.
"You won't be sent back to the Palestinians," Mosabbah was reassured, "and you won't be placed in any undue danger." But
Mosabbah looked at the dozens of police and fire department vehicles that had assembled outside the precinct and the fear began to
rock and roll inside his guts. He held his stomach and began to
sweat. He began to plead for some sort of mercy. "He didn't understand that they needed him to pinpoint the apartment and that
he'd be protected and removed from harm's way thereafter," Pascullo remembered. "He thought that we were turning him over to
his friends now that we had what we needed."

It was a struggle to get the heavy Kevlar vest around Mosabbah's midsection. He resisted the attempts by the ESU officers to fit him with the heavy and stiff dark blue protective cocoon; in Egypt, after all, the police often restrained a suspect before torturing him. Adding to Mosabbah's panic-stricken mood, the ESU cops fitted the Egyptian with a canvas black hood to conceal his identity. Mosabbah's fear was now electric. He thought, the cops believed, the hood to be an execution hood. He thought the cops were going to take him somewhere and kill him.

The Rookie, too, was given a vest—something he wasn't too happy with, either. Wherever Mosabbah went, the Rookie realized, he was going, as well.

The mood among the entry team changed dramatically, as they removed their heavy vests, helmets, and weapons from their vehicles. The officers were quiet and reluctant. The bravado and unit pride so gallantly displayed inside the squad room now turned to trepidation and the sobering notion of reality. Thoughts shifted from concern over the bomb's destructive capabilities to possible legal repercussions if the job didn't go well and some innocent people were hurt. Mostly, though, the minds were focused on survival. "I was thinking of going home to my family," Zorovic said. "As I walked down the stairs from the squad room to the parking lot, I told my partner that if anything happens to me, he should just tell my wife and the kids that I love them." Yet the fear of imminent death was blocked, albeit temporarily, by the sudden realization that this was it. "I walked out the door of the Eighty-eighth Precinct," Zorovic explained, "and never looked back. It was time to be an E-man."[3]

Pascullo, Kammerdener, and McDermott also suited up for the hit. There aren't many chiefs who would don a Kevlar vest and personally participate in a tactical operation, but Kammerdener, the marine, wouldn't have it any other way. "I just had to be there," he would later admit, "to make sure that everyone came out of this

one okay." The plan was for Kammerdener, Pascullo, and McDermott to take down the cabstand silently and quickly as the entry
team reached the location; the mysterious Middle Eastern men
who hung around the storefront twenty-four hours a day were
considered a potential threat. There was no green light issued for
the men playing cards and backgammon on Fourth Avenue. They
just had to be silenced and secured.

As he removed his helmet and vest from the trunk of his
Caprice, Pascullo rubbed his eyes and felt his tired body ache; he had
been up for twenty-one hours and this day showed no signs of ending. The thick humid July air compounded his sense of exhaustion;
the thirty pounds of Kevlar body armor wrapped over his torso
made every twitch and movement a fatigue-inducing chore. "I'm
too old for this," the forty-five-year-old sighed softly as he fastened
the Velcro straps of his ballistic vest one last time around a waist that
had spread a bit over the years, courtesy of too many Papaya King
hot dogs and too many extra-garlic slices from Patsy's Pizza. Pascullo hoped that the other cops readying their weapons couldn't
hear his quiet confessions about his middle-aged limitations. If he
was feeling like an old man, this was not the night to start complaining about it. The other cops assembled in the parking lot at
4:10 A.M. were scared and Pascullo knew that the last thing they
wanted to hear was mumblings of doubt. Pascullo wanted to smile
at the cops before he entered his car for the drive to the target; a
friendly sign of reassurance, he thought, might alleviate some of the
tension. But the officers were making every effort to avoid eye contact. A last glance might have been misconstrued as a jinx. Cops
were superstitious, especially before big jobs.

The officers had suited up quickly. Getting their Kevlar on was
second nature to the midnight veterans. They could have done it
with their eyes shut. Each officer grabbed the weapon he would
carry. The weapons were raised in the air and checked for rounds and
then double-checked to make sure they were safe. Fresh magazines

with thirty rounds of ammunition were inserted into the Mini-14 and the MP5s now nestled in the arms of the three cops. McCaffrey, English and Martinez readied their Glock 9mms, as well.

On a job where stealth was an absolute necessity, McCaffrey realized, it was virtually impossible to suppress the stampedelike sounds six heavily armed men made when bursting through a door, yet some steps could be taken. "I don't even want a chance of a radio going off," McCaffrey told the entry team, so bucking standard ESU practice, he was the only member of the team carrying a radio. McCaffrey made each officer surrender his black Motorola radio and toss it into the van. "We can't be making any noise outside the apartment," McCaffrey advised. "No keys banging against your pockets, no loose change jiggling around." Each member of the entry team also had to inside-out his pockets, and put his house keys and nickels and dimes into plastic bags. "Jump up and down," McCaffrey ordered. "I want to hear if you guys are still making noise."

"Let's cut the shit and get on with it," one of the officers moaned. "It's nearly daylight, and I have all my gear on. Let's just get it over with and if I make noise, too fucking bad!"

Pascullo understood that the cops were on short fuses. Anger in their voices signaled fear. But Pascullo chuckled to himself, hoping to dear Jesus himself that McCaffrey wouldn't join in the jumping. *I don't want the last thing that I see before I die tonight,* Pascullo prayed, trying to not to laugh out loud, *to be Owen hopping up and down in the precinct parking lot!*

As he opened the door to his maroon Chevy Caprice and sat down behind the wheel, Pascullo wanted to say good-bye to the cops, but thought it better to remain silent; the less sentiment the better, he thought grudgingly. He checked his holstered Glock 9mm semiautomatic pistol one last time, as well as the Ithaca 37 12-gauge shotgun locked in a mount just below his right hand. As he turned on the ignition and caressed the steering wheel, Pascullo glanced into his rearview mirror as Mosabbah, the Rookie, Lieutenant

McCaffrey, Sergeant English, and the four ESU cops piled into the big black armored CAT car.

Pascullo wondered if this would be the last time he would see them alive.

If the NYPD were a citywide ballet company, the department would have won accolades and awards for its vehicular choreography that night. Without fanfare, scraped fenders, or tethered nerves, each vehicle participating in the raid had positioned itself in the exact order that it would be deployed on Fourth Avenue: the CAT car, Pascullo's Caprice, and then dozens of ESU REPs, bomb squad vans, patrol cars, unmarked cars, and ambulances. By four a.m. the first federal agents from the FBI and other agencies, notified via NYPD Operations, had arrived, and now they joined the armada of law enforcement traffic. The moment the vehicles were in place, Kammerdener's outer perimeter was ordered closed. Dozens of patrol cars and nearly a hundred police officers cordoned off a five-block sterile zone around the address. No cars or people were allowed to pass through the sterile zone unless they were a part of the operation. Kammerdener and Pascullo had coordinated the resources with the borough command and the duty inspector and captain, both of whom also happened to be Housing Police alumni, and the moment the entry team and its support force were ready to roll, a slice of Brooklyn was quarantined.

At just around 4:20 A.M. something happened in Brooklyn that hadn't occurred since the 1980 transit strike—the Fourth Avenue subway line was shut down in both directions.

It was time to go. The hit was under way.

A little over two miles separated the task force from Abu Mezer and his bombs. The drive from the Eighty-eighth Precinct at 298 Classon Avenue to Fourth Avenue should have taken a matter of minutes, especially if the vehicles raced through the boulevards with lights and sirens flashing. ESU cops prided themselves on their driving abilities and for being able to negotiate their heavy vehicles through narrow side streets encumbered by double- and even triple-parked cars. But stealth was the order of the day for the two-mile journey, and the procession of police and emergency vehicles that had staged in and around the Eighty-eighth Precinct would travel to the bomb factory in a slow and deliberate motorcade. There would be no flashing lights, no wailing and yelping sirens, and, of course, no radio chatter.

Pascullo's Caprice led the motorcade, followed by the CAT car. The slow-moving, twenty-mile-per-hour cadence down DeKalb Avenue, and then on Flatbush, seemed to slow time to a surreal crawl. Seconds felt like minutes; the stalled, motionless wait at a red light seemed to last hours. Pascullo had always tried to shift his mind and his body into a zone of absolute focus before any "hit," but he couldn't find his cerebral focal point. He had been on too many jobs where the split second of a mental lapse got people killed. He had stood over the lifeless corpses of too many cops, their faces blown away by shotgun blasts, because they had glanced away from a threat for just that brief moment of opportunity that allowed the bad guy to pull the trigger.

Being in the zone was most important on this night of all, but reaching that coveted spot of mental clarity was an excruciating struggle. Each passing minute made it all the harder to forget just how tired and scared he was. He could only see Jerusalem in his mind's eye—the Jerusalem of the CNN report where emergency workers used brooms to sweep away the blood and the dead. It all seemed so Technicolor real. Pascullo thought of the talk that had gone on inside the squad room at the precinct. Would the explosives worn by a suicide bomber pierce his body armor? Probably not, he thought to himself. What was it like to be in the center of a massive explosion? He thought of his wife, pregnant and asleep in

their home, and of the two kids he adored. Looking at Kammerdener beside him, he thought of how much more careful he was
now, as a father of two and as a middle-aged man, than he was ten
years before. These weren't the thoughts one wanted to have before a fateful encounter. Doubt and thoughts of family clouded the
issue. His mind needed to be focused.

A blinking yellow light at the corner of Washington and
DeKalb Avenues should have caused him to slow down. He nearly
ran through the intersection. When the light turned red he stared
briefly into the rearview mirror, wanting to rub his salt-and-
pepper mustache, but suddenly remembering he had shaved it off
the night before, not wanting his newborn to come into the world
only to be kissed by the abrasive rub of a short-cropped mustache.
His heart sank. Shaving the mustache was an omen of bad luck.

Clutching the steering wheel as he waited for the light to turn
green, Pascullo felt his hands twitch. They were sweaty. A stream of
perspiration, dripping down the side of his head from his Kevlar
Fritz helmet, pulsated in perfect synchronization with his heavy
heartbeat. In a twenty-five-year police career that had started in the
hallways of the city's worst housing projects, he had been terrified
only one time. Just out of the academy, he was manning the police
radio switchboard as part of an apprenticeship to learn the A to Z
of being a Housing cop when he overheard the last minutes of a
fellow officer, responding to a reported burglary in a Brooklyn
housing project, shot point-blank in the face with a 12-gauge shotgun. As the officer's partner radioed frantically for backup and an
ambulance, Pascullo remembered, he'd tried to stay calm as he dispatched commands to the job, all the while hearing the gasping
moans of agony as the mortally wounded officer lay dying in a
dimly lit hallway. The awful sounds of the officer's last moments,
that gurgling sound of blood entering his lungs, would stay with
him always.

In the years from rookie to captain, Pascullo never forgot the emptiness inspired by fear as he listened to the radio. Most importantly, he never forgot the absolute horror of his utter helplessness. The helplessness, Pascullo realized as the light turned green, was infuriating, as well, and that anger, slowly, was bringing him mentally where he needed to be. The anger—the determination to not be helpless—sent a potent adrenaline hit to his system. The passing vistas of Brooklyn suddenly became focused. He was able to zero in on the flickering neon lights of the beer signs in the bodega windows with uncanny clarity.

Pascullo looked to Kammerdener and McDermott—both men had been silent since Pascullo pulled out of the precinct lot—for reassurance. There was no banter, no mindless complaining about wives, the Mets, mortgage rates, or the police department, which was so typical of cops stuck inside a car on a job. Silence meant fear—even among inspectors and chiefs.

As the convoy proceeded, Pascullo turned to his right to look at Kammerdener. The sight of his old partner brought back an avalanche of memories from the glory days of the Housing Police when the tandem was responsible for more arrests—and citations for valor—than any other policemen in the department. During any given day, Kammerdener and Pascullo would complete investigating their caseloads before noon, and then spend the rest of their shift sitting in an unmarked car outside a project waiting to catch a junkie, a mugger, a thief, or a pusher in the commission of a crime for a quick arrest. The criminals were combative back in the early eighties, and arrests came only after a chase and a fight. Almost every day, Pascullo recalled, the two men—their clothes torn in scuffles and their hands and faces bloodied—would return to the station house with a "collar" and evidence bags filled with guns, drugs, or stolen property. The desk sergeant would often yell at them, pleading with the two to slow down in order to cut down on the mountain of paperwork generated by each arrest.

Thinking of the old days brought a brief smile to Pascullo's face, and it was reassuring to see his old partner next to him once again just as he had been so many times while working in the projects. But this wasn't the good old days and the two men had aged since they'd traversed the bowels of the projects in their fancy duds in search of rapists, crack dealers, and murderers. His old partner was a chief now, and sitting next to him wearing a heavy vest and a military-style helmet. The two men weren't working a case this time. They were, in reality, fighting a war.

Kammerdener looked at Pascullo with an expression of reassurance, and spoke in the voice of a seasoned marine gunnery sergeant instilling confidence in his men before they hit a beach under fire. "If we stick to the plan, and the guys do their job, we'll be okay," Kammerdener remarked in a nonchalant tone.

What plan? Pascullo thought to himself. *What fucking plan? We have an informant nobody can understand rambling about two alleged terrorist roommates who have built an alleged bomb that they are intending to allegedly detonate on an alleged subway train. If these guys are really terrorists, then we are probably walking into a shooting gallery. If not, and the informant is a nut job, then we are about to blow away two innocent civilians. By morning,* Pascullo did the math, *I'll be either dead or indicted.*

Deputy Inspector Ray McDermott had also been silent in the backseat of the Caprice, attempting to feel comfortable in his heavy Kevlar body armor. "You guys are the experts," he now told both Pascullo and Kammerdener. "I'm just here to back you up!" Pascullo had never worked the streets with McDermott, knew little of the Special Operations Division's executive officer, and didn't know much about his reputation under fire. But McDermott could have refused to come along. He could have sent an underling, just as his boss did. "You guys are the experts," McDermott reiterated from the backseat as he leaned forward to tap Pascullo's body armor. "Ralph, we are going to follow your lead. We're counting on you."[4]

McDermott's sentiments brought confidence to the ESU captain.

Suddenly he felt as if he was the "go-to" guy. That sense of responsibility shattered any lingering feelings of apprehension. Too many people depended on him now, Pascullo realized. Being the man others turned to was what he enjoyed most.

As the convoy moved down the strangely empty streets of Flatbush Avenue, Pascullo felt the rush of adrenaline racing through his chest and arms, flowing smoothly like electric velvet. He felt refreshed and alert, though he wondered what the mood inside the CAT car was like.

Unlike the virtually silent tension that made the two-mile journey inside Captain Ralph Pascullo's unmarked Caprice seem almost unbearable at times, the mood inside the CAT car was outspoken angst. Lieutenant McCaffrey had lost the I-don't-give-a-shit-about-anything attitude that was the trademark of a man blessed to have unexplained forces in the universe just make everything go his way. Nothing pushed McCaffrey over the edge, and nothing, short of threatening his overtime, could remove the permanent smile from his cherubic face. Yet the ride toward Fourth Avenue was changing the always confident lieutenant's demeanor.

Inside the CAT car, McCaffrey wasn't calling anyone "dude" anymore. His rosy round cheeks seemed long and pale. On the ride to Fourth Avenue McCaffrey was one pissed lieutenant, and his long cold stare could eviscerate a man. Owen could not peel his eyes away from Abdel Rahman Mosabbah. The more McCaffrey thought about the task at hand, the icier the stares at Mosabbah became. *I'm a cop, not a soldier,* McCaffrey thought to himself as he looked at Mosabbah, wondering if this was some poor asshole that was doing the right thing, or if he was a dupe, luring the ESU cops into an ambush. *Is he scared because he knows that there are bombs in the apartment,* Owen wondered, *or because he thinks we'll kill him once we are hit from all sides?*

McCaffrey had a lot riding on Mosabbah. After all, of all the cops inside the CAT car, it was McCaffrey who had believed Mosabbah's story from the get-go. Now, only moments away from what he feared was going to be a terrifying encounter, McCaffrey's doubts about Mosabbah's intentions were multiplying at a violent pace. Looking at Mosabbah, McCaffrey felt his fear and frustration grow. His heart began to race and the Irish in him came to a boil. Unfastening his Glock 9mm pistol from his black leather holster, McCaffrey slid the weapon into his right hand as if he was about to aim the gun straight at Mosabbah's forehead, and ordered the Rookie to translate. "You tell this motherfucker that if he's setting us up, I am going to kill him. We might not get out of this thing alive, but he'll be the first to get blown away!"[5]

The Rookie relayed McCaffrey's warning word for word. The Egyptian's eyes began to swell with tears. He shivered with fear. Mosabbah had looked upon McCaffrey as the *one* cop who didn't look at him like he was nuts. McCaffrey had made every effort to reassure Mosabbah, even patting him on the back and telling him, "It'll be fine, dude—don't be scared" during questioning inside the squad room. Now, inside a van crammed with cops who, in their own minds at least, were resigned to the fact that they were embarking on *half a suicide operation,* McCaffrey was clutching at his service weapon, about to press it into Mosabbah's forehead. Mosabbah was free-falling in a panic. His right leg gyrated up and down. His breathing was erratic. The stench inside the van indicated that Mosabbah had indeed shit himself.

"I never saw someone that scared before in my life," McCaffrey recalled. "The sight of his bulging white eyeballs popping out of the black hood was something that I'll never forget."[6] Just to press home the point, Zorovic also asked that the Rookie translate a warning. "If we are being led into an ambush," the Eight-Truck veteran threatened, "I'll personally kill you." Mosabbah closed his eyes tightly in fear. His heart raced as the vehicles inched closer toward Fourth Avenue. He believed he was about to die.

Mosabbah's fear was contagious and unsettling in the claustrophobic confines of the CAT car. The ESU cops were used to high-pressure situations and each of the men sitting inside the CAT car had been in the thick of his share of jobs involving barricaded psychos, cold-blooded killers, and desperate suicide cases. Each of the ESU officers had participated in over a hundred warrants against high-risk narcotics and homicide suspects before. The cops had burst through doors before, throwing flash bangs into hallways and placing the barrels of their shotguns and MP5 submachine guns into the necks of some of the city's most violent felons. Before knocking down the door of an armed criminal, the cops on an entry team would always check off a series of concerns that they needed to be aware of. Before each hit, the cops would make a mental recording of the number of weapons known to be at a location, their calibers, and what the wanted suspects looked like. The cops often wrote down the address of the location on their right wrist so that in case of a shoot-out and the eruption of a life-and-death struggle, the officers could radio for help and not have to remember exactly where they were—all they had to do was read it off their hand.

There was no checklist to take care of on a bomb job. If the shit hit the fan, body parts were tossed in a violent force of energy and debris. Bombs were indiscriminate. Bombs detonated at temperatures that incinerated flesh and threw shrapnel wildly over a 360-degree frenetic field of fire at three thousand feet per second. "Bombs are something that you don't have full control of, and anything that you don't have full control of comes with great skepticism," Zorovic would reflect. "Skepticism doesn't mean that you don't act professionally. You have to utilize everything you've learned to that point until you are safely out of there. Bombs force you to put your mind on survival mode. I thought to myself, what do I need to do to make sure that I go home in the morning?"[7]

Usually, before embarking on hits, ESU entry teams would engage in biting and sometimes cruel gallows humor, which the unit was famous for. "We used to joke about everyone and everything when in the truck or CAT car toward a hit," a former unit officer explained. "We joked about one another, our ethnicities, our wives, and everyone else's wife. Nothing was off-limits. We made fun of other people in the unit, and of course, we made fun of our sergeants, lieutenants, and captains. We did whatever we could to clear our mind of the fear."[8]

The banter inside the van was just as uncomfortable as the seating arrangements; the six ESU cops, the Rookie, and Mosabbah had a difficult time squeezing into the CAT car. Just sitting inside the vehicle was hard enough, but shifting one's leg, or moving a weapon from the left side of a shoulder to the right, required cooperation from everyone. The talk was of regret and fear.

"I can't die today," Joe Dolan told Dave Martinez, his steady partner. "My two-year-old," he confided, "she was asleep when I left for work and I didn't kiss her before heading out the door. How can I die without giving her a good-bye kiss?"

"You're not going to die," comforted Martinez, angry that his partner was thinking about getting killed. "It's all going to go well," he uttered. "The informant is probably a kook and this is all a lot of nothing." *He's bumming us all out,* Martinez thought as he feigned a smile of reassurance to his partner while wanting to slap him silly. Then, as if awoken from a soft slumber, Martinez's face collapsed in fear. "I just remembered"—he looked over to Dolan—"today is my fortieth birthday. This is a bad sign. This is bad!" As Sergeant English guided the CAT car toward the target, Zorovic crossed himself.

The Rookie, too, was not handling the stress of the raid very well. A military operation was not what the rookie officer had bargained for when he joined the department. Walking into a terrorist lair was not part of the job description. He wanted nothing to do with terrorists or gunfire. Mosabbah and the Rookie looked toward one another for reassurance. Both men were awash in the trepidations of being part of this insanity.

Collectively, the cops joined one another in a group prayer. ESU cops *never* prayed before a hit. Then again, this wasn't a typical night for the unit.

The tinted windows made it almost impossible for anyone sitting inside the van to see anything but blurs of metal shutters with graffiti and the streaking trail of neon signs. Several blocks from the target, McCaffrey was calculating the risks of being aggressive, or worrying too much about the legal consequences. *If we blow these fuckers to hell and we are wrong,* McCaffrey tabulated, *I'll still have two chances to get off. The grand jury will have to indict me and a jury will have to convict me.*

Pascullo, too, was thinking about the legal and career ramifications of the job if it went horribly out of control. *What if there are no terrorists and we end up killing someone innocent? The mayor will be pissed!* Pascullo knew that being on Hizzoner's shit list was a fate far worse than death. He had been on many large jobs throughout the city—from train derailments to officer-involved shootings—when Giuliani, angered by one thing or another, went on the warpath against police captains and inspectors who provided the mayor with a wrong answer or had just happened to do the wrong thing. Giuliani demanded results—positive results. And he didn't like being overshadowed. *Look at Bratton,* Pascullo thought. *He was a success and look how he was hung out to dry.* Failure, even with mitigating circumstances, was unacceptable to Giuliani. *Shit,* Pascullo thought, *nearly twenty-five years on the job is only seconds from being flushed down the toilet.*

Pascullo knew that in the event of a cluster fuck, *he* would be the department's scapegoat—a high-ranking cop would have to fall on his sword and he was the highest-ranking ESU boss there that night. Pascullo knew that Chief William Morange, the Special Operations Division commander, would protect Inspector McDermott, his protégé, over the former Housing captain. Morange and

Pascullo often butted heads and in the world of NYPD office politics, chiefs usually beat out captains. Kammerdener was a rising star, but he was still a Housing cop, and he lacked the political juice inside the department to protect an ESU captain from a mayor desperately needing to placate the hounding media wanting to know why SWAT cops were shooting unarmed Arabs in the middle of the night.

Pascullo wished that Chief of Department Anemone wasn't on vacation. When Pascullo had been promoted from lieutenant to captain, Anemone had seen to it that he remained in ESU. "Anemone used to like saying 'square pegs in square holes,'" Pascullo reflected. "He liked having people he could trust in commando positions."[9] Being indicted or out of a job with no pension was not good, especially with a mortgage, two kids, and a wife only weeks away from giving birth to number three. *Being dead,* Pascullo concluded, *sounds better. Some world in which we live,* Pascullo thought to himself only blocks away from the target, *when cops worry more about their jobs or being sued than they do about dying in the line of duty.*

Driving past Sterling Place, the team realized that they were only two blocks from the target. Suddenly, the cold truth of reality was shoved in the faces of the men now seconds away from the encounter with the Palestinians. The cops tried to get their heads in the zone. Cops used to like saying that when you were in the zone, en route to a hit, you could tell if a penny was heads or tails just by driving over it. The rest of the convoy peeled off to wait while the CAT car and Pascullo's Caprice moved forward into the darkness.

Less than a hundred feet separated the cops from the cabstand and the alleged bomb factory. The entry team began to pump oxygen into their system with hard deep breaths; the restraining Kevlar armor made it hard to suck in a mouthful of air. The breaths were vain attempts to force down the taste of stinging bile rushing through everyone's throat. The cabstand was now twenty feet away.

"Get ready," one of the cops yelled. Two officers unlocked the sliding door, each man gripping a knob. The police officers tightened the slings supporting their MP5 or Mini-14 around their shoulders and gently caressed the triggers. Dave Martinez readied the ballistic Body Bunker shield. McCaffrey glanced at the display on the CAT car's dashboard clock. It was 4:38 A.M.

Pascullo had charged past Berkeley Place, less than thirty feet from the cabstand, taking a deep breath and exhaling slowly to shake off his last jitters as he accelerated the Caprice to forty miles per hour. The hum of the engine turned into a sharp roar. His right hand unlocked the shotgun mount, and he grabbed the 12-gauge shotgun by the trigger and raised the weapon slowly. He unlocked the doors as he passed the cabstand, and then banked a harsh right turn, pushing the car over the curb. "Here we go," he shouted. "This is it."

Entry Team

The cabstand was carved into the first-floor landing of the brooding brick tenement. The six men at the cabstand were sitting on old metal folding chairs and milk carton boxes, and were in the throes of a heated backgammon tournament. They ranged from young men in their twenties wearing T-shirts and baseball caps to middle-aged men whose better years had been spent in the capitals of the Middle East. Dozens of smoked-to-the-filter cigarette butts littered the sidewalk. Although it was nearly five a.m., the men were serenaded by the wailing chants of a female vocalist, singing what the cops thought might be a love song, at top volume, courtesy of a ghetto-style boom box. Mosabbah hadn't known if the men at the cabstand were connected to his roommates and their plans for the subway later that morning, but he suspected them to be *with* his Palestinian roommates in their political views. Asked a dozen times at the station, Mosabbah said he knew nothing of the people who dispatched rickety Town Cars to pick up Arab immigrants all over Park Slope, Cobble Hill, and Carroll Gardens. If the cabstand was part of some larger terrorist cell, neutralizing it was the key to the surprise assault on the bomb factory apartment. The cops were going to treat them as if they were hard-core Hamas killers. The cabstand was going to be neutralized at any cost.

The men in front of the cabstand were immersed in their game, deep in laughter, when the CAT car came to a screeching halt on the curb, followed by the maroon Caprice running the curb as if it was out of control and about to run them down. They immediately jumped up in fear, as if wary of a drunken driver, but they had little time to flinch or react. The six ESU cops who spilled out of the CAT car quickly rushed the Arabs, knocking them to the ground with body blows the likes of which would have made a defensive tackle from the New York Jets jealous. The brute force was designed to prevent any of the men from tripping a buzzer or even hitting a speed-dial button on his cell phone that might alert the two Palestinian bomb makers of the encroaching police action. There was nothing by-the-book about blows and kicks, but this wasn't the kind of incident that was taught in the police academy. "We pull up right next to them and we flatten them," McCaffrey remembered. "Dolan and Martinez, they are big guys, and we just get out of this van and we flatten them. We drop them to the ground and we start moving."[1]

The cops wanted to numb the Arabs and to make sure that the five men *stayed* on the ground. Once the cabstand was secure, the bosses would handle security of the men moaning in pain on the ground. Pascullo leaped out of his seat and ran around the front lights of the car, pumping one green-jacketed 12-gauge round into the chamber of his Ithaca 37 as he stared at an overweight man in his fifties wearing a pair of black slacks and a white sleeveless undershirt, who looked like he was in charge. "Stay down on the ground!" Pascullo ordered, advancing toward the man in the undershirt with his shotgun prone in textbook firing position inches from the nape of the man's neck. Pascullo motioned for the man to stay down, but the Arab balked. The terrified man lifted his head five inches off the curb, as if bench-pressing an enormous burden, to beg for his life, wanting to tell Pascullo his life story or any Arabian tale to get the barrel of the shotgun away from his face. The Arab began to cry. But Pascullo needed him to be flat on the ground and quiet. Shoving the beer-can-wide 12-gauge barrel of the shotgun into the Arab's neck, Pascullo forced the sobbing man onto the pavement and held the gun pressed against the back of his head. Kammerdener took hold of two other Arabs, pressing the barrel of his Glock into the small of the young man's back, since he looked, momentarily, as if he was trying to get up from his position on the sidewalk. Deputy Inspector McDermott, standing to the side, held his gun on the other men.

Breaking radio silence, Pascullo got on the frequency secured for the operation, and whispered, "Blockers in place."

On the corner of Fourth Avenue and Prospect Place, five blocks from the raid, a dozen police, fire, and EMS vehicles that were standing by moved into tactical position in front of the location. The convoy had followed Pascullo's Caprice and the CAT car, and then stayed blocks behind out of sight to prevent itself from sparking the interest of any possible lookouts. A handful of high-ranking police commanders, fire battalion chiefs, MTA bosses, and EMT supervisors monitored the police band broadcasting Pascullo's words. "Blockers in place" was their signal to inch closer toward the action.

Mosabbah led Lieutenant McCaffrey and the entry team into the vestibule of 248 Fourth Avenue. The building was your typical Brooklyn brick walk-up—a dirty outer facade covered with graffiti, and surrounded by piles and piles of trash that for some reason never got picked up. The hallway of the building was dark and dingy. A twenty-watt bulb, barely bright enough to illuminate a refrigerator, stood over a row of mailboxes. The floor was last tiled before the Second World War; the white ceramic squares long since dyed black by dirt and neglect. But there was no courtyard, no garbage, and no folded Ping-Pong table. *Where is the apartment?* McCaffrey thought to himself, not wanting to reveal the sinking feeling festering in the pit of his stomach that maybe the raiding team was set up. *Where is the goddamned courtyard?*

Sergeant English was getting antsy, too. So much preparation, so much angst, and so much terror while sitting inside the CAT car seemed wasted. *This location is wrong,* English concluded, clutching his Glock semiautomatic tighter with each step onto the curb, feeling as if he was being set up for something terrible. The cops raised their weapons inside the building, searching for possible traps, or the telltale signs of trip wires. *Maybe the terrorists have wired the building with explosives?*

"The informant told us that the apartment was going to be on the right," McCaffrey explained. "Sure enough, he keeps going straight down the hallway and I'm thinking to myself, what the fuck is going on? The cops were nervous. We were scared, but I told them that on the hit I'd be the only one doing the talking and *I* wanted to know what the fuck was going on."[2]

But Mosabbah had come too far this night to let everything evaporate in misunderstanding and second-guessing. Looking like a drunk caught wearing a fool's Halloween costume in his oversized flak jacket and his black balaclava mask over his panic-stricken face, he decided to seize the initiative. Mosabbah proceeded toward the back door and, almost by will alone, brought the entry team into a back courtyard. The darkness was an obstacle and the stench of urine and decaying food from the garbage that tenants threw out in the alley was overwhelming. The ESU team warily followed Mosabbah's and McCaffrey's lead, walking deeper into darkness and careful not to hit the trash strewn about the five-foot-wide corridor. Mosabbah had walked through the darkened entrance a dozen times returning from his menial jobs at all hours, so tired that his bones ached. The smell and the filth of the doorway didn't bother him. It was similar to the reek he remembered from the slums of Cairo that he had escaped only weeks before. The entrance was the gauntlet that had to be run before he could collapse on his small cot. It wasn't much, but when one was chasing the American dream working sixteen hours a day, it was just enough.

Once through the door, in plain sight under a darkened July sky was the hidden world that Mosabbah first shared with the Long Island Rail Road cops, then the Eighty-eighth squad of detectives, then the ESU. Mosabbah, grabbing the Rookie by the vest, ran ten feet into the courtyard and pointed, hysterically, toward a door. *Yallah, yallah,* Mosabbah urged in the silence he was ordered to maintain, pointing toward the small armpit apartment.

Taking one step across the doorway, McCaffrey was suddenly enraged at himself for pointing his gun at Mosabbah's head moments before. *Holy shit,* McCaffrey thought to himself, *this guy has been right on the money.* Mosabbah had been telling the truth all along. The garbage cans were where the Egyptian said they'd be. The bicycle was exactly where he said it would be, thrown against the side of a brick wall. The chalk diagram had been precise and to scale. An entire world existed behind the rear-hall doorway at 248 Fourth Avenue completely unknown to the NYPD and a multitude of other city, state, and federal agencies. The rear area of the building had been converted into a refugee camp of converted miniapartments where illegal immigrants could for ten to fifteen dollars a week find a small spot to rest their weary bones.

McCaffrey thought of David Dinkins for a moment as he paused to position the cops. The former mayor of New York City had often commented that the Big Apple was a wonderful mosaic incorporating cultures and colors from the four corners of the world. Smelling the garbage strewn about the courtyard, trash simply tossed out of small windows to the floor below, McCaffrey thought of the wonderful mosaic and the stench the mixture of Arabic, Chinese, Mexican, and African food produced as he looked at the discarded wrappers sporting a half dozen languages. Rats the size of kittens moved about the courtyard picking apart anything that was edible. McCaffrey's attention was seized by one rat, limping with a huge bite scar across his back, struggling slowly toward a pile of crushed eggshells.

"We were wary that there was something wrong with the information we had about the place," Zorovic recalled, "but the closer we got to the target, the more we felt that the danger was increasing. The closer the informant got to his front door, the more he started to backpedal. He couldn't wait to get out of there. But the more terrified he became, the more I realized that this was a real job. At this point you begin to say to yourself that you have to be the best that you've ever been on any given job, because you are only as good as your last job in ESU. I knew that if I could be the best that I can be, and I could contribute in this situation, I was going to be okay and act appropriately enough that my part of the operation would be okay. This is where everything that I had ever done, saw, and learned in ESU was boiled down to these few seconds."[3]

Mosabbah's fear level was the true litmus test. This was it for the entry team. They were in the kill zone. Only two doors separated them from Jerusalem.

The moment Mosabbah identified the correct apartment, the Egyptian and the Rookie raced back toward Fourth Avenue. "You've never seen two Arabs run that fast in your life," McCaffrey would comment. "They ran back through the front door and kept on going, for nearly two blocks, until the detectives stopped them."[4]

"Team, stop," McCaffrey demanded in a whisper, gathering the five other cops around him. "Listen, all that crap about this guy not describing the building the right way—he is describing the building one hundred percent. This is game on. This guy isn't bullshitting. This is the real deal—do you all understand me? Move forward and let's go!"

McCaffrey suddenly felt a burden of tremendous responsibility. Back at the station, he had tried to take only bachelors or married men without children with him on the raid. He didn't want to bring fathers to a terrorist job, but the rookies were not up to this, either. This night in Brooklyn required experienced veterans—and veteran cops had families. *Now what have I done?* He realized that all this was for real, like a surreal scene out of some Middle Eastern nightmare. Terrorists were in Brooklyn, and they were only yards away.

The entry team lined up in the positions they had preset back at the Eighty-eighth and silently tiptoed across the courtyard toward the Palestinians' apartment. Martinez, the Bunker man, went first, followed in a single file by Dolan, Zorovic, Keenan, English, and McCaffrey. The air was hot and putrid inside the courtyard, and the officers felt the weight of their equipment getting the better of them as they attempted to step around the rats that were lingering at their feet. Sergeant English aimed his Glock pistol at the doorway to cover the assault team. McCaffrey and English, assigned door security, were last. Dave Martinez positioned himself on the right side of the door and carefully hoisted his Body Bunker up over his face and torso while turning on his Glock's flashlight. He removed his helmet and put his ear to the door—an old trick used on drug warrants—and he heard snoring coming from inside the apartment. Joe Dolan, Mini-14 in hand, stood behind Martinez. Zorovic and Keenan were next in the stick poised to race through the doorway; they were followed by English and McCaffrey in the rear. It was 4:50 A.M.

"Team ready," McCaffrey bellowed in a low whisper.

"Team ready" was Dolan's cue to insert the apartment door key McCaffrey had taken from Mosabbah into the cylinder and to gently turn counterclockwise to open the door for the team. It was imperative for the entry force to achieve absolute surprise before racing through toward the room with the explosives; opening the door gently and silently, then flowing through the two rooms quickly, might buy the cops a few valuable seconds that would keep the Palestinians from blowing everyone up. Dolan gently removed the key from a pouch on his body armor to his left hand. The lock was low, so he lowered his six-foot frame to one knee. Martinez aimed a beam of light from the flashlight mounted on his Glock on the lock to help his partner along, watching anxiously as the key was placed inside the lock.

Closing his eyes for a brief second, as if expecting the entire building to blow up once he turned the key, Dolan followed the plan and gently shifted the key to the left. *I thought that the Arab told me the door locks to the right,* Dolan thought to himself in anger, disappointed that he just might have let his team down. "I think I locked it," Dolan told Zorovic, grinding his teeth in embarrassment and fear after realizing that he had just accidentally doublelocked the door. "Well, Jesus Christ, unlock it!" Zorovic demanded with a fed-up wince as he struggled not to laugh and wondered what else could go wrong on this midnight tour. Looking at his partner, his eyes bulging in an urgent expression, he pleaded, "Do it now!"

Dolan turned the key to the right this time, slowly turning it a full 360 degrees to first undo what he had done seconds before. Martinez offered a sigh of relief hearing the key turn the first time, though the weight of the Body Bunker was making his left arm ache. He wouldn't be able to hold it much longer. Dolan turned the key slowly one last time, and felt the bolt relinquish its hold on the door. Getting back off his knee, Dolan slid the Mini-14 slung over his shoulder back into a two-handed combat grip. The officers looked back at McCaffrey, as if seeking parental approval, before storming through. McCaffrey, eager to get the job over with, gently nodded, ushering his men forward.

With his right hand, Joe Dolan twisted the key still inside the lock ever so gently to the right, pushing the metal door open. Martinez entered first, followed by Dolan. Attempting to illustrate the chalk diagram with what he was seeing before his eyes, Martinez was struck by how small the apartment was. Just as Mosabbah had indicated, a man was sleeping on a cot along the wall opposite the door. The cot looked like the kind of bed that could have been stolen from a Red Cross emergency center. The cot sagged under the weight of the thirty-year-old man, an Arab, fast asleep in the fetal position. A bad stench of mold emanated from the shower and toilet; the smell, quite strong, seemed to battle the smell of rotting food coming from the sink to the left. The door leading to the Palestinians was directly adjacent to the sink; the door to Mosabbah's room was to the right.

Instinctively, and as they had done hundreds of times before, Martinez and Dolan wanted to burst through the door of the Palestinians' room. SWAT cops were trained to move like water, to flow into a location without stopping, filling all the gaps and leaving no stone unturned, no closet unopened and no door unchecked. But as Martinez was about to flow through the Palestinians' door, he suddenly paused. He heard two men talking and movement coming from inside the room. The targets were awake.

The Hit

Joe Dolan had been through doors with Martinez hundreds of times before. They were partners and they trusted one another's instincts. All along, the talk had always been about the bombs the two men had built, but now, inside the apartment, Martinez shuddered when he thought about guns. Were they armed? Were the bombs already attached to their waists? What was behind that door?

Dolan looked at his partner, and then looked down at the floor. Raising two fingers to his eyes and then motioning toward the bottom edge of the door, Dolan indicated to his partner that the light in the room was off. If the Palestinians were armed and the room was, indeed, dark, it would be easier for the two cops to handle them; with the lights of the officers' weapons shining brightly directly into the eyes of the other two men, the Palestinians would be blinded by the flashlight beams.

Hoisting his twenty-pound Body Bunker shield high with his left hand one last time, Martinez gave his partner one final look. There was nothing to say before going through the door. What could they say? Both locked eyes and decided this was it.

Martinez hurled his six-foot-three frame through the door, leaping in a controlled manner that would enable him to reach the other side in firing position. He opened his mouth before lunging into the Palestinians' room, hoping to clear his throat of the fear that raced up through his chest. "POLICE, GET DOWN!" Martinez shouted in a no-shit-taken-today voice. Holding his shield firmly, Martinez used his Glock like a searchlight, looking for movement, a weapon, or even a face. The room was small: ten feet by ten feet. The room felt like an oven and the stench of feet and underarms was stifling. Before Martinez could make out what he thought was the outline of a teenage boy on the bed, he felt two skinny arms grabbing at his weapon. In the blackness, with his dark hair, olive skin, and goatee, Abu Mezer looked like the kind of Hispanic street tough that usually caused the cops problems—punks who were short and wiry always felt that they had something to prove by fighting. Working in the shitty end of Brooklyn for so many years, Martinez had locked horns—and knocked down—so many young hoodlums who thought that they could beat it out with a cop covered in Kevlar, they all became faceless collages of the same idiot. But Abu Mezer was different. The empty look in his eyes was an expression of hate and determination that the veteran ESU cop had never seen before. His cold stare, Martinez would later admit, was menacing. The fight he was putting up was less a struggle of self-preservation than raw offensive violence. Abu Mezer didn't curse or growl in the brief scuffle. He was silent and unflinching.

Martinez had just made it through the door when Abu Mezer confronted him and challenged him for his weapon. Abu Mezer used every ounce of strength in his compact frame to dig into the forearm of the ESU cop, but Martinez didn't want to bother with a life-and-death struggle. He fired a single 9mm round toward the Palestinian. The gunshot popped a flash of light into the darkened room; sparks emanating from the barrel of Martinez's gun sprayed onto a blue woolen blanket on the bed. Martinez shot Abu Mezer at point-blank range; the explosion of the gunshot was muffled only by the proximity of the Palestinian's body to the barrel of the gun. The bullet, though, only grazed the right side of Abu Mezer's temple and continued straight into the drywall. Abu Mezer was undeterred. Martinez fired again, hitting the Palestinian in the midsection. Abu Mezer didn't moan when shot, even though the force of the bullet entering his body sprayed blood over the room and threw him back three feet.

The exchange between Martinez and Abu Mezer took seconds. It was over in the blasts of a muzzle flash. Lafi Khalil leaped off the mattress he was on and lunged for the black satchel bag that was on the floor; Martinez fired two rounds into him, stalling his progress as blood and bone sprayed into the wall.

Joe Dolan couldn't follow his partner into the Palestinians' room—he was blocked by Martinez's struggle with Abu Mezer at the door. The room was so small that Dolan found it difficult to get a foothold through the door to back up his partner. He pushed his way in the moment Martinez fired his first shot, and then reached around to the right to launch one round from his Mini-14 assault rifle into each Palestinian. The two rounds of M193 NATO ball 148-grain ammunition that traveled at 3,250 feet per second ripped gaping holes inside both Abu Mezer and Khalil.

Khalil turned on his side after getting shot and then he arched his back on the bed; his legs, fighting for one last gasp of energy, slipped clumsily on the blood and the shell casings on the linoleum floor.

When Mario Zorovic and Mike Keenan followed Martinez and Dolan inside the apartment, their job was to subdue the Arab man in his thirties asleep on the cot in the kitchen. Mosabbah had told the cops that the man on the cot wasn't part of the plot but another poor sucker chasing the American dream at three dollars an hour, eighteen hours a day, spending as little as he could on food and clothing in order to send the rest home. But the cops couldn't be sure that the Arab was a good citizen, or an accomplice, so he would be treated as a threat; Zorovic and Keenan were tasked with handcuffing the dazed Arab.

Zorovic felt his heart racing through his chest and out of his body armor when he walked through the door. He positioned himself in the kitchen, next to the stench of rotting food sitting in the sink, while his partner took aim with his MP5. When Martinez and Dolan went through the door to his right, Zorovic was to pounce on the sleeping Arab and cuff him. The flashlight attachment on Zorovic's MP5 was on high beam and he directed the blinding rays of light into the Arab's eyes. When the sounds of Martinez splitting the wooden door leading to Abu Mezer's room jolted the man out of a deep slumber, he was blinded by the piercing beams of light. Before the Arab could figure out what was going on, the 240-pound Zorovic was on top of him. Keenan's gun was jammed in the poor man's neck while Zorovic twisted the man's struggling arms forcefully behind his back. The hapless man must have been confused and terrified by the sudden events. He heard screams and then shots, and was restrained.

Zorovic and Keenan never expected to hear gunfire. Six earsplitting shots were above and beyond even their worst-case scenarios. Zorovic twisted his back toward the Palestinians' room the moment the gunfire erupted, in the hope of getting the fatter part of his ballistic vest between him and the unleashed rounds. *Fuck, they're shooting in there,* Zorovic thought to himself immediately, relying on all his mental resources to stay calm and follow the plan. The shots rang out so fast that there wasn't even time to yell out to see if the cops in the room were OK.

When the entry team raced into the apartment, McCaffrey and English rushed into Mosabbah's room just to make sure that there wasn't a mystery Arab hiding in a closet or under a bed. The two supervisors were tasked with a twofold assignment: first, they were to prevent anyone from getting in the apartment who didn't have business being there, which on this job meant virtually everyone in Brooklyn; second, they were to make sure, in the scenario that the entry team was cut down in a hail of gunfire, that the shooters never left the apartment alive. Sergeant English was the more pragmatic of the two men posted outside the door. Soft-spoken, English was a confident squad leader who used to assume the worst in big jobs like this one in order to be prepared mentally for the outcome. McCaffrey, on the other hand, was a wide-eyed optimist who always felt deep down in his heart something he called the "luck of the Irish"—that everything would work out in the end. The sounds of gunfire confirmed English's worst fears and shattered McCaffrey's carefree confidence. English headed straight for the gunfire and his cops.

The six shots fired ripped through the quiet Brooklyn night with an ear-shattering force. "*HOLY SHIT*," McCaffrey said to himself, recognizing the sounds of the guns and knowing that his guys had just let off six rounds. *The Palestinians must have made a move,* McCaffrey thought, *and these guys did the right thing.* Back at the Eighty-eighth, when the tactics of the night's operation were being planned, McCaffrey had told the entry team that under no circumstances did he want them letting off rounds free and clear inside a bomb factory. "I told them that I don't want more than three rounds in each guy, no more than six rounds total, because I didn't want a lot of firepower inside a bomb-making facility. We couldn't use our distraction devices or smoke grenades because we didn't know what kind of materials they had. We couldn't have a ton of fire going downrange. If one of them had let a clip go, and one of those rounds hit the bomb, we would have all been dead."[1]

McCaffrey entered the room and found English, Dolan, and Martinez standing over the two Palestinians. The room smelled of gunpowder and the sweet, sickly tang of fresh flowing blood. Both Martinez and Dolan held their weapons over the two men. Everyone stood in stoic silence gazing at the chaotic scene in stunned disbelief. "Hey, fellas, let's go and cuff these guys," McCaffrey ordered. The bleeding messes that were Gazi Abu Mezer and Lafi Khalil were dragged out of their room and brought to the kitchen area. They were searched and then cuffed.

The entry team had been inside the apartment for all of two minutes.

Pascullo was angry that he was left out in front of the car service storefront as his cops were poised to make entry into the Palestinians' apartment. Pascullo's general philosophy of being a cop was predicated on always being in the center of things. It didn't matter if he was a rookie cop walking down a flight of stairs inside a project in Brownsville, Brooklyn, or if he was on a job as the executive officer of the four-hundred-man Emergency Service Unit, standing next to Secret Service agents protecting the president. Even though, as a boss, his role was to supervise, quite uncharacteristically for someone with his captain's bars, Pascullo would often roll up his sleeves and lend a hand on jobs, getting gear off a truck, and helping out with a sledgehammer or even a weapon on an entry team if the unit was short on bodies.

Other captains and inspectors used to scoff at the ESU second-in-command when he'd pitch in to help the men. The bosses used to laugh at Pascullo for breaking a sweat. Many veteran ESU cops, primarily those who weren't fond of former commissioner Bratton's decision to merge the NYPD with the Housing and Transit Police, used to call Pascullo "Captain Chaos" behind his back. He was all over the place, they'd complain. Pascullo tried too hard to be one of the guys, because he *loved* being one of the guys. He believed cops should help one another regardless of rank. Being one of the guys, more often than not, meant doing the right thing.

As he stood over the men from the car service, Pascullo tried to assess how much time had elapsed since the cops went into the building. And then he heard a shot, and then the second crack of a bullet being fired. "Sounds like shots," he told Kammerdener, sensing an empty punch slamming through his stomach. "I don't think so," Kammerdener replied, not wanting to believe that the worst-case scenario was now becoming a reality. In the projects, adrenaline had always propelled Pascullo forward—it was a sixth sense that directed his movement. On this Brooklyn morning, a sixth sense ordered Pascullo into the courtyard.

Pascullo rushed into the building, clutching his shotgun in his right hand. For a man wearing nearly forty pounds of Kevlar he made it through the vestibule of the building quickly, hearing another gunshot as he ran. Opening the door with his left hand, Pascullo entered the courtyard not knowing what to expect. Were his men dead? Were the Arabs blown away? A million thoughts raced through Pascullo's mind inside the courtyard. All the scenarios appeared bleak.

Walking slowly into the courtyard, the ESU captain's mind flashed back to the diagram that Mosabbah had drawn so many times inside the squad room. It was like a different universe existed behind the street, where the outside world was unwelcome. Looking at the illegal structure, Pascullo raised his shotgun toward a ground floor apartment door that was partly open. *This must be the one,* he thought. *This looks exactly like the Egyptian's descriptions.* He had never fired a 12-gauge shotgun on an actual job. He peered through the sights and caressed the trigger very gently. He took a deep breath and exhaled slowly. He thought to himself that if he saw anything but a blue shirt coming through that door, he was going to fire; if anyone but a cop was going to walk out the front door, it meant that the entry team had been killed.

He heard movement inside the apartment and he heard people speaking English. It was an encouraging sign, he thought. But then he heard two rifle rounds highlighted by the simultaneous burst of muzzle flash eruptions inside the darkened apartment. *What's going on in there?* Pascullo wondered nervously. This was no longer a job. It had become an incident. Pascullo stood frozen by the thoughts of his men lying dead, killed by Middle Eastern terrorists. He stood frozen by the fear that his men might have killed unarmed civilians. Then there were two more shots, and two more successive bursts of muzzle flashes. *Damn it,* Pascullo reasoned to himself, *I'm going in.* . . .

Just as he moved toward the staircase, he heard sounds inside the apartment, and then talking. The crisscrossing beams of the officers' weapon-mounted flashlights bounced off the walls of the small apartment, creating disappearing shadows. A figure appeared in the doorway. It was McCaffrey. He was dragging Lafi Khalil by the arm, hoisting his motionless body across the courtyard, and then dropping him by Pascullo's legs. "Hey, dude." McCaffrey smiled, as if greeting Pascullo on a bright sunny day at the annual ESU barbeque. "Can you keep an eye on him?" The West Bank native was gray and bleeding profusely. His hands were cuffed behind his back.

"Keep an eye on him?" Pascullo asked in angry disbelief. "Are you fucking nuts? He looks like he's ready for the morgue. . . .

"Is there a bomb in there, Owen?" Pascullo demanded. "Is there a fucking bomb or not?"

McCaffrey shrugged his shoulders as he returned to the apartment. "I don't know, Ralph," the lieutenant replied. "I have to go and look now."

The shouts, the gunfire, and the tumult awakened most of the dwellers in the house behind 248 Fourth Avenue. They came to their windows and saw a shotgun-wielding policeman standing over what looked like the corpse of one of their neighbors. On the second floor, in an apartment to the right side, a man wearing a white Arab robe appeared at his window; a woman, veiled in black, stood next to him. Pascullo raised his shotgun at the Arab man, motioning for him to get away from the window. *This place is like the set of an Indiana Jones movie,* Pascullo thought. *Who dresses like that in New York City?* "Get the fuck away from the window!" Pascullo ordered the man, double clutching his shotgun in the process and appearing ready to fire his weapon.

By the time Pascullo lowered his shotgun and his peripheral

vision to the courtyard, Mario Zorovic was walking down the stairs dragging another body. "Can you also keep an eye on him, Captain?" Zorovic asked, offering a brief but somewhat relieved smile. It was Abu Mezer. The bomb builder who had put up such a fight against a cop who towered over him was still smiling with a sinister grin. The smirk, the cunning type of smile that a serial killer offered victims before slicing their throats, was pure evil, Pascullo thought.

Both bodies looked as if life was quickly draining out of them. Khalil moaned in a low-frequency hum; Abu Mezer looked like he was going into shock. Pascullo gazed upon the two critically wounded men, and scanned the courtyard for the rats that, smelling blood, were slowly emerging from their hiding spots behind the trash. Inspector McDermott and Chief Kammerdener both raced into the courtyard. The two men didn't say it, but their facial expressions summed it all up: "Oh, shit! What the hell do we have here?"

There was a moment of pure unadulterated silence as the two former partners stared at the two Palestinians. They didn't look like much. Didn't look like holy warriors or people capable of bringing the jihad to the subways. They simply looked like shot perps.

Suddenly, Pascullo's knees shook, as if about to crumble under the weight and the stress. Two seemingly lifeless Palestinians were at his feet, each shot three times by ESU, *his* cops, and there was no word of a weapon or a bomb. *Was this a bad shooting?* he wondered. *I should have been on the entry team*, he thought to himself. *I should have been there. At least then I'd know what's going on.* Suddenly, he also felt very tired. With the Brooklyn sky lightening to a soothing shade of royal blue over Fourth Avenue, the new day dawning sent a signal to his overtaxed brain as to just how exhausted he truly was.

Pascullo's first instinct was to race toward the apartment and see what the bomb looked like. But the Palestinians were still alive and they had to be rushed to the hospital. Looking at the blood-gurgling West Bank sons at his feet brought the ESU captain back into the game. Pascullo and Kammerdener hoisted the two shot men onto a stretcher and then helped to bring them out to Fourth Avenue, which by now was alight with the cascading red-and-white flashing lights of dozens of police and emergency vehicles. When the first two ambulances arrived in front of the location on Fourth Avenue, the EMS duty captain, an African-American man in his forties with dreadlocks and an angry snarl, walked in front of Pascullo and Kammerdener with an indignant gait. "What mess of yours do I have to clean up today?" the captain said with both hands angrily clutching his waist. The EMS captain watched as the two Palestinians were loaded into two separate ambulances with a police guard, and he then sneered at Pascullo in disdain and asked, "Did you all have to shoot these guys?"

Did we have to shoot these knuckleheads? That was a good question, Pascullo thought. *Was this a good shooting?* It was obvious that the EMS captain didn't like cops, but Pascullo suddenly wondered how many people on a grand jury set to indict him would share those same sentiments. Pascullo stared at his old partner. Kammerdener's white shirt, visible under the heavy Kevlar vest, was full of Palestinian blood. Pascullo's hands, too, were covered with blood and tissue from the shot Palestinians.

Pascullo headed back to the courtyard nervous, and wary of wiping his brow with his bloodied hands. Sweat was dripping from his close-cropped hair down into his eyes; the weight of the Kevlar helmet was becoming a nuisance—a real pain in the neck.

McCaffrey had returned to the apartment with a sigh of relief and reluctant anticipation. He walked through the door and saw Zorovic and Keenan on top of the Egyptian. The Egyptian struggled, but did not resist. There was no point in resisting—the Jaws of Life couldn't have freed him from the grips of the two ESU officers. McCaffrey walked into the Palestinians' room and tried to figure out if this was going to be an "Oh, shit, why did we shoot these guys?"

sort of night or an "Oh, shit, there is a bomb here—we need to get the hell out of here right now" moment. The crisscrossing beams of lights from the flashlights reminded some of the officers of the images of London during the Blitz. The officers didn't want to flip the light switch, not wanting to initiate a possible blast with an electrical spark. The room was awash in blood. The four 9mm rounds and two .223 slugs that had cut through the Palestinians' bodies had created an absolute mess. The smoke and dust kicked up by the gunfire and the struggle was stifling. Sergeant English gazed down at the floor, aiming his flashlight at what appeared to be a black gym bag.

What the fuck do we have here? McCaffrey wondered as he trained his flashlight on the bag; his heart began to race in a loud and unstoppable gallop. English and McCaffrey moved closer to the bag, peering inside it as gently as they could. They saw plumbing pipes covered with nails, connected to two industrial-sized batteries by red and blue wires. Each pipe was capped and fitted with hundreds of five-inch nails held together by silver electrician's tape. There were two bombs that Martinez could see. McCaffrey and English looked at one another. They didn't utter a word, but their expressions spoke volumes. "Holy shit, let's get the fuck out of Dodge," McCaffrey finally ordered. The Egyptian was removed from the apartment.

The entry team remained in the Palestinians' apartment to conduct a secondary search—albeit a hurried one. The officers were looking for additional bomb-making materials, trip wires, booby traps, or anything else that the bomb squad or other investigative personnel would need to know about. "As crazy as it sounds, I was relieved that we found a bomb in the apartment," English would admit. "Two shot perps and no weapon could have been an uncomfortable situation."[2]

Pascullo stood at the rear entrance of 248 Fourth Avenue like an expectant father. "Captain," McCaffrey informed his boss, trying to be as curt as possible, "there's a fucking bomb in there. We better get the bomb squad in here now!" McCaffrey smiled.

Pascullo was in no mood for McCaffrey's "dude" routine. "Show me the fucking bomb!" Pascullo demanded as he grabbed McCaffrey's body armor and pulled him back into the courtyard. "I want to see the fucking thing with my own two eyes."

"Dude, there's a bomb. Trust me . . . ," McCaffrey reassured his longtime boss. "I've seen it."

For the first time in a long time, Pascullo lost it with someone of a lower rank. He had always refrained from yelling at a subordinate—that wasn't how Pascullo liked to command—but he grabbed the much larger McCaffrey and yanked him into the building at 248 Fourth Avenue, and yelled, "But I haven't. Let me see it now."

Walking toward the apartment, Pascullo saw Zorovic and Keenan bringing out the other roommate, followed by Dolan and Martinez. The ESU captain could now hear people talking inside their homes in myriad languages. He heard babies crying and mothers trying to comfort them. He heard the shuffling of pots and pans and he heard dogs barking. Pascullo stood inside the doorway, apprehensive to enter. He saw the blood sprayed all over the walls and in puddles on the bed and blanket. He removed his flashlight from his utility belt, and illuminated the black canvas bag. Pascullo didn't touch the bag, but could clearly make out the batteries, the wires, and the capped pipes covered with nails. *The shooting was a good one,* Pascullo thought, smiling to himself as he removed his helmet to wipe his forehead. It was the first time he had smiled all night. He realized, or hoped, that his career, pension, and mortgage were now intact. He also realized that his men had saved the city from a calamity. Now he needed to finish the job. He felt rejuvenated—born again almost—as he realized that tonight had not been a nightmare. Not just yet.

The job was far from over. Pascullo informed McCaffrey that on the second floor of the illegal building a suspicious Middle Eastern man refused to heed his commands to get away from the window. Pascullo had taken aim with his shotgun, but the man continued to act suspiciously. McCaffrey assembled his entry team and once again the six officers burst through the front door of the second-story apartment and cuffed the middle-aged man; he was of Middle Eastern descent and spoke no English. The man's room was a small decrepit dwelling covered in filth with wall sockets and wires exposed throughout. When the team entered, Zorovic noticed a wire hanging by the door and managed to duck his head under; Mike Keenan, following closely behind, failed to see his partner avoid the obstacle and found himself with a hanging wire now taut against his forehead. He froze and, fearing it to be a trip wire of some kind, called for Zorovic to help him. Zorovic followed the wire with the flashlight mounted on his MP5 and saw that it was nothing more than an extension cord. Nerves were already frayed and there was still the basement apartment to do, as well.

The entry team, now suffering from excess adrenaline being flooded out of their systems, began to slow down. With weapons at the ready, the team garrisoned its forces and stormed the basement apartment. The entry team braced itself at the door and then burst through in the same formation. Expecting to find more Middle Easterners possibly involved in the plot, the officers entered the basement room only to find a family of Mexicans, huddled together; the parents hugged their eight children, who were cowering in fear. The officers lowered their weapons, attempting to bring some calm back to the terrified parents and their children. *These poor bastards are living in filth chasing the almighty dollar, and here I am leading them to what they must think will be instant deportation back to Taco-land,* one of the cops thought. "It'll be all right," another officer tried to reassure the family as they were led out of the apartment toward the front building and one of the waiting city buses commandeered to take everyone in the area back to the Eighty-eighth Precinct. "We aren't from La Migra!"

McCaffrey glanced at his watch. It was just after five a.m. and his entry team had been on the scene for well over a half hour. He wanted to get his cops out of there and to the hospital as soon as possible to be treated for trauma. All police officers involved in a shooting, whether they fire their weapons at a suspect or even at a pit bull, or are targeted by gunfire, are required by their union agreement to receive emergency trauma care. The trauma care was rudimentary and basic—a hearing test, a psychological examination, and a heart test—but necessary. Sometimes, the check was to see if the officer had been hurt in the gunfire but hadn't yet realized his injury; there was an actual instance when an overweight ESU officer who was shot through the vest on a job didn't realize he was shot until the end of the tour when he removed his uniform and the bullet fell to the ground. McCaffrey wanted all his cops to head to the hospital, but Zorovic wasn't leaving until the job was done. There was still a lot of work to do—248 Fourth Avenue had to be searched and evacuated.

McCaffrey saw to it that Martinez and Dolan were sent to New York Methodist Hospital up the hill on Seventh Avenue in Park Slope, while Zorovic and Keenan, along with Sergeant English, joined with the secondary tactical team that McCaffrey had assembled back at the Eighty-eighth Precinct to take down each and every apartment at 248 Fourth Avenue. "The front building consisted of railroad flats," McCaffrey explained. "Each floor had two apartments per floor, so we systematically split our strength into a left and right team and cleared the five floors of apartments." Many of the residents were rousted out of their sleep and outraged that their apartments were being searched. The cops didn't have time to play community policemen and offer explanations to everyone. The residents of the building were ordered to dress, grab ID, and head downstairs. They were placed on the buses waiting outside for transport back to the Eighty-eighth detective squad to be briefed by teams of NYPD detectives and federal investigators.

By six a.m., Fourth Avenue looked like the center of the universe. Dozens of emergency response vehicles filled the avenue and the side streets. Ambulances from a dozen volunteer corps, as well as from the FDNY, stood at the ready in case calamity still struck. A small army of FBI agents, wearing grayish blue nylon raid jackets with the letters FBI emblazoned on the backs in a bright reflective yellow, began to assess the situation. Federal agents had been alerted several hours earlier.

Back at the Eighty-eighth Precinct, LIRR police officers Huber and Kowalchuk eagerly awaited word of the raid. They felt responsible for the entire apparatus that had been put into play and they wanted to know that everything had gone according to plan. Kowalchuk asked one of the detectives if he knew anything, and the response was, "ESU raided the location and two people were shot."[3] Kowalchuk's heart sank. "You have to find out what's going on," he pleaded with the detective, desperate to make sure that no police officers were hurt.

Throughout the borough, hearts were sinking. Brooklyn woke up to no immediate news of the night's events, only massive gridlock. The Fourth Avenue subway line was shut and lines in and around the Park Slope neighborhood were diverted elsewhere. The first morning commuters raised an enormous fuss with transit workers and police officers diverting the traffic to alternate train and bus routes. It was still early. The city had yet to realize how many lives had been saved in the muzzle flash of a Brooklyn night.

On Fourth Avenue, McCaffrey's most pressing concern was getting the rest of the cops to go to the emergency room. McCaffrey and English were proud of the cops. They performed above and beyond the call of duty under the most dangerous of circumstances. McCaffrey was certain that the officers would be a lock for the department's highest decoration.

Pascullo was busy running interference between a small army of bosses, both from the borough and from One Police Plaza, who had made their pilgrimage toward what was now a confirmed terrorist job that was bound to get in-depth media play; it was always good to be seen on camera doing something when it came time for promotions. The bosses on such jobs were vultures. They picked through the carcass of police work to find a morsel that they could devour and take credit for.

The ESU cops still on the scene had moved themselves away from the tumult to bullshit and blow off some steam when one of the bomb squad detectives summoned McCaffrey with a grave look of concern blanketing his face. *This can't be good,* McCaffrey thought. *When the bomb squad guys get worried, we all better run.* McCaffrey knew Detective Richard Teemsma to be a stand-up bomb squad technician whom he had seen on numerous jobs before. "Three toggle switches are one way on one of the bombs," the detective told McCaffrey, "and one toggle is another way. The terrorists hit one of the switches. The bomb has been activated. It probably should have gone off."[4]

The bomb squad had examined the black satchel and they had attempted to ascertain just how the device worked. It was clear that this was a suicide bomb. There wasn't a fuse or a timer, just the four switches. The bomb squad estimated that the four toggle switches were needed to heat the filament to the point where it could spark the gunpowder. As long as the juice to the battery was flowing in a circuit, the device had the potential to blow. The bomb squad needed some intelligence. They needed to know how to disarm the device.

Pascullo and McCaffrey wondered if the devices would still detonate. They wondered what shit storm of criticism they would encounter from the police commissioner's office, the borough, or even city hall. They wondered if the two Palestinians were still alive.

Both men knew it was still going to be a long time before they had the chance to go home.

It was after one a.m. when the phone rang—late-night calls were never a good sign. Jeremy Yamin stumbled out of bed in his SoHo apartment to see what was so goddamned important that it couldn't wait until morning, and tried to assemble his voice and find his footing when he picked up the phone. "Okay," Yamin answered, "let me write this down and I'll be there right away." Sitting on the foot of his bed, he grabbed the mattress for support and then slowly righted himself in a clumsy attempt to stand and find his bearings after being shattered out of the peaceful slumber of a good night's sleep. Yamin grabbed his gun, his badge, and his car keys. *Where are my pants?* he thought to himself, fumbling in the closet and trying not to awaken his wife. There was a report of a terrorist cell operating in Brooklyn and it wasn't a good idea to respond to a police precinct in nothing but a pair of boxers and an undershirt.

Jeremy Yamin was a special agent in one of the least-known American federal law enforcement agencies—the State Department's Diplomatic Security Service, or DSS. Security within the Department of State was formally established in 1916 under Secretary of State Robert Lansing, and was headed by a chief special agent. The chief special agent, who also carried the title of "special assistant to the secretary," reported directly to the secretary on special matters and conducted covert investigations, especially on the movements, activities, and possible espionage operations of foreign agents in the United States. In 1918, Congress passed legislation requiring passports for Americans traveling abroad and visas for aliens wishing to enter the United States. Soon afterward, the chief special agent's office began investigating passport and visa fraud. In the entity that would eventually develop into the Diplomatic Security Service, investigating passport and visa fraud would become the staple of anticriminal activity (similar to the United States Secret Service's task of investigating currency counterfeiting). At the same time, the secretive agency also was tasked with a dignitary protection mandate, and was responsible for the safeguarding of distinguished visitors to the United States. The Diplomatic Security Service, or "SY," as it was known then, remained a relatively obscure arm of federal law enforcement until those shocking events of the early 1980s, when American embassies in the Middle East began to disappear in a cloud of smoke and the fury of a suicide bomber's truck laden with a half ton of TNT. Between 1979 and 1984, there were nearly one hundred terrorist attacks against Americans—American embassies were torched, blown up, and seized and some three hundred American citizens killed. In 1984, Secretary of State George Shultz formed an advisory panel to make recommendations on how to minimize the probability of terrorist attacks on U.S. citizens and facilities. This commission, headed by retired admiral Bobby Inman, would initiate sweeping reforms, starting with, on November 4, 1985, the creation of the Diplomatic Security Service.

DSS is a master of many trades—it provides dignitary protection to the U.S. secretary of state, as well as visiting foreign non-head-of-state dignitaries—including visiting foreign ministers, former heads of state, members of the British royal family, the secretaries-general of the United Nations and NATO, Palestinian Authority President Yasir Arafat, and even His Holiness the Dalai Lama. Domestically, the agency's primary law enforcement mission still centers on passport and visa fraud investigations. Overseas,

DSS agents are dispatched to over 150 U.S. embassies and consulates around the world to serve as regional security officers, or RSOs; RSOs and their assistants (known as ARSOs) are the sole U.S. federal agents permanently stationed in every foreign diplomatic post. They are America's liaison to foreign police agencies and, more often than not, America's eyes and ears picking up tidbits of intelligence concerning hostile intentions against American interests abroad. DSS agents work in places like Beirut, Sarajevo, and Islamabad; two DSS agents stationed in the Pakistani capital, in fact, were behind the February 1995 capture of Ramzi Ahmed Yousef, the al-Qaeda lieutenant responsible for masterminding the February 26, 1993, bombing of the World Trade Center.

It was the thought of international intrigue, and being a federal agent serving overseas, that attracted Yamin to a career inside the Diplomatic Security Service. He had worked as a part-time police officer in Wellfleet, Massachusetts, during his graduate studies and he wanted to combine his fascinations with law enforcement and international relations. Yamin envisioned Third World hot spots and being America's man inside the crosshairs of the war against terrorism. DSS had an equally exotic vision for the new special agent—they sent him to the most bizarre hot spot on the globe: Manhattan. "I joined the State Department to see the world," Yamin reminisced, "and they sent me back to my hometown, New York City."[1]

Manhattan, the heart of the New York metropolitan area, is just one of the twenty-two field and satellite offices where special agents from DSS are posted inside the United States. But because DSS special agents work as security officers in embassies and consulates around the world, their precinct was truly a global one. DSS is one of those federal law enforcement agencies that few people outside of the Beltway in Washington, D.C., know exists; many *inside* the Beltway don't have a clue as to what DSS does, either.

At the sprawling 26 Federal Plaza New York field office, over thirty agents—some new rookies straight out of the Federal Law Enforcement Training Center (FLETC) and some seasoned hands with fifteen years on the job—work visa and passport fraud cases along with the almost weekly duties of protecting the many foreign VIPs who visit the Big Apple throughout the year. The workload is enormous. New York City is the country's busiest hub of criminal cases involving the fraudulent use of passports—American and other—and visas; Los Angeles, with its South American and Asian immigrant and criminal imports, follows NYFO in the high volume of fieldwork. Illegal aliens use doctored and counterfeit birth certificates to get driver's licenses and other paper-trail necessities to establish legitimate paper identities in their adopted countries. Once an illegal has an established identity—no matter how bogus—he is one step away from acquiring a bona fide U.S. passport, which establishes citizenship and provides him with the ability to return to his homeland and not only visit family and friends, but bring them to the United States, as well.

If mere illegal aliens could use this most basic paper fraud to establish new identities, then its criminal potential was infinite. And in a city like New York, criminals of every nationality, color, and size—from Russian organized-crime groups smuggling in prostitutes to Dominican coke dealers—use fraudulently acquired passports and visas to escape the long arm of the law in the United States and overseas. Many deported convicted felons attempt to come back to the U.S.—this time in a new identity with a U.S. passport.

Because the international terrorist angle involving passport and visa fraud is so obvious, the city's NYPD-FBI Joint Terrorism Task Force, or JTTF, requested that DSS supply *at least* one agent to serve in the multiagency and multijurisdictional assembly of city, state, and federal cops tasked with investigating all terrorist activity in the New York City area. Special Agent Yamin had only three years on the job in 1997 when he was asked to assist a more senior DSS agent assigned to the JTTF—to cops in the NYPD and agents in the FBI, anyone with less than five years on the job was considered a rookie. But Yamin had proved himself to be a top-notch investigator, moving beyond passport and visa cases to smuggling and other multifaceted felony cases with international angles. Fluent in Spanish, he handled and spearheaded many of the large-scale criminal cases against Dominican, Colombian, Mexican, and Salvadorean passport counterfeiters and vendors.

"When you worked on the JTTF, it didn't mean that you just dropped everything that you were doing for DSS and reported to an FBI supervisor for counterterrorist work," Yamin recalled. "I still managed my passport cases and handled protection work for DSS, and I went downstairs to the FBI's New York Field Office, sat in my cubicle there, and handled a caseload and was answerable to my JTTF supervisor. DSS didn't have the luxury of assigning me temporarily to the JTTF because we only had thirty bodies in the field office and we were busy. The FBI, on the other hand, had over a thousand agents assigned to their New York office and they couldn't comprehend how I juggled things both here and there."[2]

On the New York JTTF, the FBI and DSS worked remarkably well together—which was an absolute anomaly for the two agencies. "If we could have given the JTTF five or six agents, they would have been thrilled because they wanted to put the DSS personnel into different squads focusing on different things. DSS just couldn't spare the bodies—our field office was so short-staffed."[3] The relationship between the two agencies was unique—especially considering that the FBI traditionally butted heads with virtually every other federal law enforcement agency. "The bureau was the largest and they thought that they owned every case, every crime, and every jurisdiction," another federal law enforcement agent commented. "They liked to assume none of the risk, take all of the credit, and make sure that their budget increased by billions of dollars every time a kilo of coke was found or a Middle Eastern male was discovered holding a gun. On incidents they would push us out of the way. They outnumbered you and overpowered you. Co-operation wasn't in their dictionary."[4]

DSS and the FBI were particularly at odds over the Ramzi Yousef affair. Even though two assistant RSOs stationed in Islamabad nurtured an informant and went on the raid that eventually led to Yousef's apprehension, it was the FBI that went out of its way to take credit for the capture, sending a team of thirty agents to bring him back to New York City. The animosity between the two agencies was absolute and real, yet in order for a multiagency beast like the JTTF to work, egos and allegiances had to be left at the door. The task force assembled talent and resources from a vast pool with one direct aim, and that was making sure that there were no more World Trade Center bombings perpetrated that would catch law enforcement completely by surprise. Beyond Yousef, DSS played an important role in the capture of conspirators involved in the plot, using their international ties, as well as skills and expertise in combating the use of fraudulent passports and visas.

On the JTTF the FBI appreciated DSS representation for much more than just being able to investigate a good or counterfeit passport or visa stamp. The FBI was a behemoth bureaucracy where every small step needed to be approved, initialed, signed off on, sent out in triplicate, and then initialed again. Field investigations were laboriously slow and tedious. Agents were never allowed to roll on a hunch, contact outside assistance, or be real cops. "The bureau liked having things run like a law firm," a federal agent commented, "and what do you have when lawyers run the world? Mental gridlock."[5]

DSS on the other hand was the complete opposite—DSS was an agency that lived in its own peculiar universe far from being encumbered by the weight of bureaucratic burden. The diplomats inside the State Department had very little use for DSS, since the notion of men and women with guns and shields cut against the grain of everything pure diplomacy stood for; of course, overseas,

DSS agents assigned to consulates and embassies often had to write up consular employees and even ambassadors for infractions as mundane as forgetting to lock away classified material and as serious as child molestation charges.

Unlike the FBI, DSS did not have a field office with a thousand agents in it—there were barely twelve hundred agents in all of DSS and they were spread thin across the United States and around the world, tasked with an enormous workload of dignitary protection assignments, passport and visa cases, and overseas duty. There was little bureaucracy in the day-to-day functioning of a DSS special agent on the street because there was so much work to do and so few ways to do it without cutting corners and being as innovative and creative as they came. DSS agents didn't need supervisors to approve every move made on a case or while protecting a principal; from the moment they left their training and were awarded their shield and gun, new DSS agents were often thrown out into the lion's den of actual operations to sink or swim.

If the FBI needed information on a potential suspect from Egypt or Pakistan, the bureau had to run through a bureaucratic minefield to get authorization, through three supervisors, a division chief, and a deputy director, to send a classified memo overseas through their legal attaché at a foreign embassy. DSS operated differently. Their special agents were as autonomous a force of federal cops as existed anywhere in the world. Agents came and went as they pleased—performance, not rigid rules, was what mattered. Agents were taught to think on their feet, to adapt, improvise, and initiate. And if an agent needed to contact the U.S. embassy in Cairo or Islamabad in the investigation of a criminal case, he didn't need departmental permission or a ream of forms filled out. All he had to do was pick up the phone. "We had no barriers," Yamin explained. "In DSS we could work anywhere we needed to in the tri-state area of New York, New Jersey, and Connecticut, and we could also work anywhere we wanted to overseas. We didn't just deal with terrorism as some sort of distant threat. We had agents who served in Beirut, who served in Saudi Arabia, who knew the dangers and the mind-set firsthand. No other law enforcement agency had that going for them."[6]

For a new agent in DSS who had yet to head out overseas, being on the JTTF was considered a plum assignment—yet it was hard work. Even though both the DSS and FBI New York Field Offices were located in the same building, Yamin found himself going back and forth between the two offices several times a day, juggling a desk and a computer at the DSS field office, and a terminal and a phone at his JTTF desk. A morning could begin with Yamin wearing his DSS hat and making the final preparations for a dignitary detail he'd been assigned to, and then have him take the elevator to his FBI desk where he was monitoring suspicious "hits" on the computer concerning some Lebanese nationals, and then before lunchtime he'd be back at DSS interviewing a suspect who was arrested for attempting to pass a phony birth certificate at the passport office.

On July 29, 1997, Yamin assisted in the Spanish-language debrief of an informant peddling information about an alleged explosive device in New York City that was related to narco-terrorism. In the New York JTTF it was always something. As Yamin remembered, "There wasn't a day when you weren't looking into something very bizarre involving a threat from overseas, or from a foreign group that involved New York City."[7]

On July 31, 1997, Special Agent Yamin was on call, up at the plate "catching" cases, when around one thirty a.m., his DSS unit supervisor, Joe Prendergast, called him with a brief and all-too-typical roundabout message about a possible incident involving Middle Eastern terrorists and explosives. Yamin was told to contact his FBI supervisor, who in turn told him to pick up the FBI's civilian Arabic translator. He was an older gentleman who worked for the bureau whenever the services of an Arabic-speaking linguist were needed. Yamin was told to drive him to the Eighty-eighth Precinct in

Brooklyn and to be ready to provide translation to the NYPD to assist in the ongoing investigation. It was as simple an assignment as a federal agent could receive in the middle of a sultry night in New York City—but nothing was ever as simple as it sounded.

Unlike many of the FBI and DSS agents who lived in New Jersey or in Long Island an hour from the office, Yamin lived in lower Manhattan and could be anywhere in the city's confines in minutes—especially with lights and sirens on his government car, or G-ride. He figured that picking up the FBI translator, who lived nearby, would be a piece of cake.

Unbeknownst to Yamin, however, this was the third night in a row that the translator, a professor whom Yamin referred to only as "the Doctor" in order to shield his identity, had been rousted out of bed on wild-goose chases by the JTTF; the Doctor was very concerned that if his identity was ever revealed, one of the many Middle Eastern groups that he had helped investigate while working with the FBI would try to exact revenge on him or his family back home. When Yamin phoned the Doctor's apartment, his wife answered the phone angrily and she yelled at the State Department special agent for waking the couple up yet again for no good reason. "This is the third night in a row you people have needed him. He's only human. He's an old man—let him sleep. You people can't be bothering him all the time!"[8]

Before Yamin could try to reason with the woman, she slammed the phone down and hung up. Again Yamin made the call and again he heard the receiver slamming down. Undeterred, Yamin phoned again and again until the Doctor's wife relented and handed the phone to her husband. "I hate to disturb you, sir," Yamin apologized, trying to sound sincere yet stern, "but I received a call from my boss and we need to head to Brooklyn because of an incident involving Middle East terrorists and explosives, and your services might be required. I can be in front of your house in a few minutes."

"That's all well and good for you, my dear man," the Doctor replied. "You may have heard from your supervisor, but I have not heard from mine and I am not going anywhere until he approves it." He hung up the phone and returned his tired head to his pillow. The Doctor was confident that this was yet another one of those nights when sleep was going to be interrupted for no reason, and he was determined to stay home at all costs.

NYPD detectives and federal agents assigned to the JTTF were old hands at dealing with "bullshit jobs." After all, many tips that the office received were unfounded. There would be the anonymous tip about Palestinian operatives in Brooklyn preparing to bomb synagogues, Egyptian terrorists plotting to blow up a bridge, or Colombian narco-terrorists determined to hijack an aircraft at JFK. Each tip, no matter how vague or bizarre, needed to be investigated. There were also the "F-U" tips—information funneled to the JTTF by the disgruntled, the malcontent, and the jilted. "My former boyfriend is this Arab and he's been stockpiling weapons and explosives to kill lots of people in a terrorist attack" was one type of these calls that would come into the JTTF. When a team of agents would make the trip somewhere into the city to investigate the claim, they'd find out that the suspected terrorist wasn't an Arab and he wasn't stockpiling weapons, but was in bed with a new girlfriend; the jilted woman wanted some payback and to screw her ex. Other F-U calls included anonymous tips by landlords wanting to get rid of tenants, fired workers trying to ruin their boss's day, and wives pissed at their husbands.

Yamin knew the clock was ticking on the case, and that he had to get down to the Eighty-eighth Precinct as soon as possible. Yamin called the FBI's twenty-four-hour command center, got approval from the Doctor's supervisor, and then called the Doctor back. He told the Doctor to stop his whining and get dressed. Yamin was in front of his house ten minutes later.

The Doctor had worked his share of unfounded F-U calls that

unseasonably warm week in New York City, and so had Special Agent Yamin. Both men were skeptical as they drove over the East River into the Borough of Kings, hoping that their late-night interruption wasn't just another exercise in futility. Both men thought little about the prospects of terrorists. They wanted to be back in their beds before dawn. But as Yamin neared the Eighty-eighth Precinct house he noticed that the redbrick building was bustling with activity. There were more white shirts than Yamin remembered ever seeing other than when the president came to town; nearly everyone was on a phone barking orders and speaking loudly and animatedly as they demanded subway lines be shut, gas mains monitored, and every available EMS crew on call to respond to 248 Fourth Avenue. Bosses from a multitude of city agencies entered the Eighty-eighth Precinct as if gearing up for a major calamity. Yet most sobering were the two-man patrol teams being pulled off the streets for emergency deployment. It was dawning on Yamin that this was no ordinary tip. He realized, feeling a cold tingle in his spine, that this time it was for real and that the NYPD was taking this job very seriously.

Yamin didn't recognize any familiar faces in the precinct—there were no detectives he knew from his time working the streets on passport cases, nor were there any cops he knew from the Intelligence Division, which he had worked with on protection details for Arafat, Mandela, and Secretary of State Albright when they visited New York. "My name is Jeremy Yamin," the three-year DSS veteran stated to anyone in authority who would listen, as he showed his badge and handed out a business card. "I'm a DSS agent assigned to the JTTF. I brought the FBI Arabic-speaking translator here. We are here to support you. What do you guys need?"[9]

Yamin introduced himself to at least a dozen NYPD bosses, each one running around more anxiously than the next as the night passed into the early-morning hours. The ESU cops stayed in their own group with their own bosses, as did the bomb squad, the major-case squad, and a dozen other smaller groups assembled at the precinct at three a.m. Yamin made a point of at least introducing himself to everyone who was there so that in case someone asked for a translator, or needed something from DSS, he would know whom to ask. "The last thing in the world that I wanted to do was flash my tin and say I am the federal agent and I am coming in here and we are going to do this, that, and the other. That's the worst thing that you could do in such a situation because then none of the cops want to work with you. But I made a point of introducing myself to just about everyone, when finally someone of rank said that the cops were about to hit the location where they believed the bombs were being built and that they would like the translator there to assist with questioning at the scene."[10]

That's all it took. Yamin was offered a spot in the motorcade headed to Fourth Avenue along with the ESU, NYPD, FDNY, and other city agency vehicles. The Doctor seemed nervous, yet remained silent. Outside the station, as the entry team suited up in their body armor and readied their weapons for the raid, the Doctor's mood became somber, then fearful; Yamin, too, realized that this was no ordinary night in Brooklyn. The NYPD was gearing up for war.

"The streets were silent," Yamin remembered. "Even though it was after four a.m. there was always traffic in Brooklyn, always delivery trucks and gypsy cabs darting in and around intersections and always some sort of movement. But the police cordoned off the adjoining streets and intersections, and it was as if this piece of New York was sliced off from the rest of the city."[11] The silence was foreboding.

"I am not an agent," the Doctor reiterated to Yamin in an animated state of fear. "I am only a translator. There isn't supposed to be any violence." But the Doctor's plea was too late. Yamin's car had followed the procession and now he was two blocks from the targeted address. DSS agents rarely phoned in to their supervisors for permission of any kind when working on a case. It was the nature of the job and the organization, but now, amid a sea of NYPD officers suited up and carrying submachine guns, Yamin felt compelled to check in with his FBI JTTF chief; after all, Yamin thought to himself, he'd been asked just to go to the precinct and see if they needed anything; he hadn't been asked to participate in a raid. Asking for permission to join the motorcade two blocks from the target was a bit after the fact, Yamin surmised, but better safe than sorry.

Inside Yamin's car the Doctor engaged in unimportant chitchat to try to wash away his jitters. It wasn't working. At just about 4:40 A.M. the ESU CAT car and the Caprice driven by Pascullo darted across toward 248 Fourth Avenue in a mad dash of speed. There were the screams outside of the cabstand, and then what appeared to be the entire NYPD moved into position in front of the location. The silence of the darkened July night was interrupted by the steps of men filtering through a courtyard and then the gunshots, when all hell broke loose. Yamin fired up his bubble light and followed the unmarked car in front of him to the cabstand. Police reinforcements started to deploy around him. Suddenly, patrol sergeants and captains began shouting to evacuate the area. For Yamin, his adrenaline fired up by the dramatic events, the entire operation was absolutely mesmerizing.

"Shit, this *is* for real," Yamin said in a muted whisper as he made sure to have one eye on the Doctor just in case his services were needed. A few minutes after six shots resonated into the Brooklyn night, Special Agent Jeremy Yamin saw the two Palestinians brought out on stretchers and quickly loaded into waiting FDNY ambulances. "They each looked like they'd been shot multiple times," Yamin remembered from that initial glance. "They didn't look like they would survive." Each of the Palestinians was taken to Kings County Hospital in a separate ambulance—each man was handcuffed to his stretcher and guarded by an NYPD detective.

A detective told Yamin, "Follow that bus—he's the bomb maker, and we need the translator to question him."[12] Yamin rushed the Doctor back into the G-ride and followed the ambulances straight to Kings County Hospital.

The Debrief

Kings County Hospital was one of those inner-city hospitals where the arrival of two multiple-gunshot patients did not spark any added concern or activity—for Brooklyn, one of the cops would say, two people shot is considered a slow night. Special Agent Yamin arrived at the hospital with the "buses," NYPD slang for ambulances, carrying Abu Mezer and Khalil. The emergency room was already an armed camp. As part of the incident contingency operation that Kammerdener, Pascullo, and McCaffrey had assembled, ESU personnel were staged at Kings County Hospital. "I had lived in New York City all my life and I had worked in the city as a federal agent for three years and I never saw cops with long guns," Yamin reflected, "but the entrance to the triage center outside the emergency room was bustling with cops who appeared to be ready for anything. The scene was surreal almost. Dozens of heavily armed ESU cops, wearing their helmets and heavy vests, deploying around the two Palestinians, and the doctors and nurses operating, completely unfazed by the two bleeding Palestinians hoisted and handcuffed to their gurney."[1]

Inside the ER Yamin hooked up with Bob Moore, the NYPD detective who had ridden in the ambulance carrying Abu Mezer and had already assembled the pedigree information on the suspect. Yamin knew it was crucial to start disseminating the information quickly to the FBI, to the State Department, and even to the intelligence agencies to try to ascertain if these guys were acting alone or if they were part of some larger terrorist cell. "We needed to know if we had come across their names before, we had to determine what country they were from," Yamin recalled, "and we had to figure out how they fit into the larger puzzle."[2]

But a more pressing concern came over Yamin's train of thought: if there were devices in the Brooklyn apartment, then it was crucial that the men lying on the gurneys—if they were still alive—assist and provide information that could help render the bombs safe. Yamin called one of the bomb techs he had spoken to at the Eighty-eighth Precinct and asked him what information he needed.

Nurses and doctors worked on Abu Mezer to stabilize him in preparation for surgery. Although shot up, the West Bank native was remarkably resilient. He did not require any emergency life-saving procedures and appeared to be resting as comfortably as could be expected for someone with two bullets in him. Yamin relayed some questions to Detective Moore that he thought should be asked of Abu Mezer; Yamin viewed the detective as the arresting officer and did not want to "flash the tin" and have a federal agent walk all over his interview—that wasn't how DSS did things.

Abu Mezer was sprawled out on a gurney, hooked on a heart monitor, covered in seeping bandages, and being prepped for surgery. He was, however, lucid, and attempting to raise his head ever so slightly to take in his surroundings. It was much different from the Israeli administrative lockups he had been to before. There were no soldiers or Border Guard policemen sneering at him; there were no veiled threats of private question-and-answer periods with the Shin Bet. The doctors and nurses racing around with charts and X-rays looked at Abu Mezer curiously, almost as if he were a UFO. The ER staff had seen hundreds of shot perps before; shootings, in Brooklyn, were part of the natural landscape. But a real live shot-up terrorist didn't land on their doorstep every day.

Yamin asked the NYPD detective to see if he could find out something about the device's construction from Abu Mezer that might assist the bomb squad. "We found the bomb," Detective Moore informed Abu Mezer. "How do you defuse it?" Detective Moore wanted one or two words that might help. Instead, he received a challenge for a confrontation.

"I made the bomb—bring it to me. I'll cut the wires," Abu Mezer responded as a small smirk began to widen across his grayish face.

Detective Moore wanted to know more. There were so many questions that the investigators needed to know quickly, and the fear was that Abu Mezer would expire right then and there before he could be of any assistance. "Where are you from?" Moore continued.

"I am a Palestinian from Hebron," Abu Mezer answered defiantly, not shielding his nationality for a second.

During a break while the doctors examined Abu Mezer, the detective turned to Yamin and told him that the agent should continue the questioning because he knew more about the devices. As a DSS agent he had received a fair amount of training in the art of improvised explosive devices, and he knew what questions needed to be answered. Abu Mezer seemed pleased by the fact that the cops were now coming to him to talk about his bomb. He had stumped them, and that satisfaction was pleasing. "You cut the wire leading from the bomb," Abu Mezer offered. "There's only gunpowder in the bomb. You flip the four switches for it to explode. All four have to be flipped. There are four switches for the bombs."

Yamin felt some sort of comfort with Abu Mezer, especially since he was offering a small bit of information about the device and admitting that he knew how to detonate it. Yamin felt that perhaps Abu Mezer would feel more comfortable speaking in Arabic—after all, Yamin was summoned out of bed in order to bring the Doctor to the scene to help out. Yamin left the triage area where Abu Mezer was lying and spoke to the FBI translator. "Just introduce yourself to him and I will start passing questions to you about the construction of the devices," Yamin instructed the Doctor. He later explained, "I truly thought that the translator would help things out and speed communications—time was of the essence."[3]

The Doctor could have been Abu Mezer's grandfather, and there was a traditional reverence for the elderly in the Arab world that was unrivaled in the modern dog-eat-dog world of Western society. Abu Mezer should have been respectful of the old man's introduction and questions, but instead, the use of an Arabic-speaking tool incensed the West Bank native. He began to gyrate violently in the restraints of his gurney, and swore that he was going to kill everyone in the room. *"Ruh min hun,"* he yelled at the Doctor. "Get the hell away from here."

The Doctor walked back to Yamin, his head held low, confessing the obvious—the Arabic routine had not been successful. The Palestinian was becoming combative; the Shin Bet and military intelligence always spoke to the detainees in their native tongue. It must have brought back memories of occupation and demands of collaboration. Abu Mezer would have none of it.

Yamin realized that it was time for him to speak to Abu Mezer directly. In his three years in DSS, Yamin had interviewed hundreds of suspects, leads, informants, and witnesses in passport and visa cases, as well as in his work for the JTTF. His medium-sized frame, calm demeanor, and general nonthreatening personality made him a natural for one-on-one sessions inside the foreboding confines of an interview room. His goatee and glasses made him look more like a young professor at an Ivy League business school than a federal agent carrying a SIG Sauer semiautomatic holstered on his belt. There was never the prospect that Yamin would yell at or threaten a suspect. It wasn't his style. He was thorough, strictly business, yet always respectful. Yamin had that unique knack of not appearing judgmental when talking to people, even when he was dealing with individuals whom he knew to be a hundred percent guilty of a multitude of federal crimes. He was a good listener. His trademark DSS personality—the one where you always got more with a smile than with a demand—was part and parcel of his interview technique.

And Yamin's appearance made Abu Mezer feel at ease. Although he's Jewish, Yamin doesn't look it and when he asked the young Palestinian if it was all right for the two men to talk, Abu Mezer reflected, staring at Yamin's lanky features, dirty blond goatee, and short hair, "You don't look like a Jew and that's good you are not a Jew."[4] Yamin's primary objective was to establish a rapport with the Palestinian. If the Palestinian thought he wasn't a Jew, Yamin wasn't about to correct his misperception.

Yamin paused, held his breath, but continued. As a cop, Yamin wanted nothing more than to wring the Palestinian's neck, but he was after information, and swallowing the bile of disgust that was assembling in his throat was a fair price to pay for the needed intelligence. "Right now I need to understand more about the bomb. How many bombs are there?"

Abu Mezer paused for a few moments, grimacing in pain, but wanting to use his last embers of energy to boast of his handiwork. "There are four bombs in all, with four switches each. You must trip all four switches."

Yamin suddenly looked concerned, thinking that the Palestinian was talking only because he knew that he had tripped one of the toggle switches and perhaps the bomb had already detonated. "The bomb won't go off with only one switch pulled, right?" Yamin asked. "How do you disarm the device?"

Abu Mezer paused, winced in pain, and responded, "You cut the wire. I've told you already." A film of perspiration covered his body, and the stubborn Palestinian struggled to retain consciousness as if taunting Yamin with his ability to withstand point-blank gunshot wounds and still talk of his device.

"But you've already tripped the switch," Yamin reminded the Palestinian prisoner. "You've already armed it."

"It won't go off—just cut the wire," Abu Mezer reminded Yamin yet again. "Just cut the wire."

Which fucking wire? Yamin asked himself, trying to draw a mental picture of a multiexplosive device with multiple wires. "Which wire, Gazi?" Yamin demanded from the Palestinian, wanting to shake him until he stopped playing around. "The blue, red, black, which wire? Are there are any timers or booby traps?"

Abu Mezer was not showing if he was in pain or not. He was defiant. "Just cut any wire. There are no booby traps."

After each and every brief exchange with the Palestinian, and whenever the doctors needed to attend to him, Yamin went to the nurses' station to call the bomb squad detectives set up outside the Brooklyn tenement. By now, FBI Explosive Ordnance Disposal technicians had arrived on the scene, as well. The bomb squad technicians weren't relying solely on Yamin's information—they had x-rayed the devices, photographed them, and examined them with their own eyes; beforehand, ropes had been affixed to the satchel and then pulled, in order to empty the bag's contents so that the technicians could have a more accurate picture of what they were facing. The concern was that the toggle switch that either Abu Mezer or Khalil had managed to trip in the struggle with the ESU entry team had initiated some sort of countdown timer.

The emergency room triage staff battled with Yamin for control of the patient, and the thirty-one-year-old DSS special agent was determined to provide Pascullo and the NYPD bomb technicians with the information they needed. Yamin thought he would use a little kindness and compassion. "Gazi, look, man, I know you are in a lot of pain, but you are the best source of information so that no one else gets hurt." Yamin paused, leaning over the gurney and offering the wounded Palestinian a smile.

"So now you are my friend?" Abu Mezer remarked sarcastically, staring at the DSS agent with contempt and anger.

"No, Gazi, we are not friends," Yamin stated, stiffening, "and we are not going out to have drinks together. We are soldiers on opposite sides. And we follow orders. But you are a soldier who was captured in battle and now we want you to get well. But while you're waiting for the test results and surgery, we need to talk. I must make sure that none of the soldiers on my side get hurt. Gazi, you are the one person who can prevent them from getting hurt. You were wounded and captured honorably, as a soldier. The best thing you can do for yourself right now is to make sure that no one else gets hurt."[5]

Yamin's appeal to Abu Mezer, soldier to soldier in a fight of East versus West, struck a chord. The Palestinian had, since his teenage years, been considered nothing but a "filthy fucking Arab" first by the Israeli secret service, then by the Toronto Police, and finally by the U.S. Border Patrol. Once addressed as a soldier, like the masked men back in Hebron, Abu Mezer opened up to the DSS agent.

"So what do you want to know? I've told you everything," Abu Mezer challenged Yamin, as if he was eager to spill the weight that the foiled operation was pressing on his subconscious.

"I have more questions about the bomb," Yamin replied. "How is the bomb made?"

"With gunpowder!" Abu Mezer replied angrily, wondering how many times he was going to have to repeat the contents of his device.

"Just gunpowder?" Yamin said. "What triggers it?"

"The switches!" the Palestinian replied, again angry to be repeating himself time and time again concerning the device's construction.

"But is there a time delay?" Yamin wondered, trying to get some information about what had become the largest piece of the puzzle missing from the bomb squad's equation back on Fourth Avenue.

"No!" Abu Mezer responded. "Flip all four switches to make it ignite."

Yamin slowed down. He realized that if the only way to activate the bomb was to manually flip all four switches, then there was no delay action designed into the circuitry. This was a suicide device. Yamin held back a bit, and looked at the Palestinian.

"So you were going to kill yourself?" Yamin asked.

Abu Mezer refused to answer the question with the fluid back-and-forth rapport that the men had established with one another. Instead, the Palestinian made the gesture of an explosion and simply said, "Poof!"

"What is in the bomb to make it explode?" Yamin asked. "A flashbulb or a blasting cap?"

"No, only wires," Abu Mezer reiterated, the pain from his wounds beginning to get the best of him. "Each little wire is connected and they heat up the gunpowder."

"What's the power source?" Yamin wondered. "Batteries?" Yamin pressed on, but Abu Mezer was writhing in pain. "I know you are in pain, but I need to know more. What kind of batteries?"

"Duracell!" Abu Mezer responded, perhaps getting fed up with the Q and A.

"Duracell?" Yamin asked. "The CopperTop?"

The Palestinian smiled. The interview had come to an abrupt end as the doctors continued their examination.

Special Agent Yamin had taken over the nurses' station. There were phone calls coming in left and right from Fourth Avenue, DSS headquarters, and the FBI JTTF. There were notices over the public-address system saying, "A call for the State Department agent on line one . . ." It was nearly comical. "At that point I was juggling a lot of different things," Yamin remembered. "Everyone wanted to know everything immediately. My priority was the bomb squad. But you still have to keep people in the loop—the FBI supervisor, the DSS supervisor, the FBI operations center, the DSS command center, everyone!"

The ER doctors had stabilized the Palestinian and were waiting for a specialist to arrive to oversee the surgery. Abu Mezer was thirsty and confused, and the doctors and nurses didn't want to talk to him. It was as if he was a strange pariah and Yamin was his only link to the outside world. Uniformed police officers in the dozens were now rushing to the emergency room. Abu Mezer felt cordoned off and threatened, as if he suddenly found himself back in the West Bank inside an Israeli detention center. The pain of the gunshot wounds would be nothing, the Palestinian thought, wondering if the Americans were as hard-nosed as the Israelis. Would they really save his life? He turned to Yamin with his questions.

Before the doctors and nurses took Abu Mezer away for surgery, Yamin reassured the Palestinian. "Gazi, they are going to take you away to surgery now," Yamin said as he walked alongside the gurney being pushed into the operating room. Abu Mezer seemed reassured by Yamin's presence. "So, Gazi," Yamin said, reaching over to the Palestinian, "I am going to uncuff you now. They are going to operate." Abu Mezer nodded, resigned to his fate.

"So maybe it wasn't my time today," he commented. "I may have a long life then?"

"Yes. They are going to operate to fix you and take out the bullets," Yamin reassured the Palestinian. "You'll be OK."

Abu Mezer felt a warrior's bond with the DSS agent. "I will see you later?" the Palestinian asked.

"Yes, I will see you when you come out of the operating room," Yamin replied.

The Palestinian smiled. "I will see you later, soldier," he told Yamin.

"Good luck, soldier," Yamin answered, slightly troubled by the strange bond developing between himself and the Palestinian terrorist. Abu Mezer disappeared behind the swinging doors of the OR.

Yamin now attempted to try his luck with Khalil, who was also handcuffed to his gurney. Khalil's English was nowhere near as good as Abu Mezer's; his injuries were nowhere as serious as those of the young man from Hebron. Khalil was angry and tearful. He appeared to be agitated about his predicament and did not have the bravado displayed by his roommate. Khalil was reticent about speaking to the State Department agent and about acknowledging the questions put forth by the Doctor. He invoked his rights and chose to remain silent. He looked as if he never wanted to say another word again.

Back on Fourth Avenue, the information Yamin was able to obtain was put to good use. Using rubber-coated cutting tools designed to slice through wires without generating a spark, the NYPD Bomb Squad tandem cut the wires leading from the Duracell batteries to the pipes. The bomb did not explode. Abu Mezer's information was genuine. The bomb disposal technicians had carefully and painstakingly handled the device whose toggle switch had been flipped; it was hoped that during the wait, the wires attached to the gunpowder had gotten as hot as they were going to get and that it simply wasn't enough to ignite the smokeless powder. As scientific as bomb disposal was, there were no absolutes. The phrase "one false move" was holy to a bomb tech—one false move, one infinitesimally small spark, could be the difference between a job well done and the force of heat, fire, and shrapnel eviscerating the massive Kevlar cocoon of the eighty-pound protective bomb suit. The most experienced techs, with the best hands, were always wary of that one call that could be their last. Improvised explosive devices were always tricky. Poor workmanship, shoddy materials, and the simple inexperience of the bomb builder made those shaky devices all the more volatile. Abu Mezer's bomb, especially hot and active, was the type of device that made even the most seasoned bomb tech very nervous, and a case of jittery nerves could be lethal in the bomb disposal business.

The bomb techs, satisfied that the devices were safe, walked the satchel outside of the illegal structure behind 248 Fourth Avenue, through the courtyard and entrance to the front building, and outside to the street where ESU personnel were waiting. One of ESU's most difficult assignments was to assist the bomb squad in all their endeavors. ESU officers walked side by side with the device until the bomb tech gingerly placed the bag inside the circular steel tub of Two-Truck's TCV; the TCV could contain the wrath of a powerful explosion inside its reinforced steel walls. Pascullo, McCaffrey, and English watched as the bombs were secured, and hoped that this was the beginning of the end of the job. The three men were tired, and they knew in their hearts that the day was far from ending.

The TCV, under heavy escort, was driven slowly through Brooklyn, into Queens, and then across the Bronx Whitestone Bridge toward the NYPD range and detonation fields at Rodman's Neck. Traffic throughout the three boroughs came to a virtual standstill as exits were blocked off, Highway Unit patrol cars secured stretches of highway, and NYPD helicopters flew overhead. At Rodman's Neck, NYPD Bomb Squad personnel, and specialists from the FBI and the Bureau of Alcohol, Tobacco, and Firearms, reviewed the devices—all the time operating at a safe distance and from behind the protective cover of heavy bomb suits.

The bombs were simplistic in design, yet each of the experienced bomb disposal technicians understood that the pipe bombs, when detonated inside the cramped confines of a subway car with passengers packed like sardines during the morning's rush hour, would have caused an astronomical loss of life. Several of the bomb techs estimated that the blast from one of the devices could have killed anyone standing within fifty feet of the detonation.

"Just by itself the bomb could have killed scores of innocent people," Ralph Pascullo would later reflect, "but when one considers the shrapnel, the fire, the choking smoke, the confusion of what it was going to be like inside the subway car in the middle of a tunnel, the death toll could have been catastrophic. And of course, if you think that the rescuers—the Emergency Service Unit, EMS, and the firemen—would be targeted by the second bomber, the destructiveness of that double bombing would have been something the city might never have recovered from—at least psychologically. Who would have wanted to take the subway anywhere after it was hit in a double bombing?"[6]

Other bomb techs stated that in an enclosed space, such as a subway, anyone inside a twenty-foot reach of the blast would have been killed, while in the open, anyone 100 feet from the kill zone would have suffered fatal wounds.[7]

Abu Mezer's bombs were detonated in a controlled explosion. The mixed audience of NYPD and federal bomb technicians was shocked by the ferocious force of the devices. New York City had truly dodged an indiscriminate bullet. The carnage would have been horrific.

Later, one of the NYPD bomb techs told Special Agent Yamin that it was the first time that the experienced explosive-ordnance technician had handled a device whose mechanism had been tripped; and of course, it was the first time that the bomb tech had worked a bomb and received instructions on how to disarm it, in real time, from the man who had actually constructed the explosive device.

End of the Day

Fourth Avenue became the capital of New York City that bright summer's morning. The police traffic alone up and down the main Park Slope thoroughfare was pure gridlock. When the bombs were removed safely from the Palestinians' home, the rotating shifts of visiting VIPs and politicians were incessant. The most important visitor that morning was Mayor Rudy Giuliani. This was the first terrorist incident under Giuliani's watch, and the prospect of two Palestinians blowing themselves up inside a crowded subway train angered the mayor. Giuliani was a strong supporter of Israel and he had traveled to Jerusalem in February 1996 to ride the same bus line that had been hit twice in one week in suicide-bombing attacks that killed over fifty men, women, and children. Giuliani had long warned that the United States was complacent in light of the threat posed by fanatic terrorist groups that would, inevitably, spread the war of Islamic fundamentalism to them.

Giuliani walked slowly up Fourth Avenue, wearing a dark blue suit. The sun squarely in his eyes, Giuliani pointed toward the car service as he was briefed on what had transpired there hours earlier before dawn's first light. Giuliani appeared surprised, almost shocked, that such a plot had been hatched and nearly executed in the heart of Brooklyn. Giuliani was joined by Police Commissioner Safir in his walking tour of the crime scene, as well as a glum-looking First Deputy Commissioner Patrick Kelleher. Dozens of chiefs and inspectors lined Fourth Avenue, eager to be seen by New

York City's commander in chief, even though most had been fast asleep when Assistant Chief Kammerdener helped to coordinate the massive early-morning operation and Police Officers Martinez and Dolan had their nearly lethal confrontation with the two Palestinians. The bosses were out in force trying to seize some sort of credit for the night's events. Had the job ended differently, the bosses would have been cowering in fear from the camera's view.

NYPD choppers, flying next to television news helicopters, buzzed the Brooklyn morning. ESU officers stood atop nearby rooftops, helmets worn tightly and Ruger Mini-14s at the ready. An army of detectives and federal investigators swarmed all across Brooklyn determined to piece together the puzzle of Abu Mezer's plot. NYPD detectives were joined by FBI agents, who were also joined by men with federal credentials from myriad intelligence agencies from the Washington, D.C., area. Nobody was sure who the Palestinians were or how deep this cell would lead. Some of the investigators hit the streets of Brooklyn armed with mug shot books containing photos of known and wanted Middle Eastern terrorists; others, looking closer to where Abu Mezer and Khalil lived, checked out livery cabs that were used by the Family Car Service, including one vehicle sporting the bumper sticker I LOVE ISLAM.

For many members of the JTTF, the investigation reminded them of the rush of activity following the 1993 World Trade Center bombing and, two years later, the aborted "Day of Terror" plot to bomb New York City landmarks by followers of Sheikh Omar Abdel Rahman. The detectives and agents understood that for whatever reasons, and there were hundreds, New York City was squarely inside the crosshairs of the terrorists' sights. And four years after Ramzi Yousef's determined attempt to destroy the Twin Towers, these seasoned cops and federal agents found that reality ever so troubling.

Police Commissioner Safir ordered Assistant Chief Kammerdener to city hall to give a press conference about the night's events.

Kammerdener was tired and drained; the white shirt he wore was stained with the blood of the two Palestinians. Kammerdener didn't have time to head back to his office at Bronx Detectives to change his clothes. When he appeared before the cameras an hour later, his police department blazer covered the stains that were a testament to the violence and bloodshed of the night's raid.

Pascullo, McCaffrey, and English were reluctant to leave the scene. They weren't waiting for accolades or a chance to shake the mayor's hand. This was their operation and they were determined to be the last men to leave. By nine a.m. the ESU day tour had already deployed to Fourth Avenue and was augmenting the remaining cops still on scene from the midnights. "Why the hell don't you guys go to the hospital? We have it from here," one of the lieutenants told McCaffrey, sensing the Irishman's exhaustion and spent emotions. McCaffrey and English looked at one another and shielded their eyes from the rising sun. By nine thirty a.m. McCaffrey and English joined Martinez, Dolan, Zorovic, and Keenan at Methodist Hospital. The six embraced one another in displays of emotion that were atypical for ESU—even on "big jobs." McCaffrey hugged the others and said, repeatedly, how grateful he was. "As far as I am concerned, and to the day I die, I know that Dolan and Martinez saved my life," McCaffrey would state. "We would have all died had they not done what they did. They did the right thing."[1]

The ESU desk had phoned the hospital and requested that each of the arriving officers be treated anonymously because there was an ongoing terrorist investigation under way and it was imperative to protect the identities of the officers involved. The six ESU cops were convinced that they had neutralized at least an integral element of a major terrorist cell operating in Brooklyn. If the two Palestinians did, indeed, have cohorts who were still unknown to law enforcement, then perhaps they would want to seek revenge against the police officers who prevented the suicide bombing from taking place. That the terrorists might be only the tip of the iceberg was what concerned the cops.

Shootings never happen in a vacuum. Each time an officer discharges his weapon at a suspect, the wheels of police department and district attorney bureaucracy are spun with rapid and unstoppable force. First, for the cops, there is departmental paperwork that they need to fill out. The "49s," as the NYPD forms are known, must be filled out in a meticulous manner—once something's on paper, it becomes a matter of public record, or as the cops liked to joke, *whatever you say can and will be used against you in a court of law!* On shootings when there was more than one officer involved, the accounts on the 49s needed to match in absolute and unflinching manner. One small discrepancy, one minor factual infraction, or even the perception of the slightest difference in accounts could make even a second-rate defense attorney salivate. Worse, the word "discrepancy" always guaranteed scrutiny from Internal Affairs. And any time Internal Affairs was involved, the district attorney's office was never far behind. As any cop knew, the DA's office was a place where the pursuit of justice was often overshadowed by political correctness and the chase for votes. No matter how good the 49s were, no matter how satisfied Internal Affairs might be that the shooting was a good one, there could always be a DA in the midst of an election campaign eager to show his Arab American constituents that it wasn't open season on Palestinians in *his* borough.

When the six-man ESU entry team members were finished having their blood pressure, hearing, and heart rates anonymously examined at Methodist, it was time to initiate the paperwork and begin logging their statements. The Eighty-eighth Precinct had become a chaotic epicenter of police and media activity by morning. Hundreds of police officers from around the city had deployed to the Eighty-eighth to support the precinct and help out with security operations throughout Brooklyn. The Red Cross had set up vehicles to help administer the displaced people brought to the precinct house to be questioned. Television news helicopters buzzed the building hoping for a glimpse of the officers involved in the shooting.

The entry team returned to the Eighty-eighth to begin the laborious paperwork that needed to get done. The duty inspector handling the 49s maintained the officers' anonymity in the official report—he referred to Dave Martinez as Officer One, and Joe Dolan as Officer Two, giving each officer a number corresponding to his position outside of the Palestinians' apartment. An attorney and a representative from the Patrolmen's Benevolent Association, or PBA, were summoned to represent Martinez, Dolan, Zorovic, and Keenan; their union, the PBA, protected all officers from volunteering information or testimony within guidelines and time frames that went against the union contract. The Sergeants Benevolent Association (SBA) sent an attorney and a delegate to represent John English, and the Lieutenants Benevolent Association (LBA) sent its legal representative to protect Owen McCaffrey's rights. It was a maddening process and one requiring immediate attention. Representatives from the Brooklyn DA's office were on hand— briefcases at the ready. According to some of the officers involved, the DA representatives looked upset.

According to the PBA, SBA, and LBA contracts at the time, the officers who discharged their weapons in the line of duty were not required to give any statements for forty-eight hours after the fact; the two-day rule was designed to protect an officer who might have undergone a horrific ordeal from saying anything that might incriminate himself (civil rights attorneys, critical of law enforcement, would contend that the two-day rule helped to bolster the blue wall of silence). Witnesses, according to the various union contracts, could remain silent for one day. The bickering and the back-and-forth conversations between the department and the DA's office over the entry team's testimony was a source of tension, but it soon became irrelevant.

Early on in the process, as morning was turning into noon on Thursday, July 31, representatives from the U.S. Attorney's Office for the Eastern District of New York arrived at the Eighty-eighth Precinct and told the Brooklyn DA's office that they were off the case—this was a terrorist incident and the federal government was taking over. A pissing contest between the local DA and the feds worried the six men from the entry team. The last thing the men wanted, after a grueling tour and a harrowing incident, was to be a football tossed back and forth between a set of politically hungry attorneys. One of the officers commented, "Terrorists flipping toggle switches are one thing. Lawyers with an agenda are far more treacherous creatures altogether."

Again, the veteran ESU cops remembered how the department and the DA's office in the Bronx had crucified the E-cops involved in the Eleanor Bumpers shooting.

By the time the jurisdictional tug-of-war began, the ESU cops realized that they had stumbled onto something quite significant. By midday the first mentions of a possible Hamas connection reverberated throughout the Eighty-eighth Precinct. The rumor mill is a vicious beast inside a police precinct, and cops were talking about things that they heard on CNN, or on NY1, the local cable all-news station, as well as things that friends had mentioned in passing. By the talk in the precinct one would have thought that the Holy Army of Islam had landed in Bensonhurst and was pushing toward Manhattan.

The rumors and the heightened security were something that the city had never seen in a regular working-class neighborhood. Counterterrorist precautions were evident in the wake of the World Trade Center bombing four years earlier, and after the Oklahoma City bombing in 1995; in these cases, or when the president of the United States came to town, most of the security blankets were cast upon Manhattan. Here, virtually all of Brooklyn became an armed camp. As DAs and federal prosecutors bickered with one another inside the precinct, train service was still out for some three hundred thousand commuters throughout the borough. Traffic throughout Brooklyn was a nightmare. Patrol cars were positioned at key intersections, and the myriad Jewish neighborhoods in the borough received massive reinforcements.

There was the belief that the interrupted terrorist plot was part of a coordinated attempt by Palestinian terrorists to link the double-tap attack in Jerusalem with a suicide bombing, or a series of them, inside New York City.

"The federal government came in, they looked at everything that had happened, and they said here's the deal," McCaffrey recalled. "They said that they had evaluated that there was, indeed, a bomb in the location, and that we know it was a justified shooting, and that they would give everyone on the entry team full indemnity if they would waive their right to be silent for a day or two, and go on the tape that day right then and there."[2] The deal, a guaranteed escape from any second-guessing or from a local DA eager to get some Arab votes, was exactly what the entry team wanted to hear. Too many times in the past, the actions of police officers, often acting above and beyond the call of duty, were Monday-morning-quarterbacked by the media, criticized by politicians, and then scrutinized in federal lawsuits. Anytime some politically minded attorney felt that he could ride the coattails of a police shooting toward higher office, the officers involved in that incident braced themselves for possible career-ending witch-hunt.

The six-man entry team knew wholeheartedly that their shooting was as justified as they came—but right and wrong often mattered little in a politically charged atmosphere. The union delegates and lawyers believed the U.S. Attorney's offer to be a good one. The cops signed off on it.

The U.S. Attorney's office took the statements of each of the six men on the entry team, along with Pascullo, the highest-ranking ESU officer on scene. The procedure was tedious. The officers were exhausted and emotionally drained. Each officer was questioned, debriefed, and asked to recount the events of the early-morning hours of July 31. "In the paperwork each man was referred to solely as your position on the entry team. They didn't even want to list your name or age on the forms," McCaffrey recalled. "In fact, the authorities went back to Methodist Hospital and pulled all the paperwork from the trauma care, even though our names weren't really on file. They went in and simply expunged any mention that we were ever there. The feds were scared about what other terrorists were out there. It didn't make us feel very reassured."[3]

For many involved in the raid on 248 Fourth Avenue, the desire to phone home and say a good-bye before setting foot inside the CAT car was overridden by not wanting a fear-filled call to be the last thing their wives and children heard from them. The first time most of the police officers managed to phone home and tell their wives that they'd be coming home late from the midnight tour was near noon, when the trauma treatment was complete and they had returned to the Eighty-eighth Precinct for the paperwork. " 'I'll be coming home a bit late' was what I told my wife," Sergeant English remembered. " 'You might be seeing some mention of this on the news, but don't worry—I'm okay.' " Every news network in the city—and the country—was following the events on Fourth Avenue. It was a story that was impossible to miss.

On a routine day, ESU cops completing a midnight tour would return to their homes at about nine a.m. There were always the bullshit sessions with the cops coming in on the day tour, a few bits and pieces of paperwork to attend to, not to mention the traffic to contend with. Few of the cops could afford to live inside the confines of the five boroughs; real estate prices within the city were just too astronomical for anyone earning the mediocre wages of a New York City police officer to afford. During the Giuliani administration, police cars were first adorned with the letters "CPR" to stand for "Courtesy, Professionalism, and Respect"—the ideal by which New York's Finest policed the greatest city in the world. Most of the cops joked that "CPR" meant "Can't Pay Rent." Many of the cops had to live thirty, forty, and even sixty miles from where they worked just to be able to afford a decent home for their families. Their commutes home were staggeringly long.

Most of the men involved in the raid on 248 Fourth Avenue returned home after ten p.m. on the night of July 31. They were exhausted and hadn't had the proper time or outlet to release their angst and anxiety. They returned home to hug and kiss their wives and to embrace their small children. Some of the officers dropped to their knees when they came home to hug their kids and thank God that they had been in the situation to do their jobs in order to save so many New Yorkers from the fate of being trapped inside a subway car with a pair of suicide bombers.

As members of ESU, the cops often found themselves in life-and-death struggles where one false move had lethal implications. On a ledge with a jumper, the E-cop had a one-on-one encounter with the person in peril, and the officer knew that his actions and his cool under fire would have direct implications upon the one life being threatened. The same was true when ESU responded to a critical accident on the roadways and the officers worked feverishly, operating the Hurst tool, in order to extricate a motorist from the mangled wreckage of a car—the contact was one-on-one; at best the officers could save one or two lives. In those cases the E-cops responded during the event or after the bloodshed had occurred.

There had never been the opportunity to stop a mass murderer before he could kill scores of victims. It was humbling for the cops to realize that their actions and their bravery helped to save hundreds of lives. When the cops took to their knees to hug their sons and daughters, holding back the tears of gratefulness, they could visualize the men, women, and children who would have been on the subway car targeted by Gazi Abu Mezer and Lafi Khalil that rush hour morning.

As the day came to an end in suburbia, it was impossible for the officers involved to mentally set aside what they had participated in earlier that morning. "I think we were close to disaster here," James K. Kallstrom, the special agent in charge of the FBI's New York Field Office, stated. "Whether it was twelve hours away or eighteen hours or twenty-four or thirty-six is irrelevant. I think we were close to a disaster and it didn't happen, and that's the good news."[4]

When they thought of the disaster that they had played a pivotal role in preventing, Pascullo and the men on the entry team shuddered in collective fear. Who else was out there? they wondered. Many headed off to bed staying close to their off-duty service revolvers. Some looked out the window every time a car passed the house. They wondered if terrorists would now hunt the men who took down their cell in Park Slope.

For most of that morning Special Agent Yamin operated from the nurses' station that he had turned into a mini-command-center. Using a bank of phones usually reserved for summoning bedpans and meals, he was in touch with Washington, D.C., Tel Aviv, Jerusalem, and Amman. "As a DSS agent I didn't need special permission or authorization to call my colleagues in the Middle East to get the ball rolling on an investigation. All I needed was to be patched through to the twenty-four-hours-a-day DSS command center and I was on the phone with the RSO in the embassy in Tel Aviv, or the RSO in the Jerusalem consulate or the embassy in Amman."[5]

All investigations had to start somewhere and Yamin passed the biographical information about the suspects to the Regional Security Officer in the embassy in Tel Aviv, who immediately passed it to his Shin Bet contacts. It was late afternoon in Tel Aviv when the RSO received his first call. He would be up all night, along with contacts inside the Israeli security hierarchy, attempting to find out who these Palestinian young men were. The RSO in the consulate in Jerusalem who maintained contacts in and ties to the security services of Yasir Arafat's Palestinian Authority was also busy on the phone. Arafat's security services maintained dossiers on everybody—especially young men once detained by the Israelis whom the Shin Bet might have flipped into becoming double agents.

The RSO's office inside the sprawling fortresslike U.S. embassy in Amman was also busy at work that afternoon, summoning its contacts inside Jordan's General Intelligence Department and Public Security Directorate to pull the passport applications and files of the two Palestinians. The world in which Diplomatic Security Service operated was, indeed, a small one. A contact, a lead, and information were never more than a phone call away.

Yamin commandeered a computer terminal at the nurses' station and began typing a log of everything he had done from the moment he picked up the Doctor, including a transcript of his conversation with Gazi Abu Mezer. By eight a.m. Yamin headed back to 26 Federal Plaza and to his cubicle inside NYFO. He not only had to begin composing his own DSS report about the incident—any time foreigners entered the United States on bad paper or on mistakenly stamped visas, it was a DSS matter—but also to work on his JTTF report; wearing two hats was an exhausting but challenging exercise. In addition to filling out forms, Yamin also followed up his phone calls to the Middle East and the RSOs to see what information they had managed to pull together on such short notice. That day Yamin was lucky if he had time to grab a stale cup of office coffee. His day was only beginning.

Hundreds of FBI agents had flooded Brooklyn, commencing the largest terrorist investigation in the city in over four years. Jeremy Yamin didn't think there would be any need for him to head back to Brooklyn, but because he had been the only federal agent to actually establish a relationship with Gazi Abu Mezer, Yamin's

JTTF supervisor wanted the DSS special agent back at Kings County Hospital to speak to the young Palestinian once he regained consciousness after surgery. The bureau felt that Yamin had established rapport, and wanted him present to assist during the next round of questions. Outside a pair of recovery rooms, Yamin was walking tiredly along the hallway on his way to attempting to once again speak to the Palestinians when he heard a ruckus.

The NYPD had been in charge of security for both Abu Mezer and Khalil. ESU counterassault teams, in full tactical gear, were spread throughout the hospital to make sure that any additional terrorist cells in Brooklyn did not try to mount an operation to either free the two Palestinians or, in the effort to ensure their permanent silence, kill both men for failing to blow themselves up on the subway train earlier that morning. ESU snipers ringed the rooftops of Kings County Hospital, the sights of their M24 precision rifles covering all points leading in and out of the hospital. It was a massive security operation—Kings County Hospital, the largest municipal hospital in New York City and one of the largest general acute-care hospitals in the nation, was spread out on forty-three acres across the span of twenty-three buildings.

By evening, though, the federal prosecutors had formally staked their claim on the case, and the FBI and the U.S. Marshals Service would now be in charge of Abu Mezer and Khalil. The SWAT team from the New York FBI field office marched up to the recovery center to relieve ESU of its burden; the FBI tactical team was supported by deputy U.S. Marshals armed with Uzi machine guns.

"It was surreal," Yamin recalled. "Inside the recovery section of the operating room you had two sets of law enforcement types all heavily armed with machine guns arguing over control of the prisoners."[6]

The cursing, the shouts, were just the beginning in what was developing as a New York-sized pissing contest that was brewing throughout the city over the "Brooklyn Bomb Job," as one New

York City tabloid called the incident. From the seat of power at the U.S. Department of Justice to the epicenter of Gotham's rule at city hall, forces were colliding over credit for and control of the ongoing investigation.

"I had never seen anything like that in my life," Yamin recalled. "In DSS something like that never happened. We just don't act that way."[7]

Special Agent Jeremy Yamin rubbed his eyes in exhaustion and then looked at his watch. It was just before eleven p.m. He had been on this job for over twenty hours.

By the time he had the chance to look in on Abu Mezer one final time, the enormity of the Palestinians' terrorist plot had become clear and there was no doubt in anyone's mind that both men had been intent on blowing up a subway train that morning in order to kill Jews. To Yamin, the plot's objective was beyond insidious. The enormity of a terrorist attack that would have killed over a hundred people was something the likes of which New York City had not experienced. The potential for two sons of the West Bank to plot and then execute an attack that would have targeted Jews inside the claustrophobic container of a subway car was knee-buckling.

Both Gazi Abu Mezer and Lafi Khalil were arraigned by U.S. Magistrate Marilyn D. Go at their bedsides that night, charged with a multitude of terrorist-related offenses. No pleas were offered to the two Palestinians. In a late-night hearing at the U.S. district courthouse in downtown Brooklyn, prosecutors charged Gazi Abu Mezer with admitting to possessing bombs that would be detonated on board a subway train; Lafi Khalil was in possession of an address book that contained the name of a member of a known terrorist group.[8] According to reports, the federal complaints had initially included the word "Hamas" in the documents presented to the judge, but were later amended with the words "a known terrorist group."

As he headed back toward Manhattan that night, Yamin

couldn't stop thinking about the intensity of being eye to eye with the man from Hebron who could have potentially flipped his four toggle switches and turned the B Train into a fireball of death and destruction. The DSS special agent had been invited to a party that night and although he needed a chance to unleash the tension riding through his system, his mind was transfixed on the face of the West Bank native and the murderous zeal he could now identify in his eyes.

At a chic SoHo party, surrounded by a small army of Manhattan yuppies, Yamin sat by himself and reflected on the past day in Brooklyn. He couldn't remove Abu Mezer's cold stare from his mind. There was no doubt that the Hebron native had the potential to kill lots of people. Thinking of how difficult it must have been for the ESU entry team, especially considering the fact that officers shot and stopped two moving targets in absolute darkness, made Yamin appreciate the enormity of the ESU operation and of the courage of six men who battled the notion of a suicide mission in order to do what needed to be done to stop Abu Mezer and Khalil from being the first suicide bombers ever to strike inside the United States. *Thank God for the NYPD and ESU,* he thought to himself.

Angst, Accolades, and Aftermath

Twenty-four hours after he had first located Long Island Rail Road police officers Huber and Kowalchuk, Abdel Rahman Mosabbah lay sleepless in a bed in a safe house somewhere in New York City. Protected by a phalanx of ESU cops, federal marshals, and detectives, the Egyptian wondered if he had, indeed, done the right thing by informing on his roommates. His world, he realized, would never be the same. He wondered if he might be deported. He wondered if he would be implicated in his roommate's insane plot.

Twenty-four hours after Police Officer Dave Martinez fired his first shots into Gazi Abu Mezer, a small army of NYPD detectives and FBI agents was still tearing through the building behind 248 Fourth Avenue searching for any clues to a wider terrorist link. The agents and detectives ripped up floorboards, sifted through personal belongings, and attempted to piece together a growingly bizarre human puzzle of not only how the two Palestinians made it into the United States, but what support apparatus was in place to facilitate their terrorist plans. Investigators realized that the two men were some sort of Islamic idealists. It was clear by Abu Mezer's statements and by the paraphernalia uncovered in their room that the two men were inspired by the desire to wage some sort of jihad. The posters and propaganda about Sheikh Omar Abdel Rahman and the need to free him from his prison sentence at the federal facility in Springfield, Missouri, were passports to the fundamentalist fringe; the first canvass of the al-Farooq Mosque also linked the two Palestinians to the most hard-core Islamic radical train of thought known to exist inside New York City.

Investigators removed photographs of the two men posing in Palestinian headdresses clutching shotguns; the photos were taken during their brief stay in North Carolina. Amid the filth and the Coke cans, empty pasta boxes, and opened tins of tomato sauce whose contents had hardened, investigators uncovered notes, wires, small trails of gunpowder, and other incriminating pieces of evidence. Some of the FBI agents, from the bureau's elite Evidence Response Team, had driven up from Quantico, Virginia, and were carefully dusting every inch of the apartment for fingerprints. Every set of prints would be run against NYPD and FBI files, as well as those on record by Interpol.

As investigators ripped through the apartment, they realized just how shaky the building was. Knowing what they did about the bombs that Abu Mezer had constructed, the agents knew that had the Palestinians successfully flipped the four toggle switches, the entire building would have buckled and collapsed, killing everyone inside it.

The investigation went far beyond the boundaries of the five boroughs. The Royal Canadian Mounted Police and the Canadian Security Intelligence Service were summoned to compile a thorough report as to how Abu Mezer managed to get into Canada in the first place and then smuggle himself into the United States. INS was put to task, as well, for permitting Abu Mezer into the country and then losing him following his bail hearings. The INS also began to review how Lafi Khalil managed to get into the U.S. and overstay his visa. Politicians began using the immigration loopholes as lightning rods for protest and disgust. "We should not parole people into the United States when they say that they are already or alleged to be part of a terrorist organization," Mayor Giuliani, a former federal prosecutor, told the media. "It is appropriate to question why this person was allowed into the country announcing he was part of a terrorist group in Israel."[1]

Much of the investigation, however, focused on the nexus between the West Bank and Brooklyn. The FBI needed to know everything they could find out about the Palestinians—from their childhood years to the time they boarded flights to North America. Creating a database profile of the two failed suicide bombers was imperative in building the criminal case that would be compiled, as well as in understanding how operational the terrorist cell actually was in Brooklyn.

Immediately after the two Middle Eastern men from 248 Fourth Avenue were identified as Palestinians, FBI agents were flown on the nonstop TWA flight from New York's John F. Kennedy International Airport to Ben Gurion International Airport near Tel Aviv to begin the investigation from Israel. The Shin Bet—upon first learning of the failed plot by the two Palestinians from their DSS contacts at the U.S. embassy in Tel Aviv, as well as their own perches in the Israeli consulate general in Manhattan and the Israeli embassy in Washington—had already commenced a far-reaching probe for any information about the two Palestinians, their families, and their clannish ties to the Palestinian terrorist groups.

Almost immediately upon learning of the intention to perpetrate a suicide bombing on board a subway train, NYPD detectives, primarily from the Intelligence Division, along with their counterparts in the JTTF, focused their train of thought on two terrorist groups—Hamas and the Palestinian Islamic Jihad. By those in the know, some sort of attack by Hamas had been privately expected for some time—ever since the organization's political leader, Virginia resident Musa Abu Marzouk, was arrested and detained upon his attempted reentry into the United States in 1995 pursuant to an extradition request by the State of Israel.

Hamas had always maintained strong ties to Palestinian émigrés in the United States—the organization raised hundreds of thousands, if not millions, of dollars ostensibly for charitable ends, such as soup kitchens, orphanages, and medical equipment. The Israelis were always convinced that a large percentage of the dollars raised by tax-exempt charity organizations, mosques and businesses, was responsible for funding weapons, explosives, and military training for Hamas operatives.

There was an unadulterated fear inside the antiterrorism offices at FBI headquarters that by placating the Israeli government's desire to bring Abu Marzouk to justice for the suicide bombings perpetrated by Hamas from April 1994 to the summer of 1995, the United States had given Hamas a green light to target American citizens and American cities. And, federal law enforcement officials knew, it wouldn't be hard for Hamas to open up an American front—operatives, sympathizers, fund-raisers, and political officers, after all, were already inside the fifty states; many of them were legal residents. Others with ties to Hamas carried American passports. To one detective in the NYPD's Intelligence Division, it wasn't a matter of when they'd be coming into the country but rather when they'd receive their orders to strike.

Hamas wasn't the only Palestinian terrorist group on the American law enforcement radar—the presence of the Palestinian Islamic Jihad, or PIJ, inside the United States was even more worrisome. The Iranian-backed, Syrian-based PIJ did not depend on donations from the Palestinian diaspora in the United States for support and political legitimacy—most of its money emanated from the Islamic Republic of Iran. Yet the PIJ maintained strong roots inside the United States—especially from its command and control apparatus.

When, in October 1995, the Mossad, Israel's foreign intelligence service, assassinated Dr. Fathi Shiqaqi, the head of the PIJ, as he stopped in the island nation of Malta while traveling from Libya to Syria, American law enforcement was shocked and horrified to learn that Shiqaqi's deputy and successor came not from Beirut or

Baghdad or even Ramallah, but rather the sunny confines of Tampa and the University of South Florida. Dr. Ramadan Abdallah Shallah, who greeted Shiqaqi's bullet-riddled body in Damascus, in a ceremony broadcast live on Syrian TV, had for several years helped to run the terrorist organization from his cushy professorial position inside an American university.

The jihad was not only inside Brooklyn and in the Sunshine State, but in the American heartland. Hamas and the PIJ ran rallies in the Midwest—from Kansas City to Oklahoma City—urging young men to fight the jihad. In these rallies young boys waved swords, martial songs were sung, and organizers wandered through the crowd with large laundry bags to collect cash.

When Abu Mezer and Khalil were shot and apprehended, federal officials naturally suspected that Hamas was behind the plot but made great efforts to not mention the group by name. It was, therefore, very foreboding when Hamas thought it needed to go on the record and to go out of its way to deny any connection to the two Palestinians. "Hamas has declared repeatedly and still that our struggle doesn't target anybody but the Israeli Zionist occupation, and its battlefield is only the land of Palestine," a Hamas communiqué issued in Gaza following the arrests in Park Slope stated, read during a press conference that was protected by armed elements of Arafat's police services. From his exile in Amman, Jordan, Hamas political director Musa Abu Marzouk went even further. "It's ridiculous and a total lie that Hamas had anything to do with these guys," the short and balding leader of the Islamic group stated. "The two men arrested were renegade revolutionaries. They were cowboys."[2]

Federal agents and NYPD detectives assigned to the JTTF were perplexed by the ready-for-distribution Hamas denial. Why deny something before the finger of blame had officially been pointed? was a question many on the JTTF wondered. The denials seemed ready-made, as if prepackaged just in case the attack ever transpired. Federal investigators wondered if Hamas would have claimed credit for the planned bombing attack had it been a success, or perhaps the Islamic resistance movement would have denied any involvement, not wanting to bring unwanted attention to itself in the court of American public opinion.

Also perplexing to investigators was a statement made by Abu Marzouk to ABC News in which Khalil in particular was singled out for comment. "Khalil," Marzouk said, "rather than being a member of Hamas, is actually an informant for Israeli intelligence."[3] Federal agents were baffled about the statement. If people were to believe Marzouk's implausible allegation that Khalil was on assignment for the Mossad, then it only added credibility to the belief that Abu Mezer was hard-core Hamas. And, if they were a true Hamas cell, then the case of Abu Mezer and Khalil was an anomaly.

Hamas cells, while very compartmentalized, were rigid in their structure and design. A high-ranking officer in the organization would seek out and recruit a potential bomber and then indoctrinate him in the practices of a martyr. The "engineer," the bomb maker, would then equip the martyr-to-be with the device and instruct him on how to operate the bomb and move about with it either tucked away in a knapsack or worn under an article of clothing. A facilitator would transport the bomber to his ultimate objective. The engineers *never* martyred themselves—bomb builders were the most revered men inside the Hamas hierarchy. So, if Abu Mezer was the bomb builder, was Khalil the one to be martyred? Or, both the NYPD and the FBI worried, if the Palestinians shot in Park Slope were bomb builders, were they building the devices for other martyrs that were to attack the subway and other landmarks?

Exacerbating concern over the motives of the two Palestinians lying in Kings County Hospital Prison Ward post-op was a mysterious letter that arrived in Washington, D.C., on Friday, August 1,

1997; the letter, postmarked July 29, had been sent from Brooklyn. The note, a photocopy of an original letter, was received at an anonymous P.O. box used by the Diplomatic Security Service's "Rewards for Justice Program." The Rewards for Justice Program was established in the 1984 Act to Combat International Terrorism, administered by the Diplomatic Security Service; the secretary of state may offer rewards of up to five million dollars for information that prevents or favorably resolves acts of international terrorism against U.S. persons or property worldwide. Rewards are also paid for information leading to the arrest or conviction of terrorists attempting, committing, conspiring to commit, or aiding and abetting the commission of terrorist acts.

The unique selling point of the program was that it was an anonymous enterprise—anyone wishing to drop a dime on a terrorist could call, fax, e-mail, or write the Diplomatic Security Service and that tip would be investigated. If the tip panned out, the informant could receive in excess of two million dollars. The State Department printed photos of America's most-wanted terrorists on pamphlets designed to look like dollar bills and on matchbox covers that were disseminated throughout the Third World—primarily the Middle East—in a multitude of languages, from English and French to Arabic and Urdu. A Rewards for Justice tip was instrumental in the seizure of World Trade Center bombing mastermind Ramzi Yousef in Islamabad, Pakistan, in February 1995.

The original letter received by the Rewards for Justice Program was found by agents amid the roaches and the filth inside 248 Fourth Avenue.[4] The letter contained no specific information about an impending attack or where it would be perpetrated. Instead, it threatened a series of attacks and demanded the release of jailed Islamic militants, including Sheikh Omar Abdel Rahman, who was serving a life sentence for a plot to blow up New York City landmarks; Ramzi Ahmed Yousef, accused of masterminding the World

Trade Center bombing, who, at the time, was on trial in downtown Manhattan; and Sheikh Ahmed Yassin, a jailed leader of the militant Hamas group, serving a life sentence in an Israeli prison.*

Some of the investigators believed that the letter, tantamount to a suicide note, indicated that the two Palestinians had carefully planned to strike at the subways: "The plot was a premeditated strike," one federal agent commented. "The note says as much." Other investigators, however, felt that the rambling note, a warning of sorts, hinted that the two Palestinians were buffoons who were involved in some sort of high-stakes extortion. DSS and FBI agents assigned to investigate the letter speculated that Abu Mezer's motive in sending the letter might have been to threaten a suicide bombing, leave the evidence of his device to be uncovered, and then collect on a four-million-dollar reward. Others assessed that Abu Mezer wanted to have the letter serve as an after-the-fact prophetic warning meant to instill fear inside the minds of New Yorkers and Americans that additional attacks were imminent.

News reports of the foiled attacks, and possible links to groups such as Hamas and the PIJ, sent shivers through the spines of New York commuters and especially residents of Brooklyn. On Friday, August 1, Mayor Giuliani traveled to Brooklyn to allay fears about the invisible enemy in their midst. Giuliani's first stop was along the Orthodox Jewish enclave of Avenue J in Flatbush. Removing his jacket, Giuliani walked up and down Avenue J in a stump reminiscent of the campaign trail rather than as a mayor eager to hold hands with a community frightened about the terrorist plot.

---

* Sheikh Yassin was freed by Israel in September 1997 following a failed Mossad operation in Amman, Jordan, in which a Hamas political leader was targeted for assassination. The Mossad hit team sprayed a lethal chemical agent into the ears of Khaled Masha'al on an Amman street and, in a comedy of errors, was arrested by cops on the beat; Masha'al, crippled by the toxin, lay in a coma inside a Jordanian hospital. Jordan's King Hussein was so outraged by the Israeli operation inside the capital of one of the two Arab nations to maintain diplomatic ties to the Jewish state that he demanded the toxin's antidote as well as the release of Sheikh Yassin to his home in Gaza in exchange for the release of the four arrested intelligence operatives. Yassin was killed in 2004 by Israeli Air Force helicopter gunships.

Surrounded by a phalanx of detectives and ESU personnel, Giuliani shook hands with Orthodox men in front of kosher bakeries and grocery stores, and he embraced old women, some of whom were Holocaust survivors, who were angry that they needed to feel threatened by men who specifically wanted to kill Jews. Giuliani was sympathetic and determined—his support for Israel and a law-and-order city made him a favorite among the city's Jewish population and he understood their concerns. Giuliani pledged that the NYPD—and federal law enforcement—would protect all of New York's citizens from terrorist attack. Women pushing strollers thanked the mayor for showing his special concern, and Ehud Olmert, the deputy mayor of Jerusalem, conveniently phoned Giuliani as he pressed the flesh in Flatbush.[5]

Giuliani did not ignore the city's Arab population. Giuliani realized that the muffled after blast of the failed attack by Abu Mezer and Khalil directly impacted the day-to-day lives of the city's Arab community. There was a danger, Giuliani understood, that *all* Arab Americans along the Atlantic Avenue corridor could now be pigeonholed as terrorists and caught up in the fear of bombers on the subway. The risk of crazy individuals seeking revenge against the mosques or other social landmarks on Atlantic Avenue was high. Giuliani wanted to mend fences and to show that he was the mayor of all New York City. Outside the al-Farooq Mosque, though, his reception differed from the embrace and applause he received in Flatbush. A cleric at an Atlantic Avenue mosque turned the mayor away.[6]

Giuliani hadn't been elected as a healer—and he was hoping to be reelected to a second term as New York City mayor that November. Giuliani ran and lost against Dinkins in 1989. He beat Dinkins in 1993, and was reelected in 1997. (Term limits law prevented him from running in 2001, when Michael Bloomberg beat Mark Green.) He was all about law and order and security. It was important that the image of Giuliani, the commander in chief of New York City and the largest municipal police department in the country, be maintained and broadcast to a national audience. Giuliani wanted to appear with the Emergency Service Unit entry team. Giuliani wanted to appear with his troops.

The NYPD, in its great generosity, had granted a day off to the entry team following the raid on Fourth Avenue. The officers, the bosses, and the chiefs needed twenty-four hours to decompress and digest everything that had happened. Ralph Pascullo was proud that his cops had performed so heroically and, most importantly, that none of them had been hurt in the raid; realizing that one of the toggle switches had been flipped, Pascullo grasped that the graceful intervention of a higher authority had turned probable tragedy into nothing more than a job well done. But the media bombardment surrounding the job was terrifying. Politicians and so-called experts—from President Clinton to former FBI agents—weighed in on the Palestinians, talking about the holes in America's immigration fence that allowed two illegal aliens to possibly conspire to kill hundreds of New Yorkers, as well as about the destructive wrath that a suicide device could inflict inside the confined space of a subway train. The news reports were interlaced by reports from Jerusalem showing shopkeepers in the Mahane Yehuda market sweeping the debris from what was left of the kill zone over there.

From CBS to CNN, reporters talked about Hamas and the organization's history and mission. Video feed of Hamas demonstrations inside Arafat's Gaza Strip showed men and boys marching through refugee camps wearing mock-ups of suicide devices strapped to their chests and chanting "Death to Israel and America"; the army of suicide bomber wannabes trampled upon Israeli and American flags and set the Stars and Stripes alight. Reports spoke of the Hamas connection to the American heartland. They spoke of Abu Marzouk and the warnings from Gaza following his arrest in 1995. The media accounts were foreboding and designed to instill fear.

The ESU cops involved in the operation were concerned about the safety of their families but were confident that their anonymity would be guaranteed—after all, if the U.S. Attorney's office went so far out of its way to conceal their identities, then the city would be equally vigilant. But the officers realized that there were never ironclad guarantees of anonymity in the NYPD. ESU, after all, was not a covert strike force. Officers in the unit wore their last names and badge numbers above their right breast pockets. They didn't wear balaclava face masks to conceal their identities when they went on high-risk warrants. ESU wasn't a typical SWAT team. Its officers helped motorists whose keys were left inside locked cars, they rescued people from stuck elevators and they pulled victims from road wrecks. They were even under great pressure from Truck lieutenants and the unit commander to hand out a quota of parking summonses every month.

"We are one of the world's elite tactical and rescue units," an officer serving in Harlem's Two-Truck once commented. "We are one of the very few units in these United States that do both SWAT and lifesaving work. We are responsible for responding to plane crashes, trains derailing, and for protecting the president and the pope, and God forbid we don't hand in parking and moving violations. We did everything and everyone knew who we were."[7]

Privately, the ESU cops involved in the operation thought they might receive a promotion out of the incident, perhaps a medal, and slaps on the back from their fellow cops back at the Trucks. "Usually, in a good shooting, the police officer involved is handed a gold detective's shield and congratulated by the police commissioner," Pascullo commented. "There were routine jobs, such as a raid on a chop shop owned by John Gotti's son, when the police commissioner handed out gold shields to the cops involved. It was NYPD tradition."[8] For the four police officers, getting a gold detective's shield meant prestige and a raise—nearly five thousand dollars more a year. Sergeants and lieutenants, higher in rank than detectives, could have received "special assignment" status, which also provided a significant increase in their salaries. Promotions and pay were always a nice reward for service above and beyond the call of duty, but foremost on the minds of the officers involved in the raid was the fact that they were still alive and could enjoy a summer's day with their wives and kids. The last thing they wanted was the press.

Late on Friday night the ESU desk called each of the six men of the entry team, along with Captain Pascullo, informing them that they were to report to the fourteenth floor of One Police Plaza, the commissioner's office, before heading to city hall and appearing in a press conference with Mayor Giuliani.

Both Pascullo and McCaffrey were untroubled by the chance to appear with the mayor and be on TV—in fact, they were excited. There were never press conferences in the Housing Police—not unless a cop had killed a suspect and there was community uproar, or if a police officer was arrested on corruption charges. McCaffrey, in particular, was enthusiastic about the opportunity for some press. He envisioned appearances on *Oprah* and on *Good Morning America* and thought that this could be a career-making move turning the entry team into celebrities. McCaffrey thought that getting the word out about the raid, regardless of what terrorists were out there, was an all-out win-win situation.

Pascullo, the more reserved of the two, was equally enthusiastic about receiving accolades from the press and from the mayor because it could mean a world of goodwill for ESU. The unit's longtime war with the fire department had resulted in ESU's losing many of its coveted rescue assignments in the city; when city hall had a meeting to cover rescue procedures in case of a disaster in New York City, the fire department would send fifty chiefs, battalion chiefs, and lieutenants, while the NYPD's Special Operations Division would be hard-pressed to send an ESU sergeant. Pascullo understood the importance of rescue work to the unit and hoped that by promoting the unit with the mayor, ESU might earn some badly needed press.

On Saturday, August 2, Pascullo arrived at One Police Plaza in his Class A uniform—he wore a white shirt, blue blazer and trousers, and the traditional eight-point hat. His captain's shield, above his left breast pocket, was laced with row after row of medals and citations. When the Housing Police Department had been disbanded, Pascullo had been the most decorated officer in the department. McCaffrey, English, and the police officers wore their navy blue fatigues. The officers met downstairs at One Police Plaza at the foot of the Brooklyn Bridge across the plaza from city hall.

The meeting with Police Commissioner Safir before the press conference should have been the officers' finest hour, but instead it was rife with angst and anger. The officers were livid that they were about to be paraded before the media. They were also livid that the *New York Post* had released their names for the day's edition. McCaffrey attempted to convince the officers that since they had been already outed, they might as well make the most of the opportunity. "And so the megillah started!" McCaffrey explained. "The cops were afraid that the Palestinians were hard-core terrorists and that terrorists would retaliate against the cops who shot them, and they didn't want their names released, and we went upstairs into the war zone because the cops were fuming. I told them that since our names had already been released to the paper, we should run with the ball. It was too late to cry over spilled milk."[9]

The officers came with a union delegate to plead their desire to remain anonymous. "I knew that there was nothing I could do once my name was released to the paper," Sergeant English reflected, "but I didn't have to help the bad guys get me, either."[10]

The fourteenth floor of One Police Plaza is the epicenter of law enforcement power in New York City. Decisions that have ramifications for some eight million residents are made from behind the police commissioner's desk. At the entrance to the commissioner's office lies a waiting room with a maroon rug and the wooden desk used by Teddy Roosevelt, the NYPD's first commissioner; "Teddy's desk" is of great symbolic importance. There is no greater honor for a cop on the street than to be summoned to the fourteenth floor to be congratulated for an act of heroism; often, in such cases, the officer is invited, along with his wife and children, to meet the "PC" or police commissioner.

Instead, the entry team sat near Teddy Roosevelt's desk feeling as if they were going to an execution. "The officers and their reps told the inspector from Public Information that these guys were not going to do the interview and he had to go into the police commissioner's office and tell him," McCaffrey remembered. "He wasn't too happy about it. He sent his driver out, who used to be in Emergency Service, to speak with us, and basically he said, 'Your names are already released, you guys don't need to be concerned, the police department will take care of you guys and protect you, there's not a big threat in this, but you are going to have to do the interview.' "[11] The cops were adamant. They feared that somehow if their pictures were released, the terrorists would find it easier to target them and, more importantly, the officers' families. The level of fear gripping the city forty-eight hours after the incident was still enormous. No one yet knew how many cohorts the two Palestinians recuperating inside the prison ward at Kings County Hospital had inside the New York metropolitan area.

The ping-pong conversation outside the commissioner's office between the officers and the detectives assigned to Police Commissioner Safir's protective detail and office was numbing. *These guys really did the right thing when the city needed them,* Pascullo thought to himself. *Why the hell are they being put through the wringer?*

"The police commissioner's driver came back and told us that if you don't do the interview, he's going to retaliate against ESU by taking all your rescues away and cutting your division in half," Mc-

Caffrey recalled. "He'll let the task force do most of the entries, and then you'll become nothing more than a glorified SWAT team responding to barricades and hostages. He's very upset that you aren't going to do the interview with the mayor and it's up to you guys. I'm just passing the information to you. . . ." Special Operations Division chief Morange went in and out of Safir's office to officially present the ESU line.

Pascullo and McCaffrey looked at one another, and they looked at the cops. This was knee-in-the-groin politics played against a team of men who were tired, frightened, and thinking of nothing more than the welfare of their families and the status of the unit they loved so much. Anger was boiling over. The cops were livid. When the police commissioner's driver left the room once again, McCaffrey spoke. "You guys are in the big leagues now," McCaffrey told them. "There are no more softballs. You better play nice in the sandbox because the guy just threw hardballs at you. I don't care what you do. You guys saved my life and whatever you vote on I'll go with. The six of us went into this together and the six of us will stick together."[12]

In the end, the officers agreed to a compromise. They would appear at the press conference, but they would remain silent when standing behind the mayor. Pascullo and the entry team headed downstairs and walked across Park Place toward city hall for their meeting with assembled camera crews and reporters. As the seven ESU officers marched toward city hall, Richard Shirer, the deputy police commissioner for administration, pulled Pascullo aside and asked him if he would answer questions. "Commissioner Shirer asked me, for the sake of the guys and the sake of the unit, to help out and not make the police commissioner look bad," Pascullo recalled. "I agreed because I thought it was the best thing for the unit."

Reporters from all over the city, the country, and even the world assembled at the Blue Room in city hall. Giuliani entered the room first, followed by a grim-faced Police Commissioner Safir and First Deputy Commissioner Kelleher. Assistant Chief Kammerdener led the procession of ESU personnel. Pascullo walked proudly into the ornate room; Special Operations Division chief Morange, looking upset, as well, walked behind his ESU captain.

Lieutenant McCaffrey walked his entry team to the podium; Sergeant English followed him. Police Officers Dolan and Martinez, the sleeves of their navy blue fatigues rolled up as if they were about to enter the street brawl of their lives, their biceps flexed and coiled, walked in last. Dolan and Martinez were angry. Their faces brimmed with rage that the police commissioner would care so little about their safety and the welfare of their families.

Giuliani spoke of the incident with the broad strokes of a commander in chief informing a worried public that disaster had miraculously been averted due to the intervention of the informant and the NYPD. Speaking of Mosabbah, who was still unidentified, Giuliani said, "The information received, some people attribute to good luck and good fortune; some people attribute it to an act of God, or maybe to an act of a conscience that ultimately unites all men and women when they realize that beyond racial, religious, ethnic, and even political differences, we are all united as people and human beings and that we have to protect each other and help each other." Giuliani's words were polished and sincere.

Speaking of the NYPD operation, Giuliani was glowing, claiming that the alleged terrorist plot had been averted due in part "to the professional, courageous, excellent police work from the very best police department in the world." Giuliani's praise for the cops continued. "The police work was really absolutely remarkable. The reality is what these police officers that you see here today faced was the possibility of a major explosion taking place within seconds, not within hours, of them entering the second room of the second building, and had the bomb gone off and blown up that building, and much of the surrounding area, these police officers that you see here with me would have had very little chance of surviving. Their quick, decisive, and enormously courageous action prevented that from happening. When people stop to second-guess police officers, maybe they should stop and have a little more humility and realize how lucky we are to have them."

Does he know what happened moments earlier on the fourteenth floor? Pascullo thought to himself as he hoped that he wouldn't stammer or make a fool of himself in front of Giuliani when the questions started. *Does he even know how worried the cops are that the Palestinians might come and hunt them down now that their faces and names have been revealed?*

From Giuliani's demeanor and absolute sincerity, it is doubtful he knew how the fear of God was thrown into the faces of the officers or how the threats of disbanding ESU and depriving the city of its emergency rescue and tactical force blackmailed the officers into appearing on camera.

Before letting Police Commissioner Safir speak and telling the assembled reporters that one and only one of the ESU officers who participated in the raid would speak, Giuliani offered the kindest words of gratitude to Pascullo and the entry team. "What I want to do is to thank these guys on behalf of the citizens of New York and really for the citizens of the United States and the citizens of the world. They prevented a major terrorist attack from taking place." Giuliani continued, "We were fortunate to get information, but a thousand things could have gone wrong, from the obtaining of that information to the execution of this and the professional, intelligent, and courageous way in which they executed it, and none of the things went wrong because of these people you see here from the commanding officer to the police officers who went in, to the police officers who supported them."

Police Commissioner Safir took the microphone and likened ESU to elite units like the Marine Corps' Force Recon and the army's Green Berets. He spoke of the operation and the events that transpired on Fourth Avenue. He spoke, iron-jawed, of the events before and following the raid. "They didn't hesitate," Safir said, speaking of the cops going up against a live bomb, "and they didn't equivocate. The six of them went into the apartment under the command of Captain Pascullo and they did an outstanding job. They could not have acted more heroically and they did so in complete disregard for their safety because this is what they do and they do it well."

Safir then, to the absolute horror of the officers, thanked each of the men personally and by name. "I'd like to thank Captain Ralph Pascullo, Lieutenant Owen McCaffrey, Sergeant John English, Police Officer Dave Martinez, Police Officer Joe Dolan, Police Officer Mike Keenan, and Police Officer Mario Zorovic." *Well,* one of the officers thought, *the police commissioner has now given out our names and our faces. Why don't we just give the Palestinians our addresses and what kind of cars we drive?* Safir then looked to his right to personally commend Assistant Chief Kammerdener, who was standing in front of the entry team, as if, with his own frame, attempting to shield the name tapes revealing the officers' identities. "I also want to commend citywide commander Charles Kammerdener, who had the citywide duty and who made a very quick and effective assessment that the information was real and needed some very quick action."

Pascullo looked at this old partner and smiled. The two Housing cops had done well for themselves and the city.

Pascullo then walked to the microphone to brief reporters about the raid. He recounted the events and spoke of how he made it into Brooklyn and conceived the entry plan with Chief Kammerdener, Lieutenant McCaffrey, and Sergeant English. Pascullo was vague about many of the details concerning the assault and the Palestinians themselves—he didn't know how much information he could reveal with the investigation still ongoing. "We responded to the location on Fourth Avenue," Pascullo explained. "The entry was quick and without incident as far as injury to police or other innocent individuals, and the bomb squad responded and was able to deactivate and remove the devices." Camera shutters snapped away furiously as Pascullo spoke. Reporters pressed him for details concerning the shooting of the Palestinians and the tripping of the one toggle switch. The questions were silly and uninformed, and Pascullo used the standard line "I'd rather not say" when answering questions that were inappropriate or foolish. Pascullo explained the difference between dynamic and covert entries and refused comment on whether or not there was an informant involved. Most of the questions revolved around what the officers on the entry team must have been thinking—questions that Pascullo had to answer in the officers' names because they refused to speak.

"Can we hear from them?" the reporters pleaded. Giuliani turned to Safir, and the police commissioner, looking disappointed and angry, simply said no. Giuliani laughed, and then turned to the officers with one mayoral look pleading that they speak. McCaffrey looked at the five other men of the entry team and then told the mayor no. There would be no *Oprah* for the men who saved Brooklyn.

Pascullo then spoke of his cops, attempting to answer the question as to what was going through the minds of the entry team. "I think everybody was frightened," Pascullo commented. "They routinely go after people that are holding hostages. We do that about ten or fifteen times a day in the city. I don't think anybody was prepared to go in with an explosive device. We certainly have tools that can prevent bullets from piercing us, but at the speed that shrapnel would have come out from the explosive device, all the tools and Body Bunkers wouldn't have done anything, and the cops realized that, and that was a frightening thought. It was almost as if we were going in naked. I am so proud of the people here behind me that I just cannot express it. I am just honored to be standing here with them."

Giuliani then spoke prophetically. He thanked the cops again and then said, "Sometimes when we honor heroes we have to do it after the worst has happened, and it is wonderful to be able to do it when it all came out the right way."

Giuliani then shook everyone's hand for the cameras while the obligatory photos were taken and backs patted heartily. Pascullo had saved the unit and the careers of the men who so proudly served that midnight tour. They had, after all, saved the city. As Giuliani said, "They delivered this city from what could have been a terrible terrorist act."

The next day the cops were all over the newspapers and they found themselves on the cover of the *New York Post*. With file images of both Dave Martinez and Joe Dolan, the headline ran: NEW YORK WOULD BE COUNTING ITS DEAD IF THESE HERO COPS HAD NOT ACTED: THEY SAVED THE CITY.

The accolades continued. In a surprise press conference held at New York's Penn Station, the main hub of the Long Island Rail Road, Police Officers Eric Huber and John Kowalchuk were honored by representatives from the Metropolitan Transportation Authority, New York senator Alfonse D'Amato, as well as Mayor Giuliani. The awards and plaques, and the letters of appreciation, came as a great surprise to the two LIRR cops. Police officers in that department rarely received credit for the difficult and dangerous work they performed, and both rookie officers were overwhelmed at being rewarded for doing what they knew all along to be the right thing.

For Pascullo, McCaffrey, and the rest of the entry team, the life of an E-cop returned to normal—well, almost—in the days after the raid and the Giuliani press conference. Dolan, Keenan, and Martinez returned to Six-Truck, Zorovic headed back to the day-to-day dangers of working Eight-Truck, Sergeant English returned to Seven-Truck, and McCaffrey returned to the mysterious and unpredictable world of midnights.

ESU is a closed society of four hundred professionals where good work is rewarded by a slap on the back, and making mistakes is rarely, if ever, forgiven. The Trucks, it has been said, resemble firehouses in their close-knit living conditions, and officers who screw up, do something stupid or funny, are berated throughout their careers; officers whose photos are in the papers for a rescue or a shooting are caricatured, mimicked, and made fun of with the cruelest of comedic sabers. The men who made up the entry team were received by their comrades as returning heroes. The job, perhaps the most important tactical assignment the unit had ever executed, was seen as a textbook example of ESU's skill, courage, and discipline. The officers involved in the operation were pressed for details, tidbits, or any advice that they could offer. After all, as an officer in Harlem's Two-Truck explained, "This was the first preventative counterterrorist mission ever executed inside the fifty states."

For ESU, life returned to normal in the summer of 1997. There were warrants, overtime fights, pin jobs, barricades, jumpers, and more parking summonses to issue. Pascullo and Kammerdener would be reunited on numerous pressure-packed jobs in search of drug kingpins and murderers. The ill will felt about being forced to appear at the Giuliani press conference dissipated with time.

Justice and Rewards

The trials of Gazi Abu Mezer and Lafi Khalil began on July 6, 1998. The proceedings were expedient exercises in American jurisprudence; the evidence against the Palestinians was overwhelming. Throughout the trial, Khalil retained his impish personality and Abu Mezer retained his arrogantly determined path, eager to prove to the court—and to the world—that he was an Islamic warrior. In the court Abu Mezer's behavior was in-your-face. He chatted to his attorney and he infuriated Brooklyn federal judge Reena Raggi by continually putting his feet on the table. He made faces at witnesses and gave others the finger. He also attempted to escape—at the Metropolitan Correctional Center, Abu Mezer managed to slip out of his handcuffs. "I come to the United States because I feel that United States is supporting the Jewish state, and United States should be punished for supporting Israel," Abu Mezer proudly boasted in open court in direct examination.

One by one the police officers involved in the raid in Brooklyn took the stand to give their testimony as to the chain of events that fateful night—both Long Island Rail Road cops and Officers Dolan and Martinez. Other witnesses, including Special Agent Yamin and FBI special agent Michael Anticev, spoke of how the Palestinians had plotted to target the B Train because so many Jews traveled the line. "He said he wanted to blow up a train and kill as many Jews as possible," Anticev explained, recalling an interview with the Palestinian in the recovery room at Kings County Hospital at 5:50 P.M. on July 31;

Abu Mezer specifically said he singled out the B Train "because there are a lot of Jews who ride that train."[1]

Mosabbah, too, testified. The Egyptian, now living in the United States with his family under an assumed identity in the U.S. Marshals Service's witness protection program, was the star witness.

In the trial the jury was told of the destructive capability of Abu Mezer's bomb. Assistant U.S. Attorney Bernadette Miragliotta told jurors that the two Palestinians "were planning to use [the bombs] in what can only be called an act of international terrorism."[2] Experts spoke, as well. An FBI bomb expert talked of Abu Mezer's explosive contraption by bringing a mock-up to court. "The model was made up of four pipes, each about five inches in length and one and a quarter inches in diameter, with a total of eighty-five large construction nails taped to the pipes, and wires running from the pipes to the switches and four large batteries. In the original, the electricity would have ignited the explosive powder that filled the pipes," the FBI expert testified. The explosives expert also told jurors that a working mock-up of the device had been detonated at the Marine Corps base in Quantico, Virginia, in which pipes fragmented and burst into metal shards, and nails were thrown in all directions.[3]

Throughout the trial, Abu Mezer emphasized that Khalil knew nothing of his intentions to become a suicide bomber. Abu Mezer, wearing an Islamic skullcap, his goatee neatly trimmed, expressed nothing but hatred and contempt for the United States. "I wanted to use the bombs against the Jewish of the United States," he told jurors in heavily accented English. "I wanted to blow myself up and take as many people with me."

Interestingly enough, Abu Mezer's attorneys hinted that Mosabbah had done the right thing that night not out of the goodness in his heart but because it was the Egyptian who was interested in collecting the four-million-dollar payoff from the State Department's Rewards for Justice Program.[4] Abu Mezer claimed that Mosabbah was a member of Egypt's notorious al-Gama'a al-Islamiyyah and had come up with the idea to set off explosions in order to collect on the State Department reward.

On July 24, 1998, Gazi Abu Mezer was convicted of conspiracy to use a weapon of mass destruction, the threat to use a weapon of mass destruction, and the use of a firearm in relation to the crime of violence. After the jury read its verdict, the son of Hebron yelled, "Palestinian children do not deserve to die! Nobody deserves to die!" He then jumped from his seat and, much to the judge's horror, began to shout *"Allahu Akbar"* ("God is great") while holding a Koran over his head as federal marshals forced him to sit down.[5] He was sentenced on March 1, 1999, to two concurrent life sentences for the weapon-of-mass-destruction charges and thirty years for attempting to grab Dave Martinez's gun during the scuffle.

Lafi Khalil, portrayed throughout the trial as an unwitting accomplice, was convicted only of possession of a counterfeit alien registration receipt card. He buried his face in his hands as the verdict was read, yet apparently the jury could not find compelling and irrefutable evidence that he was an active participant in the plot. He was sentenced to only thirty-six months in prison.

On September 15, 1998, after the trial of the two Palestinians had concluded and both men had been convicted, the ESU entry team was honored by the NYPD on Medal Day. In the weeks and months after the raid that July night in Brooklyn, the officers talked less and less of their ordeal; discussion inside the Trucks of the tactics deployed began to settle down, replaced with nitpicking of the "tidal wave" of dinners, awards, and accolades the men received from just about every civic organization in the city. The excitement slowly withered away and the unit focused its attention on the day-to-day job of emergency response. Yet the "Brooklyn Job" remained a source of enormous pride inside the ten Trucks of the Emergency Service Unit.

Most police officers in the unit were certain that the entry team would be awarded the department's highest commendation, the Medal of Honor. According to the official departmental guidelines, the Medal of Honor was awarded for individual acts of extraordinary bravery intelligently performed in the line of duty at imminent and personal danger to life. Specifically, the medal is awarded for acts of gallantry and valor performed with knowledge of the risk involved above and beyond the call of duty. "If ever there was a job that the department should have done the right thing by the cops," a former unit officer said, "this was it."[6] Even the department's second-highest award, the Police Combat Cross, would have been understood. The Combat Cross was awarded to members of the service who successfully and intelligently performed an act of extraordinary heroism while engaged in personal combat with an armed adversary under circumstances of imminent personal hazard to life.

But, in the end, the six men of the entry team each received the Medal for Valor, the third-highest award, issued to officers for acts of personal bravery intelligently performed in the line of duty at imminent personal hazard to life under circumstances evincing a disregard of personal consequences, or for conspicuous excellence in service to the community. Ray McDermott and Ralph Pascullo were awarded honorable mentions for their role in the Brooklyn Job. Pascullo was surprised that the ESU cops weren't awarded the department's top medal. "Everyone was shocked," Pascullo explained, "that the six cops weren't awarded the Medal of Honor." Pascullo reflected, "This was a textbook case for the department's highest award and it might have had to do with payback from the very top for the cops not wanting to do the press conference. There were rumors that the higher-ups did not consider the entry team's performance to be so heroic because, in their view, a bomb was not a gun."[7]

A month later, though, the NYPD Emergency Service Unit members involved in the raid received perhaps their highest reward for valor. Detective Mike Corr, a veteran ESU officer, realizing that the Brooklyn raid was a remarkable display of sacrifice and courage, nominated Pascullo and the six-man entry team for the National Association of Police Organizations' Top Cops Award; NAPO is a coalition of police unions and associations from across the United States that advances the interests of America's law enforcement officers through legislative and legal advocacy, political action, and education. Founded in 1978, NAPO represents more than 2,000 police unions and associations, 230,000 sworn law enforcement officers, 11,000 retired officers, and more than 100,000 citizens. It was a huge organization and the award ceremony was a nationally recognized event—the president of the United States himself handed the recipients their awards on the White House lawn.

"The submission process allowed anybody, from a police chief to an average citizen, to nominate a police officer or group of officers to receive the Top Cop Award," explained Thomas Scotto, president of the NYPD's Detectives Endowment Association and former NAPO president. "NAPO had no say as to which officers and which incidents were nominated. But once we received all the nominations, we reviewed each one carefully and then nominated the top ten most deserving law enforcement professionals."[8]

Thousands of entries are submitted each and every year, but in 1997, Pascullo, McCaffrey, English, Martinez, Dolan, Zorovic, and Keenan were not only nominated, but selected jointly as one of the ten finalists; finalists are flown to Washington, D.C., where they are wined, dined, and then honored by the president. The ESU nomination and selection was met by rage at One Police Plaza. "First Deputy Commissioner Kelleher called me and yelled at me wanting to know who told me that we could honor the cops from the Brooklyn Job," Scotto remembered. "I tried to explain to him that the head of NAPO had nothing to do with the submission process and that any cop and even any citizen could write in and nominate someone. He was fuming. He said that the police commissioner wanted another officer recognized for heroism and that these cops weren't going to get it. Again I tried to tell him that it didn't work that way. The exchange went back and forth for several days until the police commissioner understood that this was out of his hands. Then the word came down to me from One Police Plaza that the officers couldn't travel to the ceremony in their uniforms. This was insane, I thought. We are going to be the only police department in the country that shows up in suits and ties? Then I was told that there was an oversight in the submission process and that Deputy Inspector McDermott's name had to be added to the list of ESU nominees. Then I was told that the officers had to take a day off if they wanted to go. They couldn't go on department time. And then I was told that the officers couldn't go to Washington, D.C., with their weapons. It was all very bizarre."[9]

Adding to the politics and pettiness surrounding what should have been a shining moment of glory for the NYPD, First Deputy Commissioner Kelleher informed Captain Pascullo—three days before the award ceremony—that he couldn't go with his wife and three children to the White House because the department wanted him to travel, as part of a New York City delegation, to the Dominican Republic with New York Yankees outfielder Bernie Williams; Pascullo had traveled to the Dominican Republic on behalf of the NYPD before, as part of the city's contribution to a FEMA delegation that traveled to the Caribbean nation following a devastating hurricane, but there was nothing so urgent that Pascullo needed to attend to that couldn't wait until after he was honored for his heroism and command in Park Slope. "Exiling a captain up for the nation's most prestigious law enforcement award was very suspicious," a former ESU officer commented. "It was as if the powers that be wanted to make sure that he wouldn't be there to be part of the glory. It was the absolute definition of departmental childishness."

The Brooklyn Job was the first time in NAPO's history that the

NYPD had been honored for heroism in the line of fire. "It was surely a proud moment," Sergeant English remembered. "It wasn't every day that you were able to travel to our nation's capital, with your family, and be introduced to the president of the United States and thanked for doing your job. It was impressive."[10] Other E-cops were proud simply to be in such esteemed company. "I looked at the uniforms and the patches and medals," Mario Zorovic recalled, "and I talked to my fellow officers and I was proud to be among them."[11]

President Clinton granted a private audience to each of the law enforcement agencies represented. "Hey, guys, you are the ones who shot those terrorists," McCaffrey remembered President Clinton telling the cops as he patted them on the back, aglow with pride. "It was a great job and the country thanks you."[12]

The official NAPO account of the Brooklyn Job was dramatic, and when read aloud, it resonated throughout the White House Rose Garden.

> In the early morning hours of July 31, 1997, an informant told officers that two men with whom he resided had built four bombs and planned to blow up an occupied subway car later that morning. After formulating a tactical plan, Lieutenant Owen McCaffrey, Sergeant John English and Captain Ralph Pascullo decided on a six-person entry team for the apartment where the bombs had been built by alleged foreign terrorists. The team made a tactical entry into the apartment, and Lieutenant McCaffrey and Sergeant English provided backup, while Officers Keenan and Zorovic secured the front room. Simultaneously, Officers Martinez and Dolan advanced to the rear room where the two suspects and the explosives were located. One of the suspects grabbed at an officer's gun, while the second suspect threw himself on the switcher which partially activated the

bomb. Both suspects were immediately disabled. A search of the apartment led to the discovery of four pipe bombs, which if detonated in Brooklyn's main subway station as intended, would have been devastating. In less than a minute, these members of the elite Emergency Services Unit subverted disaster and saved countless lives.

ESU was in stellar company that day on the White House lawn. Other Top Cops finalists included the Los Angeles Police Department officers from the West Hollywood Division and SWAT, perhaps the nation's finest tactical team, who were involved in the brutal West Hollywood bank robbery and shoot-out in February 1997. Other top-ten finalists included state troopers, police officers, sheriffs' deputies, and federal agents from around the country who performed heroic deeds above and beyond the call of duty. The winner of the award was Officer Malcom Thompson of the Kissimmee, Florida, police department. After responding to a suspicious-person call, Officer Thompson was shot four times by a robbery suspect who was wanted on several felony warrants and was being sought by the Osceola County Sheriff's Office in relation to two armed robberies that had just occurred that same night; the suspect was also wanted for a carjacking and a home invasion. Two rounds struck Officer Thompson's head; another struck his neck, severing his carotid artery; another round went into his right chest area, collapsing his lung. Officer Thompson, critically wounded, pursued the suspect and managed to fire his weapon and kill him before collapsing.

Standing behind President Bill Clinton, the NYPD officers were beaming and proud. They knew that they were in elite company. They knew how special the honor was.

After the award—and his return from the Caribbean—Pascullo was promoted to the rank of deputy inspector and appointed the executive officer of the Special Operations Division. It was perceived as a gesture by Police Commissioner Safir to correct his Dominican Republic banishment during the Top Cops ceremony.

The six ESU officers accepted their medals and returned to their Trucks. Over time, some would eventually leave ESU altogether and expand their horizons in elite units outside the Special Operations Division. Others remained at their posts performing the impossible and saving lives on the midnight tours. The slights and pettiness they encountered after their harrowing midnight tour mattered little to the officers a year following the job. They were grateful that they'd had the chance to, in the flash of a courageous instant, do their jobs and, in the process, save so many lives from imminent destruction. They were grateful to have survived those horrifying seconds and their encounter with suicidal terror.

Postscript

Lieutenant Owen McCaffrey pulled into Fort Totten, set to start yet another midnight tour. It was a sparkling autumn night and a mild breeze gushed in across the bay. The sky was clear and the cascading headlights moving all along the Throgs Neck Bridge provided a mesmerizing backdrop to what McCaffrey knew would be a peaceful night in New York City.

McCaffrey changed into his fatigues, fastened his utility belt around his midsection, and grabbed the division mail along with a cup of coffee. A reporter on NY1, the local cable news station, was talking about Mayor Giuliani's divorce proceedings and the upcoming election campaign for a new mayor. McCaffrey sat down to take care of some administrative work and saw an old coffee-stained copy of the *New York Post* on the table; the paper was over a week old. McCaffrey flipped through the pages as he took a sip from his cup and saw a story about Police Commissioner Bernard Kerik, who had replaced Safir as the PC a year earlier, and his trip to Israel to show the NYPD's solidarity with the Jewish state in its time of absorbing what had become a lethal string of suicide-bombing attacks. In June a teenage suicide bomber had flipped a toggle switch on an explosive charge he was wearing outside a Tel Aviv discotheque, killing twenty-one teenagers; in August, only days before Commissioner Kerik's trip, a Hamas suicide bomber dressed as a hippie blew himself up inside a Jerusalem pizzeria, killing fifteen people, including five children and seven members of a single family. Police Commissioner Kerik toured Israeli police facilities and walked through Jerusalem, visiting the crime scene, marked by shrapnel-scarred concrete, boarded-up windows, and candles to remember the dead.

Rereading the reports from the PC's Middle Eastern trip, Mc-Caffrey immediately thought of the apartment behind 248 Fourth Avenue. He thought of the cold stares from the Palestinians as they were brought bleeding into the courtyard. They didn't cry or beg for help. They were stoic and determined. They had the cold eyes of men who wanted to die. How do you defeat a foe driven by such hatred and religious conviction? the ESU lieutenant wondered. McCaffrey asked himself if New York City would ever be ready for fifteen or twenty dead in incessant suicide bombings outside nightclubs or restaurants. How would the city have reacted that morning had the informant never come forward? McCaffrey wondered. How would ESU have responded, walking into a darkened tunnel filled with smoke, fire, and the gasping lungs of the dying, knowing that a second bomber targeting the rescuers might have been there waiting? How many ESU cops would have been killed in the double tap?

Each day that passed since the Brooklyn Job was a day removed from the potential horror that was to have been inflicted on New York City. Four years had passed since that morning when a part of Brooklyn was supposed to have gone up in flames. A lot had changed. The back building where the bombers lived had since been torn down. As time went on, the stark and bloody reality of that night became less daunting. McCaffrey thought if time permitted, he would take a drive to the Seventy-eighth Precinct and sit in front of 248 Fourth Avenue just to remind himself how lucky his men were, and how lucky New York City was, to have dodged a bullet that night.

McCaffrey finished his coffee, finished some paperwork, and checked the roll call to see who on the midnight crew was working that night. Tapping his holster and grabbing his keys, McCaffrey signed out at Fort Totten. He checked his watch—it was eleven p.m.—and jotted down the time and the day's date. It was September 10, 2001.

Most of the ESU cops who worked the midnight tour that night were halfway home when American Airlines Flight 11 crashed into the North Tower of the World Trade Center at 8:46 A.M. on September 11. By the time United Airlines Flight 175 hit the South Tower some fifteen minutes later, those cops had turned around and were heading back to their Trucks. The Emergency Service Unit's Third Squad was working that fateful morning—some of the best and brightest in the unit along with many of its most experienced personnel. The moment the first reports of an aircraft slamming into the World Trade Center flashed over the Special Operations Division frequency, the entire unit rushed to lower Manhattan from the ten Trucks throughout the city. The officers grabbed their oxygen masks and Scott packs to breathe inside the smoke-filled furnace of the raging inferno, and they grabbed their ropes and rescue gear. The E-cops were determined to do what ESU did better than any unit in the world—save lives.

As tens of thousands fled the Twin Towers, racing out of the buildings in the desperate attempt to escape the destruction and fear, ESU joined other emergency workers—EMS workers and firemen—and rushed into the devastation. When those trapped on the floors directly above where the hijacked aircraft had slammed into the towers began to leap to their deaths rather than incinerate in the heat, ESU cops rushed to their trucks to don body armor and grab their assault weapons—the bodies crashing on the pavement sounded like bombs detonating and the E-cops were unsure as to how this invisible enemy would strike next.

When the towers collapsed in a fast and furious display of cascading steel and disintegrating concrete, the NYPD and the Emergency

Service Unit would pay a heavy price. Fourteen members of the unit perished the day America was attacked—the officers included newcomers to the unit and men with a combined total of over a hundred years of rescue and tactical experience between them; some of the men were only months away from their twenty years of service and the chance to retire. The dead included sergeants, detectives, and police officers. Some of the fallen had started their careers inside the ranks of the NYPD; others had begun their path toward ESU in the Transit and Housing Police Departments. Some were snipers. Others were former marines and volunteer firemen. The Emergency Service Unit did not waver in the face of the billowing danger—they excelled above and beyond the call of duty.

The NYPD lost twenty-three members of the service that fateful morning. The Port Authority Police Department, the agency responsible for airports and bridges in New York and New Jersey, whose headquarters was inside the Twin Towers, lost thirty-seven officers, including many of its senior commanders. The FDNY lost an astounding 343 firemen when the towers collapsed.

None of the Emergency Service Unit police officers who had answered the challenge of storming a Palestinian bomb factory that July night four years before September 11, 2001, were killed in the attack on the Twin Towers. Each man responded to the call and worked the "pile," as the mountain of debris and death at what would become known as Ground Zero was called. They worked atop the smoldering ashes of what had been two of the world's tallest structures to look for their brothers-in-arms in the desperate hope that miraculously they could pull a survivor out of the rubble.

The attacks of 9/11 devastated the NYPD and the Emergency Service Unit—and in those desperate hours after the towers came crashing down, New York City's Kevlar shield would be needed more than ever. Retirees were even pressed back into service. Deputy Inspector Ralph Pascullo, who had retired in 2000 after suffering a massive heart attack, raced down to Floyd Bennett Field to assist in the security and recovery operations down at Ground Zero. ESU cops who had retired and had moved far away made their way back to New York City to roll up their sleeves, recall their training, and lend a hand on the pile. The bond of the brotherhood of being a member of the Emergency Service Unit was reinforced during the unit's time of need.

The attack on September 11, 2001, was the largest event in the history of the NYPD and the Emergency Service Unit. The unit's illustrious history was now marked by all events before 9/11 and everything thereafter. But to the cops who coordinated, planned, and executed the raid on 248 Fourth Avenue, the sorrow felt after seeing their city besieged and having to salute their fallen comrades at heart-tugging funerals and memorials was compounded by a sense that the case of Gazi Abu Mezer and Lafi Khalil was a wake-up that, tragically, went ignored. Because law enforcement had acted so decisively that night, the rage, fanaticism, and devastation that the two Palestinians wanted to inflict on New York City was averted. That prevention, inevitably, was nothing more than a delay. It brought about a false sense of security that "it," the indiscriminate desire for killing and carnage in the name of God, could not and would not happen here.

Nearly all the officers who took part in that remarkable night's events have since retired from the NYPD. Charles Kammerdener, the former Housing cop who used to run up darkened staircases with Ralph Pascullo in the anonymous crime-ridden world of the projects in search of killers, muggers, and pushers, is still on the job and is now a deputy chief and the commander of the NYPD's Special Operations Division. His mission is to ensure that ESU and the department's other specialized units are trained, equipped, and ready to respond to the Brooklyn Jobs and 9/11s of the future.

Abdel Rahman Mosabbah ended up living out the American dream. His moment of righteous conviction—and desire for self-preservation—set into motion a chain of events that exploded out of his control but eventually awarded him millions of dollars in State Department reward money and an honorable spot in the witness protection program. He still lives in the United States with his family, under an assumed identity—still in fear for his life.

Lafi Khalil spent thirty-six months inside a federal lockup and was deported back to the Palestinian Authority. His whereabouts today are unknown.

In the end, Gazi Ibrahim Abu Mezer, the son of Hebron, received his two wishes. The United States endured a horrific attack at the hands of Islamic warriors, and he earned the right to stay in the United States for the rest of his life. Gazi Ibrahim Abu Mezer, inmate number 48705–053, is currently—and will be until the last day of his life—a resident of the U.S. "Supermax" prison in Florence, Colorado.

Acknowledgments

I was sitting inside a cramped office at the Royal Jordanian Special Operations Command in Amman, Jordan, when I first heard of the double suicide bombing in Jerusalem's Mahane Yehuda market on July 30, 1997. I had spent the better part of the morning with a team of Jordanian counterterrorist commandos, watching them train on a sunbaked field just outside the capital, and I had met with then-prince Abdullah, the commander of Jordan's arsenal of special operators, and we chatted over glass after glass of boiling sweet tea. The mood inside the HQ was one of guarded optimism, which was refreshing in a region where optimism was a commodity few realists shared. It was two years since Israeli prime minister Rabin's assassination and even though the peace process under Israeli prime minister Benjamin Netanyahu had stalled, the feeling was that the region had turned a corner of no return. The old ways, the wars and the terror, just could not continue. The entire region, the feeling persisted, was long overdue for a renaissance of sanity and calm. I had been in Jordan for a week, covering Jordan's special forces and elite counterterrorist unit for a series of articles I was writing, and I was enjoying the last few hours in the Hashemite Kingdom, shooting the shit with several officers whom I had befriended, swapping jokes, drinking more sweet tea, and, as when anywhere in the Middle East, always having one eye on the color TV set in the office tuned to CNN. And then it came . . . breaking news from Jerusalem.

Two Hamas suicide bombers striking in the center of the Israeli capital, in a market where thousands of the city's dwellers shopped for their fruits and vegetables, had killed over a dozen men, women, and children. The first images from the crime scene were ghastly and gruesome. Body parts were strewn about the market, and bloodied victims, walking aimlessly in their state of shock, wept as they searched for friends and loved ones. There were the initial claims of responsibility from Gaza and Damascus and a vow, from one of the Israeli prime minister's spokesmen, that revenge would be swift and severe.

The mood inside the Special Operations Command HQ in Amman turned from jovial to rigid. There were no more jokes thrown around about mothers-in-law. Cell phones began to ring and pagers began to buzz. The HQ, located in the Wadi Sir section of town, was adjacent to the headquarters of the Public Security Directorate and the GID, Jordan's intelligence service. Hamas was strong in Jordan, a legal political entity, and the roar of engines departing the Wadi Sir parking lot was proof that Jordanian intelligence officials feared the order for the Jerusalem attack might have emanated from inside the kingdom.

The next afternoon, as I started a new day across the river in Tel Aviv, the first news reports began to filter through that the New York City Police Department's Emergency Service Unit had shot and seriously wounded two Palestinians in Brooklyn who were *allegedly* en route to blow themselves up on a subway train underneath the East River. I had been covering the terrorist wars in Israel since 1988 and I was sure that the next salvo of this latest battle would be launched in the Gaza Strip or the West Bank. I thought, as someone who could be considered in the loop on how this war was being fought, that one of the Israel Defense Forces' elite counterterrorist units, or the Mossad or Shin Bet, would seize the initiative and avenge the seventeen people killed in the Mahane Yehuda bombing. I never thought that the Palestinians would attempt to strike again the next day and in, of all places, Brooklyn. And I never thought the NYPD's elite Emergency Service Unit, a unit about whom I had written two books and over a dozen articles, would be the ones to prevent New York from turning into Jerusalem.

In the five years that I had spent writing about ESU prior to the incident in Brooklyn on July 31, 1997, I had come to know a good many of the four hundred men and women inside ESU. Writing about the unit was a learning experience, filled with excitement, joy, and a lot of laughs. I've met some of the most remarkable people in the world visiting the ten ESU Trucks spread throughout New York City. They were professionals who valued human life more than any emergency room surgeon, and who could endure the most difficult of human experiences—from apprehending psychos who killed their families to peeling the remnants of a family off a stretch of highway following a particularly vicious car wreck—with skill, compassion, and humor. I have had the privilege to visit a great many SWAT and counterterrorist units around the world but I always knew that ESU was different.

ESU was a tactical unit and a rescue force—their passion, their calling, was to save people. I often suffered the razor-sharp sarcasm of an angry ESU cop when I mentioned some of the units I had visited and how they trained and prepared for those what-if situations when lethal firepower must be returned. A cover story I wrote about LAPD SWAT for *Popular Mechanics* earned me particular antagonism, but the most veteran of officers would always come to my defense and say that "we aren't a SWAT team." I always wondered how ESU would respond when confronted with a true tactical challenge. And now, when the unit faced its litmus test, I was six thousand miles away.

Even before details of the incident in Brooklyn were released and before my friends in the unit called me in Tel Aviv to tell me what had happened, I knew that Captain Ralph Pascullo *just had* to be in the thick of it. Few men worked harder; few men were as brave and self-sacrificing. This book is, in many ways, the story of Ralph Pascullo, and I owe my good friend a debt the likes of which I can never repay. I first met then-lieutenant Ralph Pascullo in 1994 while I was working on my first book on the NYPD's Emergency Service Unit. He was a newcomer to the NYPD, a rollover from the New York City Housing Police, and the enthusiasm and pride he displayed were infectious. My ESU "rabbi," Lieutenant Bob Sobocienski, introduced me to Ralph Pascullo, telling me he was "good people"—NYPD code that Ralph could be trusted. While other ESU lieutenants wanted nothing to do with the writer seeking a patrol car to sit in for a shift, Lieutenant, and then Captain, Pascullo always enthusiastically let me watch him at work. Pascullo came from the Housing Police, a little-known force of cops who worked the most dangerous, depressed, drug-infested precincts in the five boroughs—the Housing Authority projects spread throughout New York City. In its heyday, the Housing Police was the eighth-largest police department in the United States, but the NYPD, the gargantuan law enforcement body in the city, looked at the cops from Housing with disdain and disregard. When, under an ambitious and long overdue initiative from then-mayor Rudolph Giuliani and his wunderkind top cop, Police Commissioner William Bratton, the NYPD took over the smaller Transit Police and the Housing cops, ESU absorbed the emergency service units from both the smaller agencies into its ranks. Pascullo, who had founded "Housing Rescue," entered the NYPD's Emergency Service Unit as a lieutenant and he left Housing as its most decorated officer ever.

No ifs, ands, or buts . . . this book could not have been written without Ralph Pascullo's generous support, friendship, and guidance! His honesty, integrity, and tenacity in the face of sometimes enormous bureaucracy and ambivalence are a source of great inspiration to me. The fact that he would be one of the commanders of the sole counterterrorist operation against suicide bombers in U.S.

law enforcement history comes as no surprise and is a fitting chapter in a distinguished and epic career of service and sacrifice.

Special thanks also belong to Lieutenant (Ret.) Owen McCaffrey—the "dude." Like Pascullo, Owen McCaffrey was a veteran of the Housing Police. McCaffrey was stereotypical NYPD—Irish, boisterous, larger-than-life, and always ready to share a story. He knew the ins and outs of the society that was the NYPD, and he knew, perhaps better than anyone I had ever seen, how to make the most of that system. Yet unlike many an NYPD stereotype, when the word came down that two Palestinians were preparing to blow themselves up on a train between Brooklyn and Manhattan, McCaffrey made sure that his men were looked after, that they were safe, and that at the end of the day, regardless of how the political pendulum at One Police Plaza would swing, his men made it home to their wives and kids. In addition to Owen McCaffrey, my thanks go to the other members of the entry team for sharing their lives and experiences with me—Sergeant (Ret.) John English, Detective Dave Martinez, and my good friend Detective (Ret.) Mario Zorovic. This book could not have happened without their friendship, courage, and support.

I also thank the current commander of the NYPD's Special Operations Division, Deputy Chief Charles Kammerdener. An old partner of Ralph Pascullo's who fought and survived the war on crime inside the housing projects of New York, Chief Kammerdener generously gave of himself to help me piece this story together. I give my thanks to Chief of Department (Ret.) Louis Anemone, one of the most charismatic, dynamic, and far-thinking "bosses" New York's Finest will ever have. I graciously thank NYPD police commissioner Ray Kelly for his assistance and kind support of this project, and I would like to thank Deputy Commissioner for Public Information Michael O'Looney for his assistance in this endeavor; special thanks, as well, to Detective Walter Byrnes, in the NYPD's DCPI office.

Very special words of thanks are owed to U.S. State Department Diplomatic Security Service special agent Jeremy Yamin—as always, whenever the U.S. has found itself inside the crosshairs of the terrorist's evil plans, it has been agents from this remarkable law enforcement force who have been there on the front lines. And as I have done on numerous documentary and book projects that I have created on the Diplomatic Security Service, a special word of thanks is given to its spokesman, Andy Laine.

There is also a not-so-small legion of very good friends in law enforcement and security services throughout the U.S., Canada, Europe, Israel, and Jordan whom I would like to thank. For the obvious reasons, these frontline combatants in the new World War against terrorism need to remain nameless.

I also thank my agent, Al Zuckerman. Agents today like to think of themselves as sharks—Al is a King Solomon. His tempered and cunning insight and his higher-ground vision of what the literary business is all about are things that I respect greatly and admire. I would also like to thank Ron Martirano and Doug Grad, my editors at Penguin, for their patience and input.

Finally, I offer special—and loving—thanks to my wife, Sigi, for her understanding and that most important trait needed for the wife of a writer—a hell of a lot of tolerance. Thanks, Sigi, I owe you!!!

Samuel M. Katz
May 2004

Appendix

When ESU deploys—whether for people stuck inside an elevator or people trapped as hostages inside a room with a gun-wielding psychopath—it comes prepared to handle virtually any and all emergency situations.

Much of the unit's emergency rescue equipment, protective body armor included, is carried in each REP that patrols stretches of the city.

- General equipment: two high-intensity portable lights, two gas masks, two sound barriers, two goggles, jumper cable, Slim Jim, two heavy vests, two construction helmets, two ballistic helmets, two ballistic shields, ballistic blanket, battering ram, two shotguns and ammunition, two batons, two hand lights, HAZMAT book, rescue harness, Larakus belts with carabiners, webbing, and binoculars
- Nonlethal weaponry/EDP equipment: Tasers and darts, Nova stun device and pole, water cannon, shepherds crook, Kevlar stainless steel gloves, Mace, pepper gas, EDP bar, mesh restraining blanket, Velcro restraining straps, fifteen-inch chain handcuffs, and plastic shield
- Hurst tools: gas motor Jaws of Life, cutters, chains, gas can aviation tips, ram, twenty-six-inch hoses
- Pneumatic tools: pneumatic-saw kit, paratech air guns

- Air bags: inflatable air bags in three sizes, air bag bottles, air bag regulators, train kit, assorted chocks, cribbing
- Gas-powered chain saw: Stihl chain saw with tool kit, spare chain, fuel
- Scuba gear: two Viking dry suits, two pairs open-cell thermal underwear, two AGA masks with regulators, two scuba tanks and backpacks, two sets fins, gloves, knives and compass, two weight belts, two BCD vests, two rescue lines, two underwater lights, two 150-foot polypropylene lines
- Tools and other equipment: bolt cutters large and small, wire cutters, ring cutter, lock buster, sledgehammer, large Haligan tool, ax, bow saw, come-along tool, small Haligan, toolbox, hacksaw, pry bar, gas key, crowbar, "J" hook, assorted small tools, lock cylinder tool, two "J" chains, chain with hooks, radiac kit, Kelly tool, lanterns, dosimeters, isolation kit, flares, circle cord, reflective tape, oil
- First aid kit: resuscitator, two O_2 tanks, demand valve, suction, assistant masks, cervical collars, KED extrication, spare O_2 bottles, sterile water, OB kit, burn kit, Stokes Basket, scoop stretcher, folding stretcher, backboards—long and short, blankets, assorted splints, disposable body bags, canvas body bags, DB-45 deodorizer
- Other equipment: two Scott packs, two one-hour bottles, "B" suit, rubber gloves, electrical gloves, magnet, elevator and electronics kit, two waders, exposure suit, fifty-foot line and life ring, kapok vests, work line: work line assorted, lifeline, dog noose, animal control kit, "Hot Stick," gas masks, goggles and work gloves, reflective tape, sound barriers, sixteen-foot extension ladder, fire extinguishers, four six-by-six hardwood chocks, four three-by-three chocks, assorted wedges and chocks, shoring and cribbing for vehicle stabilization

During any given shift the REPs are out patrolling the city while the unit's larger vehicles, also known as the "Trucks," contain the majority of a squad's rescue equipment. The Truck is a hulking $250,000 vehicle ($1,000,000 when fully equipped) the size of a garbage truck that is usually dispatched to large-scale jobs and as a backup for the REPs; the squad's supervisor, a sergeant, and a "chauffeur," a police officer, respond with the Truck. In 1997 the equipment carried in this hulking emergency response station included everything carried in the REP as well as

- Gas-powered chain saws: Stihl chain saw, with tool kit, spare chain, fuel; K–1200 saw with wood blades, steel blades, masonry blades, tool kit, and fuel
- Electric power tools: reciprocating saw, circular saw, high-torque drill, all of which have spare blades and bits of all sizes
- Radiac equipment: Two Geiger counters, four dosimeters, twenty film badges
- Electrical and emergency lighting equipment: four one-hundred-foot electrical reels, four one-thousand-watt portable lights, two five-hundred-watt portable lights, two one-thousand-watt light towers, two four-thousand-watt light towers, assorted adapters and plugs, two multiport junction boxes
- Hand tools: forty-piece toolbox, two sets bolt cutters large and small, five- and ten-pound sledgehammers, Haligan tools large and small, two pike head axes, two flathead axes, three bow saws (small, medium, large), carpenter saws, pry bars (twelve-, eighteen-, and twenty-four-inch), lock buster (duckbill), hydraulic bolt cutters, "rabbit tool," various gas and utility shut-off keys, shovels (trench, spade, flat), various hydrant wrenches, lock puller, "K" tool kit, Kelly tool, grading hooks, "Hot Stick," assorted spikes and nails, rakes and brooms, twenty-four-foot extension ladder, pike polls, twelve-foot closet ladder, portable vise, winch (come-along), assorted hand tools

- Truck-mounted equipment: five-ton winch, air compressor, twenty-four-kilowatt generator, light towers, PA radio system, spot- and floodlights
- Cutting torches: Caldo torch with rods, oxyacetylene backpack, assorted tips, and connecting ten-foot hoses
- First aid: major-trauma kit, backboards, cervical collars, resuscitator, spare O_2 bottles, KEDs, blankets, assorted splints, burn kit, Stokes Basket, scoop stretcher
- Pneumatic tools: pneumatic-saw kit (Wizard), Paratech air gun, pneumatic jacking bags, pneumatic air chisel
- Hydraulic tools: ten-ton Porto-Power kit, Hurst 5000 gas motor, Hurst electric motor, Hurst-150 cutters, Hurst model 32-B, Hurst model 26 champ, Hurst model 16 ram, Hurst model 30 ram
- Specialized equipment: metal detector, train kit, two ten-ton jacks, hydraulic bolt cutters, electric jackhammer, line gun, Porta-lights (hand lights)
- Heavy weapons and ammunition: Ithaca 37 pump action 12-gauge shotgun, Heckler & Koch MP5 9 mm submachine gun, Ruger Mini-14 5.56 mm assault rifles, Glock and Beretta 9 mm semi-automatic pistols, Federal 37 mm tear gas projectile gun
- Tactical equipment: six ballistic helmets, six ballistic vests, one Body Bunker ballistic shield, two ballistic-barrier blankets, one forced-entry door ram, six MSA gas masks with filters, one Kwik-View mirror, one spotting scope
- Rope: two 200-foot ½-inch lifelines, 220-foot ⅝-inch lifeline, 100-foot ⅝-inch work line, 100-foot ½-inch work line, 100-foot ⅜-inch work line, 500-foot ¼-inch polyprop cord, four Morrisey life belts, two rescue harnesses
- HAZMAT kit
- SCBA equipment: two SCBA Scott packs in case, six spare sixty-minute bottles, six spare thirty-minute bottles

- Hydraulic tools: Hurst hydraulic manual pump, post support plate, two chains with clevis hooks, two clevis links, clevis pins, assorted tips, fuel, oil, two spare sixteen-foot hoses
- Vehicle stabilization equipment: six six-by-six hardwood chocks, six four-by-four hardwood chocks, assorted wedges and chocks, shoring and cribbing
- Fire-extinguishing equipment: two pressurized water extinguishers, dry chemical extinguisher, two CO_2 extinguishers, two fifty-foot rolls, half-inch fire hose with attached nozzles
- Elevator and electrical equipment: elevator and electric kit
- Water rescue equipment: six kapok vests, two ring buoys with eighty feet of rope, two shepherds hooks, exposure suits, two sets waders, four-man inflatable raft (AVON) with oars, four-horsepower outboard engine
- Scuba gear: four eighty-cubic-foot scuba tanks, four Darrel-Allen underwater lights, two sets 150-foot water rescue lines, two sets weight belts

Notes

CHAPTER TWO: THE FEDAYEEN ON FREEDOM'S DOOR

[1] Robert D. McFadden, "Suspects in Bomb Plot Took Two Paths from the West Bank," *New York Times,* 3 August 1997, p. C1.
[2] Interview, Jerusalem, 28 August 2003.
[3] McFadden, "Suspects in Bomb Plot," p. C1.

CHAPTER THREE: AMERICA, AMERICA

[1] Interview, Tel Aviv, 14 August 2003.
[2] Interview, Toronto, 15 June 2003.
[3] Interview, Toronto, 16 June 2003.
[4] Dan Barry, "Bomb Suspect Was Detained by U.S. but Released," *New York Times,* 2 August 1997, p. B2.
[5] Interview, Sioux Falls, 13 November 2003.
[6] Interview, Toronto, 14 June 2003.

CHAPTER FOUR: BACKDOOR ENTRY

[1] Interview, Tel Aviv, 20 August 2003.

CHAPTER FIVE: THE BOROUGH OF KINGS

[1] John Kifner, "Two in Bomb Case Appear More Aimless Than Ardent," *New York Times,* 5 August 1997, p. B3.
[2] Ibid., p. B3.
[3] Gerald Posner, *Why America Slept* (New York: Random House, 2003), p. 73.
[4] John Kifner, "Bomb Plot Investigators Are Puzzled by New View of Suspects," *New York Times,* 7 August 1997.

CHAPTER SIX: THE EGYPTIAN

[1] Dan Barry, "Police Break Up Suspected Bomb Plot in Brooklyn," *New York Times,* 1 August 1997, p. B4.
[2] Interview, Amman, Jordan, 24 August 2003.
[3] William K. Rashbaum, Austin Fenner, and Don Singleton, "Their Goal: Kill Americans," *New York Daily News,* 2 August 1997, p. 3.
[4] Robert D. McFadden, "Suspects in Bomb Plot Took Two Paths from the West Bank," *New York Times,* 3 August 1997, p. B4.
[5] Ibid., p. B4.

CHAPTER SEVEN: ANYTIME, BABY...

[1] Interview, Washington, D.C., 1 June 2003.
[2] Interview, New York, 15 December 2003.
[3] Interview, Washington, D.C., 30 January 2004.
[4] Interview, Washington, D.C., 29 January 2004.

CHAPTER EIGHT: MORNING AFTER JERUSALEM

[1] Interview, Jerusalem, 18 August 2003.
[2] Serge Schmeman, "Suicide Bombers Kill Thirteen in Jerusalem Market," *New York Times,* 31 July 1997, p. A10.
[3] Ibid., p. A10.
[4] Interview, Miami, 14 August 2002.
[5] Robert D. McFadden, "Suspects in Bomb Plot Took Two Paths from the West Bank," *New York Times,* 3 August 1997, p. B1.
[6] Helen Peterson, "Bomb Diagram Found in Trash," *New York Daily News,* 16 July 1998, p. 38.
[7] From material captured from the Hamas Student Association at al-Najah University in Nablus.

CHAPTER NINE: INFORMANT

[1] Christopher Davis, "Fear on Fourth Avenue," *Reader's Digest,* October 2000, p. 117.
[2] Interview, New York, 20 February 2004.

CHAPTER TEN: THE BOMB JOB

[1] Interview, Washington, D.C., 29 January 2004.
[2] Interview, New York, 12 December 2003.
[3] Interview, Washington, D.C., 29 January 2004.
[4] Interview, New York, 20 February 2004.

CHAPTER ELEVEN: THE TAC PLAN

[1] Interview, Palm Beach, Florida, 29 January 2004.
[2] Ibid.
[3] Interview, New York, 20 February 2004.
[4] Interview, Palm Beach, Florida, 29 January 2004.
[5] Interview, Washington, D.C., 7 January 2004.
[6] Interview, Palm Beach, Florida, 29 January 2004.

CHAPTER TWELVE: GREEN LIGHT

[1] Interview, Palm Beach, Florida, 29 January 2004.
[2] Interview, Queens, New York, 6 February 2004.
[3] Interview, Palm Beach, Florida, 29 January 2004.
[4] Ibid.
[5] Interview, New York, 12 December 2003.
[6] Interview, New York, 20 February 2004.
[7] Interview, Palm Beach, Florida, 29 January 2004.
[8] Ibid.
[9] Interview, New York, 12 December 2003.
[10] Ibid.

CHAPTER THIRTEEN: CAT CAR

[1] Interview, Middle Village, Queens, New York, 8 February 2004.
[2] Interview, New York, 12 December 2003.
[3] Ibid.
[4] Interview, Queens, New York, 12 December 2002.
[5] Interview, Fort Totten, Queens, New York, 20 January 2003.
[6] Interview, Palm Beach, Florida, 29 January 2004.
[7] Interview, New York, 12 December 2003.
[8] Interview, Washington, D.C., 8 January 2004.
[9] Interview, Queens, New York, 18 February 2004.

CHAPTER FOURTEEN: ENTRY TEAM

[1] Interview, Palm Beach, Florida, 29 January 2004.
[2] Ibid.
[3] Interview, New York, 12 December 2003.
[4] Ibid.

CHAPTER FIFTEEN: THE HIT

[1] Interview, New York, 12 December 2003.
[2] Interview, New York, 20 February 2004.
[3] Interview, New York, 20 February 2004.
[4] Interview, Palm Beach, Florida, 29 January 2004.

CHAPTER SIXTEEN: JTTF

[1] Interview, Montevideo, Uruguay, 11 December 2003.
[2] Ibid.
[3] Ibid.
[4] Interview, Miami, 18 February 2003.
[5] Ibid.
[6] Interview, Montevideo, Uruguay, 11 December 2003.
[7] Ibid.
[8] Ibid.
[9] Ibid.
[10] Ibid.
[11] Ibid.
[12] Ibid.

CHAPTER SEVENTEEN: THE DEBRIEF

[1] Interview, Montevideo, Uruguay, 11 December 2003.
[2] Ibid.
[3] Ibid.
[4] Ibid.
[5] Ibid.
[6] Interview, New York, 1 June 2003.
[7] Al Baker, "Powder and Death," *New York Newsday,* 1 August 1997, p. A11.

CHAPTER EIGHTEEN: END OF THE DAY

[1] Interview, Palm Beach, Florida, 29 January 2004.
[2] Ibid.
[3] Ibid.
[4] Dan Barry, "Bomb Suspect Was Detained by U.S. but Released," *New York Times,* 2 August 1997, p. B2.
[5] Interview, Montevideo, Uruguay, 11 December 2003.
[6] Ibid.
[7] Ibid.
[8] "Terror Averted," *New York Newsday,* 1 August 1997, p. A3.

CHAPTER NINETEEN: ANGST, ACCOLADES, AND AFTERMATH

[1] "Unaware of Suspect's Past, INS Sez," *New York Daily News,* 3 August 1997, p. 3.
[2] Uri Dan, "Hamas Honcho Denies Link to Brooklyn Cowboys," *New York Post,* 3 August 1997, p. 2.
[3] Brian Hartman, "Note Threatened More Bombs," ABC News, 4 August 1997.
[4] John Kifner, "State Department Got Bomb Note, but Doesn't Know Why," *New York Times,* 6 August 1997, p. B1.
[5] Lisa Rein, "Good-Will Tour of Brooklyn," *New York Daily News,* 2 August 1997, p. 7.
[6] Ibid.
[7] Interview, Washington, D.C., 7 January 2004.
[8] Interview, New York, 11 January 2003.
[9] Interview, Palm Beach, Florida, 29 January 2004.
[10] Interview, New York, 20 February 2004.
[11] Interview, Palm Beach, Florida, 29 January 2004.
[12] Ibid.

CHAPTER TWENTY: JUSTICE AND REWARDS

[1] Helen Peterson, "FBI: B Train Bomb Plot Eyed Jews," *New York Daily News,* 15 July 1998, p. 6.
[2] Helen Peterson, "Israel Bomb Inspired Brooklyn Plot, He Sez," *New York Daily News,* 7 July 1997, p. 13.
[3] Joseph P. Fried, "Agent Testifies on Content of Pipe Bomb," *New York Times,* 17 July 1998, p. B6.
[4] Ibid.
[5] Joseph P. Fried, "Jury Convicts Man in Scheme to Set a Bomb in the Subway," *New York Times,* 24 July 1998, p. B6.
[6] Interview, Washington, D.C., 7 January 2004.
[7] Interview, Brooklyn, New York, 27 February 2004.
[8] Interview, New York, 16 February 2004.
[9] Ibid.
[10] Interview, New York, 20 February 2004.
[11] Interview, New York, 13 December 2003.
[12] Interview, Palm Beach, Florida, 29 January 2004.

Index

Samuel M. Katz has written more than twenty books and over one hundred articles on Middle East security issues, international terrorism, and police and military special operations and counter-terrorism. His books include *The Night Raiders: Israel's Naval Commandos at War; Anytime, Anywhere!: On Patrol with the NYPD's Emergency Service Unit; The Hunt for the Engineer;* and *Relentless Pursuit: The DSS and the Manhunt for the al-Qaeda Terrorists.* His articles have appeared in magazines around the world, from *Playboy, Esquire,* and *FHM* to *Popular Mechanics* and *Jane's Intelligence Review;* Katz is also a frequent contributor to the *Washington Times* and is the editor-in-chief of *Special Operations Report.* Katz has also worked for television, creating award-wining documentaries for the Discovery Channel, A&E, and TLC.

Katz also lectures law enforcement agencies around the world on counterterrorist matters, as well as on the history of Palestinian and Islamic fundamentalist terrorism. Agencies represented at his courses have included the Department of Justice, the State Department Diplomatic Security Service, the FBI, the Secret Service, the BATF, the U.S. Customs Service, INS, DIA, the NYPD, the Royal Canadian Mounted Police, Canada's CSIS, the Miami–Dade Police Department, the Royal Netherlands Marine Corps, the Dutch Ministry of Justice, Belgium's Police Fédérale, the Royal Bahamian Constabulary, and dozens of other federal, state, and local law enforcement departments.